D1606102

Lewis Milestone

Lewis Milestone

Life and Films

Harlow Robinson

UNIVERSITY PRESS OF KENTUCKY

Copyright © 2019 by The University Press of Kentucky

Scholarly publisher for the Commonwealth,
serving Bellarmine University, Berea College, Centre
College of Kentucky, Eastern Kentucky University,
The Filson Historical Society, Georgetown College,
Kentucky Historical Society, Kentucky State University,
Morehead State University, Murray State University,
Northern Kentucky University, Transylvania University,
University of Kentucky, University of Louisville,
and Western Kentucky University.
All rights reserved.

Editorial and Sales Offices: The University Press of Kentucky
663 South Limestone Street, Lexington, Kentucky 40508-4008
www.kentuckypress.com

Library of Congress Cataloging-in-Publication Data

Names: Robinson, Harlow, author.
Title: Lewis Milestone : life and films / Harlow Robinson.
Description: Lexington, Kentucky : University Press of Kentucky, [2019] |
    Includes bibliographical references, filmography, and index.
Identifiers: LCCN 2019023542 | ISBN 9780813178332 (hardcover) | ISBN
    9780813178356 (pdf) | ISBN 9780813178363 (epub)
Subjects: LCSH: Milestone, Lewis, 1895–1980. | Motion picture producers and
    directors—United States—Biography.
Classification: LCC PN1998.3.M5547 R63 2019 | DDC 791.4302/33092 [B]—dc23

Member of the Association
of University Presses

For Bob

Contents

Photographs follow page 143

Introduction

When, over the course of the last eight years, I would tell students, friends, and colleagues that I was working on a biography of Lewis Milestone, most often their response would be a blank look and then a question. "Who is Lewis Milestone?"

> "He directed *All Quiet on the Western Front,*" I would reply.
> "Oh, yes, of course, I saw that in school. An amazing film."
> "And *Ocean's 11.*"
> "You mean the original one, with Frank Sinatra?"
> "Yes, that one."
> "Oh, wow."
> "And *Of Mice and Men.* And *Mutiny on the Bounty.* And *The Front Page.*"
> "Really? Of course I know these films, but didn't know he made them."
> "Really."

Film historians and critics regard Lewis Milestone (1895–1980) as one of the major directors of the "golden age of Hollywood." But his long, eventful, and influential career has not (before now) received the sort of scholarly or popular attention paid to many of his contemporaries: George Cukor, William Wyler, Frank Capra, John Ford. Only a single slim volume (long out of print) has been published on Milestone's life and work: Joseph Millichap's *Lewis Milestone*—and this one appeared nearly forty years ago.[1]

Meanwhile, many of Milestone's movies have become classics. If imitation is the highest form of flattery, he has been duly flattered: since 2007, Stephen Soderbergh has directed three highly profitable spin-offs (and produced another) of *Ocean's 11*, featuring some of Hollywood's most popular stars—George Clooney, Matt Damon, Julia Roberts. *All Quiet on the Western Front* consistently ranks as one of the most important films ever made, and sits at number 54 on the American Film Institute's list of the greatest American movies of all time. The folksy music Aaron Copland wrote for Milestone's adaptation of John Steinbeck's *The Red Pony* has become one of the most frequently programmed works of American "classical" music, often used to convey the essence of American frontier culture.

Among the most consistent and productive directors of his era, Milestone, known in the business affectionately as "Millie" (or "Milly"), completed thirty-eight films over a period of thirty-seven years, during which cinema's technical possibilities underwent unprecedented change and development, from silent to sound and from black-and-white to color. Milestone's artistic excellence was recognized by three Academy Awards, including one for Best Comedy Direction (for *Two Arabian Knights*) in 1929, the first year that the Motion Picture Academy awards presentation was held, recognizing films made in 1927 and 1928. *All Quiet on the Western Front* (1930), his poetic and disturbing adaptation of Erich Maria Remarque's novel about World War I, won two Academy Awards, for Best Direction and for Best Picture. In total, Milestone's films received a total of twenty-eight Oscar nominations in various categories, over an impressive span of thirty-four years beginning in 1928 and ending in 1962. Few Hollywood directors can match that score or that kind of staying power.

The galaxy of major stars who worked with Milestone testifies to his stature in Hollywood. They included Emil Jennings, Gary Cooper, Al Jolson, Joan Crawford, Walter Huston, the Three Stooges, Bing Crosby, Ethel Merman, Akim Tamiroff, Ginger Rogers, Errol Flynn, Anne Baxter, Dana Andrews, Lloyd Bridges, Barbara Stanwyck, Kirk Douglas, Judith Anderson, Charles Boyer, Ingrid Bergman, Robert Mitchum, Karl Malden, Michael Rennie, Sylvia Sidney, Patrice Munsel, Dirk Bogarde, Gregory Peck, Frank Sinatra, Dean Martin, Sammy Davis Jr., Peter Lawford, Angie Dickinson, and Marlon Brando. And yet Milestone said repeatedly that he did not like the "star system," and that he found working with lesser-known talent more rewarding. Along the way, he nurtured numerous young actors who later became stars, such as Lew Ayres, Dana Andrews, Kirk Douglas, and Farley Granger.

A serious artist who believed in film's power not only to entertain but to convey messages of social importance, Milestone gained a reputation as a man of principle in an industry not known for an abundance of virtue. In his *History of Film,* David Parkinson notes that Milestone's films "managed to combine the kind of characters usually associated with Howard Hawks with the themes beloved of Frank Capra."[2] His encyclopedic command of the machinery of cinema, and his ability to command the respect of actors, even the most difficult, became legendary in Hollywood. As the popular film historian and critic Leonard Maltin has written, "Milestone was a skilled craftsman who fully understood both the technical and aesthetic tricks of his trade, and utilized them well."[3] Whereas other directors prominent in the silent era fell by the wayside when sound arrived, Milestone embraced innovation, astonishing audiences with the sonic revolution of *All Quiet on the Western Front.*

One of the most impressive qualities of Milestone's career was his ability to work successfully and on a high artistic level in a wide variety of genres: film musical (*Hallelujah, I'm a Bum, Anything Goes*), comedy (*The Front Page, Ocean's 11*), film noir (the provocative and underappreciated *Strange Love of Martha Ivers*), war drama, exotic adventure (*The General Died at Dawn*), and historical costume drama (*Mutiny on the Bounty*). This wide range, in fact, may well be one of the reasons Milestone's work has not attracted the same sort of critical and scholarly attention as that of his director contemporaries. His very diverse body of work is difficult to categorize.

Milestone's proud independence, which led him repeatedly to challenge the men in the front office, also led to frequent conflicts with studio management that gained him a reputation for being difficult. By nature antiauthoritarian and outspoken, he resisted accepting the subordinate role directors were usually assigned under the rigid Hollywood studio system. He did not always try to ingratiate himself with the studio bosses, and he paid a price for that. Supremely confident in his own powers of judgment, he occasionally stumbled in choosing projects. Late in his career, Milestone's old friend Darryl Zanuck, vice president for production at 20th Century Fox, advised him to focus on directing and not to spread his energies too broadly into other aspects of filmmaking. "You were blessed with the talent of directing and the ability to enthuse a company. You know your job in this category and you know it well. You do not have to take a back seat to anyone."[4]

That Milestone turned repeatedly to the theme of war (in *Our Russian Front, Edge of Darkness, The North Star, The Purple Heart, Arch of Triumph, Halls of Montezuma, They Who Dare, Pork Chop Hill*) is not surprising. He had ample experience of the personal and national devastation of military combat. Having witnessed the violence of the anti-Jewish pogroms and the Revolution of 1905 as a boy growing up in Russian Bessarabia, Milestone (who changed his name from the original Milstein at some point before he moved to Hollywood) also served in the U.S. military in World War I and lived through World War II, the Korean War—and the Cold War. The bitter and destructive ideological conflicts of the twentieth century repeatedly touched Milestone and resonate repeatedly in his films.

Throughout his career, Milestone brought to the screen work by some of the most important writers of the past and present, including Ring Lardner, Erich Maria Remarque, Ben Hecht and Charles MacArthur, Somerset Maugham, Clifford Odets, John Steinbeck, Lillian Hellman, and Victor Hugo. His sensitivity to the literary text was one of the most distinctive features of his style: "Throughout my career I've tried not so much to express a philosophy as to restate in filmic terms my agreement with whatever the author of a story I like is trying to say."[5]

To illustrate and comment on the emotional effect of these stories, Milestone used music by some of Hollywood's most prominent and imaginative composers, including his "discovery" Aaron Copland (*Of Mice and Men, The North Star, The Red Pony*), Richard Rodgers and Lorenz Hart (*Hallelujah, I'm a Bum*), Cole Porter (*Anything Goes*), his fellow Russian émigré Dmitri Tiomkin (*Our Russian Front*), Franz Waxman (*Edge of Darkness, No Minor Vices*), Alfred Newman (*The Purple Heart*), Miklós Rózsa (*The Strange Love of Martha Ivers*), Alec North (*Les Misérables*), Bronislau Kaper (*Mutiny on the Bounty*), and even Nelson Riddle for the jazzy, innovative, and influential score for *Ocean's 11*.

Milestone's life story and his films provide a compelling chronicle of the very eventful times through which he lived. Like other prominent Hollywood directors, Milestone came under suspicion in the late 1940s when the Un-American Activities Committee of the House of Representatives (HUAC) initiated hearings into alleged Communist influence in the film business. Since he was known to have immigrated to the United States from Russia (although before the 1917 Bolshevik Revolution) and for having leftist sympathies expressed in some of his films (*Hallelujah, I'm a Bum; The North Star*), Milestone became an obvious target. In fact, he was among the original nineteen "unfriendly" individuals subpoenaed to give testimony before the HUAC in late 1946. It was at Milestone's Beverly Hills mansion that these nineteen gathered for strategy sessions.[6] His dignified behavior during this period, and his unwavering loyalty to friends, set him apart from many of his contemporaries who lacked the moral courage to withstand the onslaught. Like others, he saw his career derailed by the HUAC inquisition, and for a while he sought refuge abroad.

When he returned to Hollywood in the late 1950s, Milestone found a radically changed landscape. Television had disrupted the studio system in which he had operated for so many years. Even so, he managed to revive his career and complete several more important films before his retirement.

My hope is that the pages that follow will stimulate renewed appreciation of Milestone's large and influential body of work and his important role in building the Hollywood film industry. His is also a compelling personal story of the pursuit of the American dream. Like so many other immigrants from countries where they feared religious and ethnic persecution, Milestone arrived in the United States with the hope of re-creating himself and living up to his fullest creative potential in an environment promising equal opportunity. Unlike his brother who remained in Kishinev and eventually perished in the Holocaust, Milestone grew and prospered in America, sharing his talents with the widest possible audience. He appealed to our better selves, and to the necessity of treating all people with respect, whatever their status. His best films uplift, enlighten, and—yes—entertain us.

1

"Nobody Asked You to Go to America"

How many years did it take me to become an overnight success?
—*Lewis Milestone*

On the biggest night of his life, Lewis Milestone skipped the party. While a glamorous crowd of Hollywood celebrities gathered for the hotly anticipated premiere of his film *All Quiet on the Western Front* at the Carthay Circle Theater on April 21, 1930, the young director sped eastward on a train bound for New York. His ultimate destination was even farther from Hollywood: Europe. Milestone missed the opportunity to reunite with the actors he had so carefully guided through a difficult shooting process and to see the corps of U.S. Marines assembled to greet the well-wishing members of the Hollywood elite (including Louella Parsons and John Barrymore) who turned out to celebrate one of the major events of the season. Nor did he attend the fancy invitation-only party hosted after the screening by the film's producer, Carl Laemmle Jr., of Universal Studios. Milestone did listen to a broadcast of the premiere in the train's observation car, and "at almost every stop the train made crossing the continent he received congratulatory telegrams."[1]

His failure to show up was, of course, noted by Hollywood gossips and journalists, who had already labeled Milestone (age thirty-four) one of the most promising directors in the industry and "one of Hollywood's most eligible bachelors."[2] When he reached New York, Milestone was interviewed by a *New York Evening World* reporter, who speculated on the director's strange absence from the premiere: "This implies, of course, that he doesn't care for ballyhoos, for there isn't a doubt that he would have been called upon to take a bow, and taking bows is decidedly not in his line. He believes, on the contrary, in letting his work speak for itself."[3]

6

"Letting his work speak for itself." This was Lewis Milestone's credo. A serious and intellectual artist, he shunned the trappings of Hollywood fame. At least initially, money meant surprisingly little to this Jewish immigrant who had arrived in the United States in 1913 with a few dollars won from gambling during the passage from Germany. "I was only interested in creating motion pictures and not the business end of it."[4] Although he eventually became a wealthy man with a Beverly Hills mansion and many A-list friends, he never forgot where he came from. And his underlying goal as a director was always to use film as a medium for messages of social relevance. This tendency branded him as a "lefty" early on, an identity that landed him in the thick of the anti-Communist witch hunts of the late 1940s and early 1950s.

In an interview conducted in 1969 to mark the fiftieth anniversary of his arrival in Hollywood, in 1919, Milestone said, "I don't see how you can ever make anything on screen without a message."[5] Milestone's idealistic belief in film's ability to do more than simply entertain was noted by many who knew him and was reflected in his best films: *The Front Page, Rain, Hallelujah, I'm a Bum, The General Dies at Dawn, Of Mice and Men, A Walk in the Sun, The Strange Love of Martha Ivers, The Halls of Montezuma,* and, yes, even *Ocean's 11,* in which a group of former army buddies turn the tables on the Las Vegas casinos in an elaborate heist scheme. But like most Hollywood directors, he also produced his share of movies made for money or simply to fulfill contractual obligations—this was a reality of the business he worked in.

"I want to say a word here about Milestone," wrote Louella Parsons in her column in early 1931. "We were on the same house party over New Year's and I never had a chance before to really know him. What an intellect, what a brain and what a background and what modesty! If Lewis Milestone doesn't make another *All Quiet on the Western Front* then I am all wrong about my estimate of him."[6] By this time, *All Quiet on the Western Front* had won the 1929–30 Academy Awards for both Best Picture and Best Director. Milestone skipped that party, too. Absent from the Academy Award ceremony on November 5, 1930, in the Fiesta Ballroom of the Ambassador Hotel, he instead accepted the Best Director award remotely by the futuristic means of a "talking picture" from New York. He had stopped there on his way back from his five-month-long trip to Europe, during which he made his first visit to his family since arriving in Hoboken from Hamburg seventeen years before.

Milestone once observed of the stubborn success and staying power of *All Quiet on the Western Front*, "You hate to live on one picture," as though he were haunted by its specter. This film, he remarked tartly, "proved to have a longer life than many a politician." After completing this exhausting and cathartic epic, one of the most powerful and highly acclaimed antiwar films ever made, and the film by which he would be celebrated and judged ever after, Milestone apparently felt the need to return to his roots in Kishinev, Romania. He was hoping that after its premiere and reception, he could move on to the next phase of what would prove to be a long, varied, and eventful Hollywood career. In New York, Milestone admitted that he was "exhausted" after the filming of *All Quiet on the Western Front*. "War is hell, and he wants to forget it," a journalist wrote.[7]

In a tribute to Milestone's impressive rise, Mark Hellinger of the *Daily Mirror* wrote: "You arrived in this country from Russia only sixteen years ago with nothing but the will to succeed between you and starvation. Unable to speak English, you handled a broom by day and a book by night. You drifted to Hollywood and fought your way to the top while hundreds of others, with more pull and greater educational advantages, were falling on the way up. A toast to you, Milestone. You deserve it richly."[8]

In most accounts of Milestone's life, his place of birth (on September 30, 1895) is given as Odessa.[9] This lively port city, today in the independent country of Ukraine, was founded during the reign of Catherine the Great to consolidate Russia's military and trading position on the Black Sea, in competition with the Ottoman Empire. Always a very cosmopolitan metropolis, it had large minority populations of Jews, Greeks, Armenians, Ukrainians, Romanians, and Russians, "a melting pot of many nations" as Milestone told one journalist.[10]

Odessa has also furnished the world with a remarkable number of creative artists, especially writers (Isaac Babel and Ilf and Petrov) and musicians (the pianist Emil Gilels and the violinists David Oistrakh and Nathan Milstein). It has been an important center of Jewish culture for many generations. In Odessa, according to most accounts, Milestone's father first established his retail and wholesale clothing business and began to raise a family that eventually included five daughters ("that meant you had five blabbermouths")[11] and two sons. But when Milestone was about five years old, the family moved to the city of Kishinev, the capital of the Russian tsarist province of Bessarabia (today known as Moldova). Both Odessa (in Ukraine) and Kishinev were part of the enormous Russian empire, and they were ruled, often ruthlessly, from the tsarist capital in St. Petersburg. After World War I and the 1917 Bolshevik Revolution, most of Bessarabia (including Kishinev) became part of the independent country of Romania.

In the early twentieth century, Kishinev had a population of around 125,000 residents, half of them Jewish. The city was an important center of Jewish culture and learning. Milestone's family was Jewish, and his real name (later changed in America) was Lieb (or its Russian version, Lev) Milshtein. Years later, he told the Soviet writer Ilya Ehrenburg, "I'm no Lewis Milestone, I'm Lenya Milstein from Kishinev."[12] One of his cousins was the violinist Nathan Milstein, who also emigrated to the United States. Culturally and linguistically, Kishinev was closely related to Romania, its neighbor to the west, and many of the city's inhabitants spoke Romanian. Milestone's family, however, was Russian-speaking, and Russian was his native tongue, as Russian was the language of education, culture, and administration throughout the Russian empire. He also knew some Yiddish, spoken among the Jewish population.

In Hollywood, Milestone was friendly with numerous other Russian émigrés, and throughout his life he maintained a strong interest in Russian literature and culture. Indeed, he worked persistently on several film projects based on works of Russian literature, although none was completed.

One of Milestone's earliest and most traumatic memories—he was seven years old at the time—was of witnessing the tragic Kishinev anti-Semitic pogrom of 1903. Under the reigns of Tsars Alexander III (1881–1894) and his son Nicholas II (1894–1917), the pro-Orthodox Russian government discriminated against Jews in all areas of life, restricting them to living in certain areas and enforcing quotas on Jewish participation in education and in various professions. Even worse, there were sporadic violent raids by tsarist soldiers and Cossacks against Jewish communities along the western borders of the Russian empire.

One of the worst of these pogroms occurred in Kishinev on Easter Sunday 1903. As often happened in such cases, the pogrom started as an act of revenge. The deaths of two young local Christians were blamed on Jews who allegedly were using the blood of the victims to prepare matzo for Passover. Between April 19 and 21, forty-nine Jews were killed, nearly one hundred were seriously wounded, five hundred were slightly injured, and hundreds of Jewish homes and stores were pillaged or destroyed. According to reporting in the *New York Times,* "The Jews were taken wholly unaware and were slaughtered like sheep. The scenes of horror attending this massacre are beyond description. Babes were literally torn to pieces by the frenzied and bloodthirsty mob. The local police made no attempt to check the reign of terror. At sunset the streets were piled with corpses and wounded. Those who could make their escape fled in terror, and the city is now practically deserted of Jews."[13]

The consequences of the 1903 Kishinev pogrom (another one took place in 1905) were profound. It caused international outrage and led President Theodore Roosevelt to register an official protest with the Russian tsarist government. Many Jews left for the West; thousands went to the United States, and others to Israel. By the end of 1903, the number of Jews emigrating from Kishinev and the surrounding area to America had more than doubled. Even more important, this pogrom led many Jews to support the idea of creating their own homeland in Palestine, a project promoted by Theodor Herzl and others. As the historian J. J. Goldberg writes, the Kishinev pogrom of 1903, "and the worldwide wave of Jewish outrage that it evoked, laid the foundation of modern Israel, gave birth to contemporary American-Jewish activism and helped bring about the downfall of the czarist regime."[14]

In his unpublished autobiography, prepared with the help of Donald Chase, Milestone remembered his experience of this event. He had been taken by his nanny to a fair held in celebration of the Easter holiday. "There was a merry-go-round, a Punch and Judy show, and various other amusements, most of them for children. We were walking from one place of amusement to another when suddenly a kind of sharp wind came up. It grew stronger and stronger, blowing papers, sand, hats and other objects across the square. I heard shouts and sounds of firing. In no time people were in a full-fledged panic. Nanny grabbed my hand and we ran all the way to our house. Once in the house, I was locked up and not allowed to go out again. My home arrest lasted for something like four or five days. Some time later I learned that the disturbance we escaped from was the first pogrom. The year was 1903. The city was Kishinev, the capital of Bessarabia."[15]

Although Milestone never embraced the practice of Judaism and did not attend services regularly, this early experience of racial and religious discrimination clearly had an enormous influence on his development as a person and an artist. It helps explain why later he was drawn to make films that deal with the persecution or exploitation of the less privileged by those in economic or political power (*All Quiet on the Western Front, The Front Page, The General Died at Dawn, Of Mice and Men* especially come to mind). As O'Hara, the hero of *The General Died at Dawn*, Gary Cooper may well have been speaking for Milestone when he exclaimed: "Why am I for oppressed people? Because I have a background of oppression myself."

On his trip to Europe in 1930 after the premiere of *All Quiet on the Western Front*, Milestone was also able to see for himself the rising tide of anti-Semitism in Germany as the Nazi Party gained increasing popular support. He crossed the continent from London to Kishinev, now a city in an independent Romania after the realignment of European borders following World War I. There he visited his parents. In London he met his brother, an engineer, and warned him to stay away from Kishinev because he feared the situation could become dangerous for Jews there. But his brother did not want to leave their parents alone in Kishinev, and so he returned there. Tragically, he would be killed early in World War II when Nazi forces invaded Romania. "He was massacred there, no reason," Milestone later told the film historian Kevin Brownlow. "They walked in and he opened the door—there was a knock, he opened the door and bang! and he was dead."[16]

When Brownlow asked him how he viewed Kishinev upon his return there as an adult, Milestone said, "I didn't see a hell of a lot of changes—I felt the place was much bigger than it actually was—but that's what happens to you. You leave a place as a juvenile and you come back, it does look so damn small to you, in your own mind you know you felt it was much bigger."[17]

As a boy growing up in Kishinev, Milestone battled with pervasive anti-Semitism. His parents wanted him to enroll in the *Realschule,* which trained students in engineering, but a strict quota decreed only 10 percent of the students could be Jewish (despite the fact that half of the city's inhabitants were Jewish). Only intervention by some friends of his father made it possible for him to be admitted. "They would much rather get rid of you than give you an education," he remembered later.[18] But Milestone never cared much for engineering, or, for that matter, for education in general. His real passion lay in the world of the theater. With friends, he began working as a super in the state theater, but he had to keep it a secret because the school prohibited such activities. The theater performed classical Russian plays, as well as operetta and musical comedy. One of the leading actors was Victor Petipa, brother of the famous choreographer Marius Petipa. Milestone "attended every rehearsal; everything that happened in the theatre was much more interesting than dry old school."[19]

Eventually his sister happened to come to one of the performances in which he was cast as an extra, a café habitué. When he saw her in the audience, he tried to hide behind a newspaper, but she recognized him and told his parents. To escape their wrath, he left town to stay at the country house of a friend's father. When they pleaded with him to return, he proposed a deal: "'I'll come back if you give me 50 roubles that I need to settle a feud.' They gave me the money and I came home."[20] Milestone's natural ability to make and keep friends became one of his greatest assets in Hollywood, where he was well known for his personal charm, hospitality, and deal-making skills.

Milestone continued to appear at the theater throughout his childhood and early teen years. "I knew that sooner or later that's where I wanted to be—in the theatre."[21] As he said later, the film business eventually became "a pretty good substitute."

The details of how Milestone decided to leave Kishinev and make his way to the United States remain somewhat murky. At different times in his life, he provided different accounts of the voyage, to the point where he may not have remembered himself exactly how it happened. In most versions of the story, he was sent by his father to study engineering at a college in Mittweida, Germany, in 1913. (In another version, he was sent to study pharmacy and did so poorly that his parents sent him the money for passage to the United States. On his way to Hamburg he met up with a fellow from Prague, and they "stopped at various places and had some fun, met some dames and so on.")[22] With him there in Mittweida were two other school friends from Kishinev. Bored with his studies and eager for an adventure, the seventeen-year-old Milestone decided to spend the money his father had sent him to go home for the holidays instead of booking passage to the United States. At the time, of course, thousands of immigrants from all over Europe were traveling to America in search of a freer and more prosperous life. In the end, the idea of returning to

Kishinev and its oppressive anti-Semitism did not hold much appeal for Milestone. "I decided to leave Russia because things were beginning to get a little too narrow for me."[23]

So Milestone and his two buddies made their way to Hamburg, where they boarded a ship headed for Hoboken, New Jersey. Because they were considered Russian and there was an epidemic in Russia at the time, they were placed in steerage. To be allowed to enter the United States, each passenger had to have at least twenty-five dollars. So, according to Milestone, they persuaded a fellow Russian to lend them that amount so they could get off the ship, with the condition that they would return it to him on the dock. Between them, the three young men had eight dollars when they landed at Hoboken. At the customs and immigration processing center at Hoboken they chose the German-speaking desk "because we felt it would probably be easier to negotiate whatever we were doing in German than it would be in Russian."[24] When Milestone changed his name from Lieb Milshtein to Lewis Milestone is not clear; it may have happened at immigration processing, when new arrivals were often assigned Americanized names. In any case Milestone proved to be a fortuitous choice for a future film director, with its connotation of strength and accomplishment. Later, he would choose "Milestones" as the title of the autobiography he never managed to complete.

But to his Hollywood friends, he would soon become simply Millie.

Milestone and his buddies spent their first cold night (like many other new immigrants) in New York in Central Park. Milestone would revisit the world of the Central Park homeless with notable compassion twenty years later in his quirky Depression-era musical film, *Hallelujah, I'm a Bum,* starring Al Jolson.

Milestone knew that his aunt, his mother's sister, lived in New York and set out to find her. First they located her son. He took Milestone to her door—and she promptly fainted, having received no warning that he would be arriving. At this point, Milestone still wasn't sure if he would stay in America. After he had spent the money his aunt had lent him, he wrote to his father asking for more financial support. "Nobody asked you to go to America. Now you are in the land of liberty and labor try rolling up your sleeves and go to work," his father replied. "You've tried everything else." As it happened, Milestone's timing in leaving Europe for the United States was fortunate, since World War I would break out in August 1914, making travel across Europe extremely difficult. "Had I not gone to the States when I did, Germany, because of my Russian citizenship, would have made me a prisoner of war."[25]

During his first few years in the United States, Milestone worked at a variety of menial and physically demanding jobs. ("I had about fifty different jobs" he said with characteristic exaggeration.)[26] The first was in a raincoat factory on the Lower East Side, where he would haul barrels of naptha and mix rubber cement. There he became involved—not for the last time, to be sure—in a dispute between management and labor. When the factory went on strike, he compiled a list of scabs who were working and gave it to the strikers. As Milestone later proudly told the story, the foreman found out and hit the youth with a yardstick, and he responded by stabbing the foreman with a pair of scissors and running away. Throughout his career in Hollywood, Milestone would defend the rights of workers and unions, repeatedly siding with them in conflicts with studio management, most notably in 1945 when the International Alliance of Theatrical and Stage Employees and other unions staged a violent strike during the shooting of his film *The Strange Love of Martha Ivers*.

But it did not take Milestone long to gravitate toward the world of cameras and photography. In 1915 he found a position as an assistant to a Russian-born photographer who took sentimental society and family portraits. At first he worked in the darkroom, learning the technical and aesthetic aspects of photography. But he found his real niche as a salesman, visiting prospective clients in the suburbs. He would present to the mistress of the house an album featuring the work his boss had done. At first, according to Milestone, his boss's business partner viewed him as an unwelcome competitor, but he eventually offered to show him the ropes. Young and sure of himself, Milestone demanded that he be given a suite at a theatrical hotel, plus some spending money to buy "a couple of suits from Brooks Brothers."[27] The investment paid off, and Milestone was soon generating more business than any of the other salesmen, working on a generous commission basis. He was even sent on the road to places where the wealthy spent their summers. "My frequent visits to the homes of the wealthy introduced me to their collections of paintings, to period furniture, and to many phases of gracious living. All this I found very useful when I picked up the megaphone."[28]

This work led to another position as a theatrical photographer working in a lively studio run by a Russian émigré. "Champagne, vodka and caviar became the usual fare at our studio's cocktail parties. Before long

Lumiere Studio became the gathering place for Russians of every description: vaudevillians, dramatic actors, painters, agents, and with the beginning of the year of 1916, Russian generals, colonels and lesser ranks, all from the Russian Military Purchasing Commission. These gentlemen created quite a sensation on Broadway. The newspaper columns in that year carried numerous stories of their love escapades, their night club parties, their extravagances and their idiosyncracies [sic]."[29] Milestone also relished the chance "to rub shoulders with the actors, listen to the stories of their adventures on the road, their experiences with various audiences, and their many theories on comedy, melodrama and drama presented in their skits and sketches. It was an education no school could provide."[30]

From the very beginning of his life in the United States, Milestone excelled at meeting people who could help him move up the social and financial ladder, and he moved easily and happily in the world of the creative arts.

World War I brought further opportunity. Soon after the United States entered the war, in April 1917, Milestone decided to enlist in the army, in part to repay the debt he felt he owed the country for giving him a home and refuge. With his keen interest in photography, he chose to join the Signal Corps, in the Aerial Photography division of the Aviation Section. The army captain recruiter explained what aerial photography was, and "it sounded dramatic as hell."[31] Despite his still limited command of English (Milestone would eventually gain complete fluency, with only a trace of an accent), he managed to pass the induction examination. "When we reached the visual test which would determine whether I was color blind I didn't wait for his questions of what color this or that ball of cotton was, but I picked them myself out of the box, calling the colors as I picked them. . . . What the sergeant didn't know was that there were many colors the names of which I didn't know in English."[32]

At the time Milestone was twenty-one years old, stood five feet six inches tall, and weighed 185 pounds, although he dropped to 155 during the war after basic training. Throughout his life, Milestone struggled to control his weight.

He also loved to play practical jokes. The information that he had enlisted for the Signal Corps had not reached his local draft board. When he was summoned to appear, he informed the draft board chairman that he was already in the army. The draft board chairman wanted to know why he was not in uniform, as Milestone later remembered.

"Because," I continued with a smile, "they didn't give me one."

He pressed on, "Why not?"

I looked around the room before landing my next blow. "I don't know, sir. I'm not running this war." The laugh I drew from the crowd was rewarding.[33]

Eventually Milestone did get his uniform and was assigned to the New York City section of the Army Signal Corps for a year. He volunteered to be transferred from the still photographic section to the moving picture section. There he worked with several young men who would also become prominent Hollywood directors, including Wesley Ruggles and Victor Fleming.[34] "Soon our outfit was composed of propmen, grips, cameramen, cutters and a few directors, all from Hollywood. I didn't know it then but that was my entrance into the world of motion pictures."[35]

Later he was sent to the army's lab and medical museum in Washington, D.C., where he was assigned to edit footage of combat sent back from Europe and to make training films. (One of his colleagues was the future film director Josef von Sternberg, then known as Joe Sternberg of Brooklyn.)[36] In one of the training films, Milestone took an acting role as a German soldier. So successful was his portrayal that some local boys threw stones at him during the filming in a Washington park. In Washington, Milestone and a fellow soldier, Richard Wallace, a film editor with experience in movie business, lived with an African American family. "We had to have a special pass to cross over to that neighborhood," he recalled.[37] Milestone was later a pioneer in casting African Americans in his films, including Edgar Connor in *Hallelujah, I'm a Bum,* Leigh Whipper in *Of Mice and Men,* and Sammy Davis Jr. in *Ocean's 11.*

This wartime introduction to filmmaking, and particularly to editing scenes of war, would prove invaluable to Milestone, who would become strongly identified with war films—not only *All Quiet on the Western Front,* but also *Our Russian Front, A Walk in the Sun, Halls of Montezuma,* and *Pork Chop Hill.* He knew what war really looked like. While stationed in Washington, Milestone spent several months at the War College,

> where all the big high ranking officers meet. So we used to run a lot of film and I saw battle stuff. They would send us huge china barrels and we had to open them up and extract arms, legs, torsos,

that were shipped from the battlefield to the War College. We would wash the stuff off, put it in formaldehyde and then photograph it. So this gave me a feeling for how to show it on screen. Later, after *All Quiet on the Western Front*, people assumed that I had all the battle experience in the world. But I never saw a battle other than on the screen. I imagined what it should be.[38]

As a mature director, Milestone was drawn to stories of male camaraderie and bonding, whether in war or journalism (*The Front Page*) or crime (*Ocean's 11*) or labor (*Of Mice and Men*). And the process of directing a film has often been compared to the work of a general commanding an army. The psychological and anatomical lessons Milestone learned during his eighteen months in the military were an important component in his education. A naturally gregarious individual, someone who could turn almost any situation to his advantage and who clearly enjoyed the company of other men, Milestone looked back on his service fondly. "The war was far away and I was too damn young to understand it or to imagine that anything serious could ever happen to me. It was the romantic war. I accepted the idea that I was in the Army for the duration of the war and that the war would never end. So I just settled down to having as much fun as I possibly could. Some of my friends, however, longed for the day when the war would end. They made themselves miserable. For them, peace was very slow in coming."[39]

Milestone also used his theater connections to get tickets for his squad to a matinee vaudeville show, demonstrating his generosity and gift for cultivating popularity and goodwill. The future director later admitted that at the time, those who knew him considered him "just a good-time Charlie."[40]

By the time Milestone was discharged from the army in February 1919, he had become an American citizen. He had also gained significant practical training in photography, editing, and moviemaking. He had learned from movie veterans like Wesley Ruggles that there was good money to be made out West in Hollywood in the film business. When Ruggles told Milestone that he had earned as much as $1,500 a week before the war, he didn't believe him at first. But he was hearing similar stories from other Hollywood veterans and theatrical friends. "By the time I was discharged from the Army my future career appeared very clear to me. It was Hollywood. Originally I wanted to have something to do with the stage. I was on the stage from the time I was about fifteen years old till I left Russia at about seventeen. I started as a "super" and graduated to small parts. The theatre remained my ambition until the Army switched me to motion pictures. 'So be it,' I thought. 'It may do very well as a substitute.'"[41]

Milestone never regretted that decision.

2

The Constructive Cutter

The first punch almost always wins a street fight.

—*Lewis Milestone*

In early 1919, when Milestone arrived in Hollywood, the film industry was entering a period of rapid growth and increasing cultural and political influence. Over the next decade, until the stock market crash of 1929, the size of the audience for the movies and the profit they generated rose dramatically. By 1926, 100 million Americans attended the movies each week, generating an annual income of $750 million for the industry.[1] The film sector employed 350,000 people. Most studios produced around fifty films per year and supplied 90 percent of the world's movies.[2] Increasingly, Hollywood movies were being seen all over the world. During this period, the technology of moviemaking and distribution also underwent rapid transformation, spurred by the introduction of sound in the late 1920s and the building of ornate movie palaces in burgeoning cities.

American confidence soared in the aftermath of World War I as the country became an international symbol of modernity and industrial progress. Since it was an art form made possible by technology, the cinema represented these values better than any other. The automobile, aviation, and the movies were the faces of American ingenuity and entertainment in a new era, representing an energetic challenge to European cultural supremacy. Wrote F. Scott Fitzgerald: "We were the most powerful nation. Who could tell us any longer what was fashionable and what was fun?"[3]

The Hollywood film industry had also become a magnet for immigrants. Indeed, the major studios were created largely by recent arrivals to America, especially from areas in Eastern Europe formerly dominated by the Austro-Hungarian and Russian empires, both destroyed by the First World War. Unfettered by the class system of the Old World and energized by the huge financial rewards possible under capitalism, these producers relished the opportunity to create something new according to their own rules. Many were Jews who had been marginalized and discriminated against in the Old World.

This New World was attractive for actors, too. In the days of silent cinema, until the late 1920s, it didn't matter if actors and actresses had strong foreign accents, or if they could speak English at all. What mattered was whether they could act, whether they looked good onscreen, and whether they were already popular onstage (like the Russian star Alla Nazimova) and could attract their fans to the cinema.

In the aftermath of the collapse of the tsarist regime and the 1917 Bolshevik Revolution in Russia, however, American attitudes toward immigration shifted. Fear of the spread of Communism gave rise to a new isolationism and the passage of anti-immigrant legislation. As the historian Frederick Lewis Allen has written, Americans "were listening to ugly rumors of a huge radical conspiracy against the government and institutions of the United States. They had their ears cocked for the detonation of bombs and the tramp of Bolshevist armies. They seriously thought . . . that a Red revolution might begin in the United States the next month or next week."[4] This first "Red Scare" would not be the last, of course, and American anti-Communist paranoia would eventually have a devastating effect on Milestone's own career.

Milestone had grown very fond of New York since arriving there in 1913, and he was at first unsure whether to leave for the West Coast. Throughout his life, he retained a love for New York, traveled there frequently, and eventually married a Manhattan socialite. "New York is like home to me perhaps because of its cosmopolitanism."[5] "I'm through with small towns," he had allegedly said when someone suggested that he move to Boston. "I'm in a big city now and I want to stay."[6]

But he realized that to make it in the film industry he had to be in Los Angeles. In the Signal Corps, Milestone had struck up a friendship with A. E. Smith, the visiting general manager of Jesse D. Hampton Studios in Hollywood. Over a drink, he asked if there might be a job for him there. A skeptical Smith warned him that studio work was highly specialized. But Milestone had a specific position in mind: to work in the cutting room as an editor. Even the low pay of twenty dollars a week failed to dampen Milestone's enthusiasm, and he agreed to meet Smith one week later to travel together by train to California.

To buy a train ticket, Milestone put together his meager savings. But on the appointed day, his taxi was delayed and he missed the train at Grand Central Station. The two men did meet up in Chicago, however, and arrived in Los Angeles together. Within a month, Milestone had started working as an editor for J. D. Hampton: "It was before unions, so you walked in and got a job and that was it."[7] He shared an apartment with his army buddy Richard Wallace in downtown Los Angeles at La Belle Apartments on Fourth and Grand. Other graduates of the Army Signal Corps also ended up working in Hollywood, including Milestone's former sergeant Lucien Andriot (for whom Milestone worked as a cameraman) and Josef von Sternberg.

Milestone also soon discovered that there were many other Russian émigrés employed at all levels of the film industry. One of his duties at J. D. Hampton's was to pick up daily rushes from a film lab. The lab was run by a Russian émigré named Joe Allen. Milestone recalled:

I was always amused because when I came in I heard nothing spoken but Russian, but they didn't know that I was Russian and that I could understand everything they were saying. I used to raise hell just to tease them, and as I came in I'd hear them say in Russian, "Here's that little son-of-a-bitch again—give him the stuff and get rid of him." One day after this had been going on for a little while, I came in there whistling a very famous revolutionary tune called *Warszawianka*, a Polish composition. The root of the word was Warszawa, or Warsaw. Suddenly they all stopped and listened. Then Joe came over and said, "Where the hell do you know that from?" So I answered him in Russian, "You idiot— what do you think I am?" Well, they cheered, and by the next day I couldn't get any service at all. "You can wait," they said. "You bullied us for some time, so now you can wait." That was when Joe and I became really close, when he found out we had a common background.[8]

In a pattern that would repeat itself throughout his Hollywood career, Milestone managed to irritate his employer with his independent behavior. Despite his lowly status, he would frequently arrive at work by taxi, which his supervisors found inappropriate. They told him he should come by streetcar. But Milestone refused, and he was fired. Over the next few years, he worked in various low-level positions, ranging from editing to sweeping floors and splicing films. At Mack Sennett's Keystone Studios, he did gags with the comedian Harold Lloyd. "On the first day I worked as a Keystone Cop, we were chasing a steamroller, and every place we grabbed was hot, so we fell off repeatedly," Milestone remembered.[9] The director Henry King discovered Milestone's versatility and hired him to assist on two films for Pathé Studios. For a while he worked at Fox Film Corporation, receiving a raise to twenty-eight dollars a week. Then he was hired by the Japanese matinee idol and director Sessue Hayakawa as an assistant editor at forty dollars a week.[10] (To supplement his income, the inveterate gambler "got into crap games," an activity he enjoyed for his entire life.)[11] Milestone thrived in the fast-changing environment of the film business in the early 1920s, where rules were few and initiative and chutzpah prized. "Everyone was starting out then," he later recalled. "But even as early as that, there was a wariness on the part of California movie people towards anyone who had just arrived from New York."[12] Milestone set about proving his worth and mastering all the skills of filmmaking.

Eventually Milestone ended up at Ince Studios, where he met the director William A. Seiter. The men became good friends, and Seiter took Milestone on as an editor and assistant. By day he was on the set, and by night he cut what had been shot. With time, he gained Seiter's trust and started to do pickup shots—especially entrances and exits—that were sometimes used in the completed film. Seiter specialized in light comedies, such as *The Foolish Age* and *Up and at 'Em,* on which Milestone served as general assistant and story assistant, respectively. In 1923 he moved with Seiter to Warner Bros., where he assisted the director on several films and fulfilled various editing assignments. Eventually Milestone collaborated with Seiter on nine films, as editor, assistant director, and screenwriter. Milestone's reputation as a "film doctor" grew, especially after his work on salvaging *Where the North Begins,* a "celluloid disaster" directed for Warner Bros. by Chester Franklin, featuring the canine star Rin Tin Tin. Soon he was the "head cutter" at Warner Bros.

For Milestone, editing was the key to filmmaking. "The cutting room is an excellent place to learn the rudiments of direction; my background there gave me a firm grasp on the mechanics of picturemaking. As an editor, you had to be sure that your entrances and exits matched. If you go out on the right you're supposed to come in on the left, and so on."[13] So adept did Milestone become at fixing movies that Warner Bros began to lend him out to other studios at rates higher than his salary, a practice he found deeply offensive and unfair.[14]

By 1925, after only five years in Hollywood, Milestone had learned the fundamentals of the business (camera, editing, scenario) and was poised to fly solo. He received his first scenario credit for a slapstick satirical farce produced by Warners, *Bobbed Hair,* directed by Alan Crosland, who would make his name as director of the "first talking picture," *The Jazz Singer,* two years later.

But Milestone wanted to direct, not only write, because he believed, as he told friends, that being a director was "the easiest job in the world," an assertion he later came to question.[15] He told Jack Warner that he had a good story idea and needed a writer to help develop it. When Warner objected that the writers he suggested were too expensive, Milestone proposed that they use a young man always hanging around the studio who claimed to be a writer. "If you take him," Jack Warner is alleged to have said, "I'll pay *you.*"[16] That insistent young man was Darryl Zanuck. It also helped that Milestone had been having Friday night dinners with Warner's Old-World parents, fellow Jews who, like him, were immigrants from the tsarist Russian empire. (They came from Krasnashiltz, Poland, but their son Jack was born in Canada.) Their good opinion of Millie helped grease the wheels at the studio, very much a family business.[17] And so, as Milestone later observed, "I was off to the races."[18]

Darryl Zanuck, later to become one of the most powerful men in Hollywood as the founder of 20th Century Fox, was at the time an ambitious twenty-three-year-old with big dreams. Even then he was very much concerned with the financial aspect of the business. The year 1925 would be a very good one for Zanuck: he would write nineteen film scripts for Warner Bros. (including two for Milestone) and by the end of the year become production head of the studio. His first collaboration with Milestone was a comedy (like most of Milestone's silent features) titled *Seven Sinners.*

In the absence of the owners, seven imposters (two thieves, an elderly couple impersonating pious houseguests, the owners' black sheep family member masquerading as a cook, a notorious safecracker, and a rogue pretending to be a doctor) take over a Long Island mansion during a police strike. Like so many of Milestone's films, it revolves around the interaction of a team of characters, rather than one or two central stars. Headlined by Marie Prevost and Clive Brook, the film employs the standard comedic conventions of impersonation and disguise as the seven vie to outdo each other in obtaining a fortune in gems. Much of the humor stems from the inability of the fake servant to perform his duties, and the order of the "doctor" to quarantine the mansion. In a rather forced ending, with the help of the elderly houseguests, sweethearts Prevost and Brook decide to go straight, turn themselves in, do time in jail, and then start a new life selling burglar alarms.

According to reviews published at the time, the film found considerable favor with audiences, eliciting "roars of laughter."[19] Another reviewer noted that Milestone "has almost succeeded in making 'Seven Sinners' seem new, which is not faint praise in this case, considering the number of crook melodramas which have already been turned out of the studios."[20] In the *Telegraph*, Alma Talley wrote that "Lewis Milestone, who is comparatively new at the business of directing, shows a flair for light comedy and a definite talent for clever details."[21] Like so many of Milestone's films, *Seven Sinners* critiques the inequalities of capitalism, and the endemic corruption of the police, who are easily bought off by the crooks.

Milestone's second effort for Warners, *The Cave Man,* used another familiar story line adapted by Julien Josephson and Darryl Zanuck from a story by Gelett Burgess: a bored society lady takes up with a coarse worker to pass the time. Marie Prevost starred as Myra Gaylord, the wealthy jaded socialite, who throws one-half of a hundred-dollar bill out the window of her Park Avenue apartment with her address written on it. Mike, a burly coalheaver (Matt Moore) returns it, and, for a joke, she reinvents him (Pygmalion-style) as an eccentric visiting sociologist from London. One of Myra's friends, the desirable Dolly Van Dream, even falls in love with him, and their crowd starts imitating his primitive dance steps. But when Mike reveals his true identity, Dolly drops him, and he must return to his coal wagon.

Unable to readjust to his former proletarian life, he comes back to visit Myra, and she realizes she loves him. "He takes her over his shoulder and carries her to the coal wagon and they drive off together. . . . Their lips meet in a long, sincere caress—the barrier between them has gone forever, crushed and trampled under by a real understanding. . . . A LONG SHOT reveals the coal wagon, with its galloping steeds, and Mike and Myra at the helm, plunging down the street at a furious pace, and off into the distance."[22]

Once again, *The Cave Man* exposes (admittedly, through the lens of comedy) the unfairness of capitalism and the cruelty of the entitled wealthy, while championing the downtrodden laboring class. Numerous reviewers compared Milestone's directing style to that of F. W. Murnau and Ernst Lubitsch, two other masters of social satire with a romantic twist. Lubitsch, just three years older than Milestone, had arrived in Hollywood from Berlin in 1922, and they met soon afterward. As Milestone later recalled, Lubitsch "was a very good friend of mine because he first arrived when I was cutting at Warner Brothers. . . . I was sitting in the vestibule of the studio on Sunset Boulevard when Lubitsch arrived. Somebody mentioned his name and looked at him as he passed by and said, 'Just arrived from Germany, huh? Clothes by Krupp?' Lubitsch wore a horrible-looking suit."[23]

The Cave Man also introduced to the screen in the role of Myra's maid a young actress, Myrna Loy, who would go on to a long and brilliant career; she would also work with Milestone again years later, on *The Red Pony*. Like *Seven Sinners*, *The Cave Man* was a solid success both critically and financially.

By now Warners had recognized that Milestone was a valuable and bankable asset—so valuable, in fact, that he could be lent out to other studios at a profit. His editing skills were particularly prized. As one reporter noted: "He was a cutter, but not just an ordinary cutter. Directors called him 'the constructive cutter' because of the adroit way he could tighten up their stories. Many times it was generally known that he went out and directed extra scenes to bolster up a sagging story but you could never get him to admit it. Far from being a credit grabber, he modestly discredited the stories of how he was really responsible for the good touches in many films."[24]

In 1926 Warners lent Milestone to Paramount Studios to work on a comedy with one of the biggest stars of the silent cinema, Harold Lloyd; they had worked together several years earlier at Keystone. For Milestone's work as director, Warners was to receive $1,500 a week from Paramount— but Milestone was to receive only his usual $400 a week.

When Milestone discovered this discrepancy, he demanded to be paid the difference, but Warners refused. Angry and offended, Milestone walked out and broke his contract with Warner Bros. after only four days of work on the film (originally entitled *The Mountain Man*, it was eventually released as *The Kid Brother*). Warners responded immediately by suing Milestone for $200,000 and asking for an injunction preventing him from working with any other producers for the next four years of the original contract period.[25] In the *Hollywood Filmograph*, a writer asked:

What is to become of our congenial Lewis Milestone who just walked out of the job of directing Harold Lloyd owing to a difference with his bosses, Warner Bros.? Ordinarily no director would walk out on Harold and many would give their right hand to direct him. But be this as it may, it's the talk of the town. Some say that "Lew" was wise in so doing, others say he was wrong. It remains to be seen. At any rate it doesn't pay any director to stay off the screen any more than it pays an actor to remain idle and not be seen on the silver sheet.[26]

In the end, Warners prevailed and Milestone lost the suit, in a vivid exhibition of the enormous power that the studios wielded over their employees during this early period in Hollywood. A story published immediately after the verdict in *Variety* claimed that "Milestone will not endeavor to obtain more work in America. He is planning to leave next week for Europe where he will remain for four years or until such period as the Warners claim he was under contract. It is understood Milestone is figuring on directing for UFA in Germany."[27] (This did not happen.) Having been through many reversals in the past, Milestone did not lose heart. He declared bankruptcy, temporarily modified "his newly acquired taste for good living," and within months he was back at work, this time at Paramount.[28] Apparently, Warners did not carry out their threat to pursue legal action against other studios that employed Milestone.

During this period, he lived "in a couple of rooms" with his friends Myron and David Selznick. Myron would later become a Hollywood agent, and Milestone his first client.[29] David would later become one of the most powerful producers in Hollywood history, with such credits as *King Kong* and *Gone with the Wind*.[30]

This was only the first of many battles the fiercely independent Milestone would wage with corporate Hollywood in these years, and it established him as a maverick unafraid to challenge the industry status quo.[31] As Milestone explained years later, "I'd become a slave to Warner Brothers, and something in my nature rebelled against that lowly status."[32] Nor would this be the last time he would be blacklisted. Perhaps in an attempt to protect his reputation, Milestone put out the story that the reason he broke his contract with Warners was that they had failed to send him his paychecks while he was working at Paramount. In any case, the incident—and his willingness to stand up to the absolute power wielded by the studio bosses—seems only to have increased his personal and artistic stature in the film community, and especially among other creative people. Producers, however, considered him a difficult troublemaker. Milestone's behavior led a certain "leading producer" to tell the Hollywood columnist Jim Tully that "Milestone would wreck any company to have his own way."[33]

Through the star of *The Cave Man*, Matt Moore, Milestone met the actor Thomas Meighan, who, as Milestone remembered years later, "was at a crucial stage in his career because his contract was about to expire and he had nothing to go on to negotiate a new one." Meighan already had the idea for a new project—*The New Klondike*—based on a story by Ring Lardner about the 1920s real estate boom in Florida. With the producer Tom Geraghty, a former journalist, Milestone traveled with a crew of forty to Miami, where they researched sites and developed the concept into a script. "When we arrived we found they were selling real estate off pushcarts. Men were going through the streets ringing a big bell, and they sold you a lot right off the back of the cart from a map spread out between two sticks. When you went there you sometimes found the land still under water, not yet pumped up." To house the crew, they set up cots in a garage.[34]

Location shooting was still a rarity at the time, and it gives the film an undeniable authenticity and immediacy. Meighan played a washed-up baseball player dropped from his team in spring training. To reverse his fortunes, he turns to real estate. Although initially successful, he is swindled into buying a swamp. But in the end he gets his money back, wins the girl, and even gets hired as the manager of the baseball team that fired him. Like *Cave Man*, the story critiques the excesses of capitalism and the victimization of the ordinary Joe. In a particularly successful scene, a player rounds the bases unnoticed by the members of the opposing team, who are engrossed in studying maps of local properties for sale. The reviews were generally positive: "Lewis Milestone, a new young director, wielded the megaphone and got some of the best and most interesting 'touches' we have seen in a picture in a long time."[35] Meighan was also apparently happy with the project, since he and Milestone would work again together on *The Racket* two years later.

Also for Paramount, Milestone later in 1926 began working on another comedy, *Fine Manners*, with the megastar Gloria Swanson. But he and Swanson argued over the script. "She was being advised by a lot of

Yale boys, and they kept stressing the fact that they were Yale men—practically college professors—and I was not." When Swanson refused to accept his revisions, Milestone left the project. It also irked Milestone that Swanson was getting the enormous sum of $22,000 a week, "and I still wore a hand-me-down suit."[36]

At this rather perilous moment in Milestone's career, when studios and producers were wary of engaging him for fear of incurring the wrath of Warner Bros., an unlikely savior came to the rescue: the oil tycoon Howard Hughes. The twenty-year-old Hughes had moved to Los Angeles in 1925 with his new wife, Ella, having recently inherited his father's substantial fortune. Eager to prove himself in the glamorous world of the movies, he plunged into the business with characteristic bravado. His first effort was a comedy, *Everybody's Acting,* directed by Milestone's acquaintance Marshall Neilan, which turned a modest profit after its release in 1926.

Early in 1927 Hughes met Milestone at a Charleston dance party at the Ambassador Hotel, one of Hughes's favorite Los Angeles haunts. At the time, Hughes was already obsessed with the world of aviation, and he was impressed that Milestone knew quite a lot about it from his time in the U.S. Army. According to Hughes's biographer Charles Higham, Milestone proceeded to persuade him to back a new project that he wanted to shoot, a wartime adventure-comedy titled *Two Arabian Knights.* They obtained the rights to the story from Jesse L. Lasky. Through his lawyer Neil S. McCarthy, Hughes signed Milestone to a three-picture contract with his film production enterprise, the Caddo Company.[37] It would prove to be a beneficial deal for both parties, and it produced three features over the next four years that were successful both financially and artistically: *Two Arabian Knights, The Racket,* and *The Front Page.* All three were nominated for Academy Awards.

In his 1932 story "The Boy Pirate," the writer Ben Hecht, Milestone's friend and frequent literary collaborator, described Hughes's arrival in Hollywood with his usual cynical eye. "When Phillip Warrren [Howard Hughes] came to Hollywood and announced his entry on a large scale as a producer of motion pictures, the czars and sachems of that fabulous town smacked their lips as if confronted by a large succulent herring, winked knowingly at their subsidiary potentates and fell to day dreaming. The arrival in Hollywood of so famous a bankroll was regarded as legitimate manna. . . . He turned out to be a tall, lean aimless looking bonanza with a certain callow and effacive charm, a high-pitched, indecisive voice and full of a peculiar wall-flower modesty."[38]

The Hughes-Milestone partnership emerged at a crucial moment for both men. New to Los Angeles and the movies, Hughes needed to find a director with a strong artistic reputation and experience in the business. Milestone needed a new backer, and preferably one without a lot of baggage in the world of studio politics following his highly publicized legal problems with Warner Bros. As Milestone said later, "Since Howard Hughes was at that time a young producer just coming into the business, he didn't have to respect any agreement that the other producers had among themselves."[39] Milestone, usually a defender of the common working man, was apparently willing to overlook the fact that Hughes belonged to the American capitalist elite. At this early point in his career, Hughes was rather apolitical and not yet the active and outspoken anti-Communist he would later become.[40]

When interviewed by the *Los Angeles Times* at the time of Hughes's death, in 1978, Milestone recalled that he was "one of the young Texan's first friends in Hollywood." The interviewer continued: "Milestone thinks Hollywood was a kind of 'classroom' for Hughes, where young Howard, still called 'Sonny' by his family, learned to fight off their influence. His relatives, Milestone recalls, warned him he was going to lose all his money. 'They obviously didn't know their own relative,' continues Milestone, who, having directed a half-dozen or so pictures for Hughes, must have learned something about his psychology. 'All Howard needed was for someone to say he couldn't do something. Then he'd spend a fortune proving that they were wrong, and he was right.'"[41]

Hughes put $500,000 of his own money into the production of *Two Arabian Knights*, a rather large budget for the time. The subject of the film was frankly derivative of a 1924 Broadway hit play, *What Price Glory?*, by Maxwell Anderson and Laurence Stallings, adapted for film in 1926 by the director Raoul Walsh. Milestone even used one of the screenwriters of Walsh's film, James O'Donohue, along with Wallace Smith, to adapt a story by Donald McGibney. Set during World War I, the comedy revolves around the rivalry between two American soldiers—a working-class Irish sergeant (Peter O'Gaffney) and an upper-class private from Philadelphia (W. Daingerfield Phelps III)—for the affections of a young Arabian princess (Mirza) they meet on a steamer to Constantinople after escaping in disguise (as Arab POWs) from a German POW camp. Arriving at Jaffa, they engage in various escapades, outsmarting the girl's father, her fiancé, and other villains. In the end the three of them manage to escape in a carriage driven by O'Gaffney.

Mary Astor, then an ingenue twenty years old, took the role of the princess. The well-known stage actor Louis Wolheim (he had appeared in the Broadway production of *What Price Glory?*) was the coarse, world-weary sergeant (a role he would repeat in *All Quiet on the Western Front*). William Boyd (later to become famous as Hopalong Cassidy) played the handsome, brainy private. Several other recent Russian émigré actors took small parts. Michael Vavitch, born, like Milestone, in Odessa, played the role of Mirza's father, the Emir, and Michael Visaroff brought a zany humor to his scenes as the ship's leering, pipe-smoking captain. The English actor Boris Karloff, soon to become famous for his roles in horror films, appears briefly as the ship's purser.

Two Arabian Knights represents a significant artistic advance over Milestone's previous films. The camera work is more original and ambitious, including a dazzling overhead circular shot of the two protagonists being captured in a trench at the front, surrounded by a row of rifles pointing at them. There are numerous large crowd scenes, such as the city square in Arabia filled with Muslims whose praying allows the two Americans to escape. Sight gags abound. The two Americans manage to escape from the POW camp by robbing two Arab prisoners of their white robes, which help them hide undetected in the snow. When they have to jump into a cold stream, the robes freeze into hoop skirts that later defrost, leading the German guards to think the men are urinating.

But what distinguishes the film is the real on-camera chemistry between Astor and Boyd. Their characters meet when Mirza has been cast into the sea from the small boat in which she and her attendants are sailing. When retrieved from the water by two nearby valiant Americans and brought on deck, she wears a veil concealing nearly her entire face. At first both men try to win her affections, but O'Gaffney's crude attempts at wooing fail. His coarse remarks (conveyed in titles) about her appearance are frankly sexist and offensive: "If the face is anything like the chassis—me for her!" and "I wish I could tell you in Arabic what I think of you in English." It turns out, of course, that Mirza is fluent in English, having been educated in Constantinople, and much more susceptible to the suave charms of Boyd's college graduate. They fall for each other during an extended close-up scene. Daingerfield Phelps plays with her veil, finally persuading her to let it fall, revealing her lovely face and mouth. Their interaction packs a real erotic punch and sets up the rest of the film's action.

Other "off-color sexual gags" were added, according to Milestone, at the suggestion of Hughes.[42] In one scene, Wolheim tries to milk a goat, but he discovers the animal is male. Much cheap humor is generated from the presence of Mirza's manservant (played by another Russian character actor, Nicholas Dunaev), who is a eunuch. This serves as an unending source of amazement to O'Gaffney, who assumes a look of exaggerated sympathy and pity whenever he sees him—a gag that serves as the last shot of the film as well. In one of the POW scenes, the prisoners are deloused in showers, and we see numerous naked male bottoms pass by at the back of the shot.

In essence, *Two Arabian Knights* is a buddy movie. The joking, competitive, physical relationship between O'Gaffney (the earthy, crude proletarian, known for playing confidence games on unsuspecting ladies back home) and Phelps (the sensitive, intellectual artist who draws caricatures in his spare time) drives the narrative. They become fast friends at the outset when they return to each other items taken from them by the Germans, which they later pickpocketed from their guards. These two optimistic, never-say-die Americans triumph over every adversity, and in the familiar tradition of Orientalism they show up the rigid, wicked, bumbling Arabs as inferior beings who are easily outsmarted. When they find the American consulate, O'Gaffney reads from the flag and declares: "*E pluribus unum!* That means you eat!"

The film has no shortage of American patriotic chauvinism and racism, especially in its representation of Mirza's evil fiancé (who loses her in a climactic sword fight with Phelps) and her hierarchical father. In the end, Mirza vastly prefers the freedom and fun offered by the two Americans. Ever the good sport despite his gruff manners, O'Gaffney is even able to overcome his own disappointment at losing her to Phelps, and he is content to assume the role of loyal sidekick as he drives their carriage into a happy ending.

Hughes pressed Milestone to make the film look rough and realistic. The script called for Mary Astor to be fished from the sea onto the steamer, nearly drowning. The scene was shot not in a studio tank, but in the polluted, cold waters of San Pedro Harbor south of Los Angeles. Astor was dunked repeatedly in her heavy gold-beaded gown even though she could hardly swim. Milestone recalled, "The crew pulled her back, time and time again, dripping wet; they gave her shots of brandy, and Hughes massaged her—with understandable enthusiasm, since she was gorgeous—and then dunked her again." He reported years later that Hughes so enjoyed this sequence that he would view and review it with voyeuristic pleasure in his private screening room in the early hours of the morning.[43]

The crew spent more than eleven weeks in Truckee, California, near the Nevada border, to shoot the few scenes requiring snow. Hughes spared no expense during the shooting, which was extended by several weeks at Milestone's request. Each day Hughes would go to the set wearing a new outfit, eager to learn about the movie business.[44] According to a report in *Variety,* "After the picture was completed and previewed, Hughes tendered a banquet to the entire production company and cast at the Cocoanut Grove in the Ambassador Hotel, Los Angeles, and is said to have given presents to each one present which totaled around $10,000."[45]

To Hughes's delight, *Two Arabian Knights* (financed by Hughes but distributed by the new independent consortium United Artists) turned out to be a huge hit with audiences and critics. Hughes's accountant, Noah Dietrich, reported that the film turned a handsome profit of $614,000.[46] The premiere in Los Angeles was one of the most glamorous events of the season, "one of those friendly, home-town-boy-makes-good occasions, as everyone had known and plugged for Lewis Milestone, the director, ever since he was a cutter years ago. Of course, he isn't really a local product—he's Russian—but he has been around the studios for so long that everyone looks upon him as one of the film colony's own sons. . . . You should have seen the clothes that night!"[47] According to *Photoplay* magazine, Milestone was so excited at the opening that "he arrived with a party of twenty celebrities more than thirty minutes late, dug in his pockets and found he had forgotten his tickets." Since all the seats were occupied, Milestone "stood dejectedly in the rear of the building and watched his picture carry the crowd into roars of laughter, while he remembered with longing the irresponsibilities of being a whistling cutting-boy."[48]

Two Arabian Knights established Milestone as a director particularly gifted in portraying the wide range of emotions and adventures associated with war onscreen, and especially the dynamics of friendship that developed between soldiers in wartime.

Later in 1927, Hughes lent Milestone out to a project that had originally been developed by Joseph M. Schenck, president of United Artists, with the legendary Russian stage director and writer Vladimir Nemirovich-Danchenko during his sojourn in Hollywood in 1926–27. From the beginning, *The Tempest* was intended primarily as a vehicle for John Barrymore. Set in Russia around the time of the Bolshevik Revolution, it focuses on a soldier-turned-revolutionary who betrays his political ideals for love. Dramatic films about the fall of the Romanovs and the resulting turmoil (such as Josef von Sternberg's 1928 *The Last Command*) were quite popular in Hollywood at the time. But Barrymore, eager to be shown in a heroic light, disagreed with Nemirovich-Danchenko about the script, and production was repeatedly delayed.

Finally the Russian émigré director Viktor Tourjansky was engaged, then quickly replaced by Milestone and finally by Sam Taylor. The screenplay was revised at least five times, leading to near chaos on the set. "There were days of complete confusion, when the shooting was being directed simultaneously by Tourjansky, Milestone, Schenck's representative Considine, Barrymore, Taylor and even on the telephone by the director von Stroheim, who was working for another studio."[49] Milestone's contribution was minimal.

Much more successful was Milestone's direction in 1928 of the charming romantic comedy *The Garden of Eden*. Shot to a screenplay adapted by Hans Kraly from a popular Viennese play, it bears a strong resemblance to the kind of scripts Kraly had been creating for Ernst Lubitsch, such as *Kiss Me Again* and *So This Is Paris*. Yet another iteration of the timeless Cinderella story, it starred the popular Corinne Griffith as a poor aspiring opera singer who is befriended by a fairy godmother (the venerable Louise Dresser) in the guise of a wardrobe mistress/baroness. Once a year, the baroness spends all her money on a lavish vacation at the Hotel Eden in Monte Carlo. Taking pity on the young singer, she invites her to join her. At the hotel the singer meets a handsome young man (Charles Ray). After numerous humorous misunderstandings, obstacles to their romance are overcome.

Milestone makes clever use of sight gags, particularly the flashing of electric lights switching off and on as secret signals for the lovers. Tart, well-paced, and a bit risqué, with lavish art direction by William Cameron Menzies and nicely nuanced performances from all the principals, *The Garden of Eden* is perhaps Milestone's most successful romantic comedy, without the heaviness and longueurs of such later efforts as *The Captain Hates the Sea*. It was a commercial success, earning more than $750,000 for United Artists, and has remained the most popular and enduring of all of Milestone's silent features.[50]

As Betty Colfax wrote of *The Garden of Eden* in *New York Graphic*: "With Milestone, who is fast reaching the front ranks of Hollywood's best directorial talent, it is no haphazard use of unique camera angles, no momentary shot of satirical purpose. His whole picture is distinguished by an individuality of treatment, a smoothness of action that works as an asset not only for the star but for the entire cast."[51]

Milestone's next film, *The Racket*, also produced by Howard Hughes for Paramount, was something entirely different: a tough crime drama about police corruption and bootlegging in Chicago. All three of its stars had previously worked with Milestone, who always enjoyed a strong reputation as a director sympathetic to actors. Thomas Meighan was cast as the mostly honest Chicago Captain McQuigg, manipulated by crooked politicians; Louis Wolheim as Nick Scarsi, hard-bitten kingpin of the bootleggers; and Marie Prevost as Helen Hayes, a whorish chorus girl with a heart of gold. The screenplay adapted the Chicago society reporter Bartlett Cormack's Broadway play of the same title, which Milestone had seen in New York. According to a report in the *Los Angeles Record*, the film employed a thousand extras for the mob scenes, which were filmed in Westwood, where "an entire section of a metropolitan city has been reconstructed."[52]

Milestone uses startling, gruesome lighting effects achieved by the cinematographer Tony Gaudio to convey the claustrophobic, dark underworld atmosphere. In one memorable scene, at the funeral of a man Scarsi has killed, we see guns concealed under the hats of the seated mourners, in a clever double-exposure shot. In its portrayal of journalists as often drunk, gullible, corruptible, and eager for the next sensational scoop, *The Racket* prefigures *The Front Page*. The only exception is a baby-faced cub reporter (John Darrow) just arrived from Omaha, who has a boyish crush on Helen Hayes. When he continues to show his naive affection, she cracks: "Didn't your mother tell you not to speak to strange ladies?" Politicians, too, including the district attorney, are shown as corrupt, subject to blackmail, and afraid to challenge the power of the mob, here known as "The Organization." Although in the end Scarsi is killed and justice prevails, the message of *The Racket* is profoundly cynical and dark. Critics considered it among the best of the many gangster films made in the late 1920s.

Milestone's business relationship with Hughes proved to be advantageous, as one Hollywood observer noted: "With young Howard Hughes, who has more wealth than some of our most extravagant companies have spent in three years, Milestone has rather a free hand."[53] Under the terms of a renegotiated contract, Milestone was to receive half of the fee that Hughes received for lending him to other studios. His basic salary was the large sum of $1,500 per week. Milestone told an interviewer later that he had been approached at the time to do a picture for Sam Goldwyn, and he demanded $5,000 a week. Goldwyn refused and even threatened to blackball him in the industry. "'Look,' I said, 'this is getting boring, this goddam story: everybody threatens you with blackballing. I'm an expert on that now—Warner Brothers blackballed me, the whole Producers' Association blackballed me. Blackball me! I'm not scared. Now I don't want to do a picture with you even if you meet my terms!' And I walked out of his office."[54]

His rift with Goldwyn, Milestone claimed, led other producers to learn that he was available. One of these was B. P. Schulberg, head of production at Paramount, who offered him another project. This would be his last silent film, *Betrayal*. The impressive cast included the German icon Emil Jannings, regarded as the greatest actor of the late silent era, and Gary Cooper, by then an established screen idol from *Wings* and eighteen other films. Despite the assembled talent, problems plagued the film from the start. It was intended to be Jannings's first sound film after five silents in Hollywood (including the fine *Last Command*, directed by Milestone's army buddy Josef von Sternberg), but his heavy German accent proved incomprehensible to audiences in test screenings. In the end, *Betrayal* was released as a silent film, with some synchronized music and sound effects. (In the late 1920s virtually all talking pictures were also released in silent versions, since many movie theaters, especially those in rural areas, did not yet have the expensive and complicated sound technology necessary to screen them.)

It didn't help that the melodramatic screenplay, by Hans Kraly (who had also written *The Garden of Eden*) provided only sketchy characterizations of the main characters. Jannings played the mayor of a Swiss Alpine village who marries a local beauty (Esther Ralston), unaware that she is already pregnant by a bohemian artist, Andre (Cooper). Andre returns and tries to persuade the girl to run away with him, but he manages instead to kill her and fatally injure himself in a toboggan accident.

Meanwhile, the mayor has come to believe that his own son is the father of one of his wife's children. Some scenes were shot at Lake Tahoe, but others done in the studio look obviously fake, and the film (Jannings's last Hollywood effort) was a box-office disaster.

The main problem was that Milestone found it very difficult to work with the egomaniacal Jannings. "He would cry real tears at the drop of a hat, whenever he was presented with some obstacle that displeased him. I knew that trick and I could perform it just as well as he could. Any time he cried, I cried with him. As a result he stopped, cut it out completely."[55] "You had to know how to handle him. Like most Germans, he could understand a shout, bark or command, but if you tried to be a gentleman with him he would mistake it for weakness. He always referred to himself in the third person. If he asked you to lunch, and they served soup, he would taste the soup and say: 'That's wonderful soup—the best thing for Emil.' And he kept telling you that if it was good for him it must be good for everybody."[56]

But working with Gary Cooper was a different matter. "With Gary, all you had to do was to put him some place—on a chair, or in bed—light him, and tell him what he was supposed to think about. . . . He was so photogenic it was fantastic. There were no broad gestures in *The Betrayal*. We tried to stay on the subtle side, and yet Gary Cooper's personality would always come through. He was excellent. He was a natural screen personality."[57]

By 1929 sound had taken over the film industry. At first primitive, sound technology developed rapidly from the groundbreaking immigrant drama *The Jazz Singer* in 1927, a combination silent and sound film, to Rouben Mamoulian's much more sophisticated *Applause* in 1929. Milestone's first entry into the sound film world was not auspicious. *New York Nights*, produced in 1929 by Joseph Schenck for United Artists, with his wife, Norma Talmadge, in the leading role, attempted to fuse a gangster film with a backstage musical—with decidedly mixed results. Like many early sound films, it was shot with a single stationary camera, the actors all too obviously speaking with exaggerated elocution into hidden microphones. According to Milestone, one of the producers also "injected himself into the editing—or re-editing—of the picture. His revisions didn't meet with my approval, so I asked him to remove my name from the screen."[58] Milestone's name did remain on the film, however. Despite its shortcomings, *New York Nights*, released in December 1929, grossed $711,838 in the United States.[59]

But the most important event of 1929 for Milestone had taken place seven months earlier. At the very first Academy Awards ceremony, held in the Blossom Room of the Hollywood Roosevelt Hotel on May 16, 1929, his 1927 film *Two Arabian Knights* received an Academy Award. In a letter sent from the Academy of Motion Picture Arts and Sciences (AMPAS) a few months earlier, Milestone had been informed that he would receive what would become a symbol of the Academy: an "artistic statuette of bronze and gold."[60] AMPAS had been established only two years earlier, to promote the idea of motion pictures as a serious art form. Milestone was present to accept the award for *Two Arabian Knights* for Best Comedy Direction, a category that would be eliminated after this first year's award ceremony. Subsequently, only one award was given for Best Direction, and no distinction was made between comedy and drama.

The atmosphere at the awards party was intimate and familial, as only 270 invited guests were in attendance. After a fancy dinner, the Academy's President Douglas Fairbanks handed out the statuettes. In fact, *Two Arabian Knights* was not the only Milestone film made with financing from Hughes's upstart Caddo Company that was nominated this first year. *The Racket,* released in 1928, was nominated for Outstanding Picture, but it lost out to *Wings.* (The first Academy Awards ceremony honored films made from 1927 to 1929.) Despite his squabbles with studios, producers and stars, Millie had become an industry insider, one of the founding fathers of the movie business.

3

"The Greatest Picture Ever Made"

I don't want to marry pictures, I just want to live with them.
—*Lewis Milestone*

During the filming of *New York Nights* in 1929, one of the actors gave Milestone a book that would change both his professional and personal life: *All Quiet on the Western Front*.

First published in serial form in a German journal in 1928 as *Im Westen nichts Neues* (literally, *Nothing New on the Western Front*), Erich Maria Remarque's gritty antiwar novel depicted the horrors of World War I combat from the viewpoint of a group of "average" young soldiers in the German army. It became an immediate global best seller. Within fifteen months of its appearance in book form in early 1929, over two million copies were in print around the world. Twenty translations had appeared by May 1930. So enormous was the novel's significance that Remarque was even nominated for the Nobel Peace Prize in 1931.

Although many books dealing with the lasting psychic damage the war inflicted on soldiers were appearing around the same time (including Ernest Hemingway's *A Farewell to Arms*), *All Quiet on the Western Front* (as translated into English by A. W. Wheen) resonated with readers—and especially with war veterans—for its uncompromising refusal to romanticize the conflict. Considered by many critics to be the most powerful antiwar novel ever written, it demythologized front-line combat and conveyed the utter senselessness of the suffering and trauma endured by its participants. Even more important, *All Quiet* showed how difficult it was for those who fought to reenter civilian life, how their souls had been irreparably damaged by the experience of war.

Just three years younger than Milestone, Erich Maria Remarque (1898–1970) grew up in Germany and was drafted into the army at age seventeen. A committed pacifist, he never actually served at the front—like Milestone. But his experiences in the war (including an extended period of hospitalization) only strengthened his antiwar views and gave him a deep understanding of the difficulties veterans faced in the aftermath of war.

> Our generation has grown up in a different way from all others before and afterward. Their one great and most important experience was the war. No matter whether they approved or rejected it; whether they understood it from a nationalistic, pacifistic, adventurous, religious, or stoic point of view. They saw blood, horror, annihilation, struggle, and death. . . . I [have] avoided taking sides from every political, social, religious or other point of view. . . . I have spoken only of the terror, of the horror, of the desperate, often brutal impulses of self-preservation, of the tenacious hold on life, face to face with death and annihilation.[1]

Remarque, already the author of two rather unsuccessful published novels, finished *All Quiet* in a mere six weeks, working at night while holding a full-time position as a magazine editor. On the first page, he wrote that his goal was simply "to tell of a generation of men who, even though they may have escaped shells, were destroyed by the war."[2] The novel is narrated in the first-person voice by Paul Bäumer, a sensitive gymnasium student and aspiring poet who is sent off to war with his hometown buddies. Their authority figures (teachers, policemen, parents, government officials) for the most part are portrayed as nationalistic and vain, willing to send their students and sons off to fight without considering the consequences. "We had fancied our task would be different, only to find we were to be trained for heroism as though we were circus-ponies."[3] As the novel progresses, Paul loses his comrades to wounds, death, and madness, and he becomes increasingly unsure why he is fighting "enemies" who have done him no personal wrong. On the last page, Paul is killed, in October 1918, just one month before the Armistice that ended the war, "on a day that was so quiet and still on the whole front, that the army report confined itself to the single sentence: All quiet on the Western Front."[4]

Two of the most powerful scenes in the novel (both included in the film) show Paul's interaction with the French "enemy." With his friends, he swims across a river to a French village where they meet a group of

French girls who offer food, shelter, and sexual comfort. Their national differences disappear as they embrace: "The words of this foreign tongue, that I hardly understand, they caress me to a quietness, in which the room grows dim, and dissolves in the half light, only the face above me lives and is clear."[5] Later, Paul is trapped in a foxhole with a French soldier whom he has stabbed and mortally wounded. Because of the incessant machine-gun fire, he is unable to escape and must stare at the man for hours as he slowly dies in agony. Desperate, Paul goes through the soldier's papers and imagines his life in France with his family. "Why do they never tell us that you are poor devils like us, that your mothers are just as anxious as ours, and that we have the same fear of death, and the same dying and the same agony—Forgive me, comrade; how could you be my enemy?"[6]

Given its enormous popularity and topicality, *All Quiet on the Western Front* was bound to attract the attention of Hollywood producers and studios. By this time, films about World War I (*The Big Parade, Wings,* Howard Hughes's aviation spectacular *Hell's Angels, The Dawn Patrol*) had proven to be successful at the box office. Carl Laemmle, president and founder of Universal Pictures, and his son, Carl Laemmle Jr., were particularly enthusiastic about the potential appeal of a film version of Remarque's novel. Like Milestone, Laemmle was a Jewish immigrant to the United States (from Germany), who had worked his way up from nothing to become one of the most powerful men in the American film industry. One of Universal's representatives in Berlin had recommended *All Quiet* to Laemmle and obtained an option for the rights.[7] Laemmle and his son, recently appointed as the studio's new head of production at age twenty-one, encountered considerable resistance from Universal executives opposed to the project, considered to be too bleak and depressing. They were also concerned that American audiences would not want to see a German view of the war, and that the story lacked romance and female presence.

But the Laemmles were insistent. Carl Jr. saw the project as an opportunity to launch his new career with the sort of big-budget feature Universal had not yet attempted. And his father strongly believed in the importance of the novel's message, as he wrote in a column in the studio's newsletter:

> Nothing like it has ever been done before. It is not a sermon or a preachment, but a simple record of war in its most intimate

close-ups—and its very simplicity and lack of adornment make it all the more gripping. . . . The world will discuss *All Quiet on the Western Front* for generations to come. It will sink into the consciousness of men and nations. . . . Read it regardless of our business interest. Read it, and once having read it, I defy you to put it out of your mind. It will start your thoughts flowing in a new direction![8]

So the Laemmles pushed the project through despite the objections of the Universal board—a decision they would never regret. Indeed, Carl Laemmle Sr. later called the film "his greatest achievement."[9] Making *All Quiet* also turned him into a committed pacifist.

Milestone was not the Laemmles' first choice to direct. Paul Fejos and Herbert Brenon were both considered and then dropped. Given his previous experience in directing a highly successful film about World War I, *Two Arabian Knights*, Milestone was a logical candidate for the job. It seems that Laemmle, a strong and independent personality, also respected Milestone's work and his reputation as an artist with principles. Milestone received the large sum of $5,000 per week during fourteen weeks of shooting, which made him a wealthy man. Originally budgeted at $891,000, the film eventually cost more than $1.4 million to make, a significant sum for the time.[10]

By the time Universal hired Milestone, the playwright Maxwell Anderson had already been brought on to prepare the screenplay from Remarque's book. Remarque had chosen not to participate. Anderson (1888–1959) was a natural choice, since he had recently collaborated with Laurence Stallings on the 1924 Broadway hit *What Price Glory?*—another World War I story, filmed in 1926 by Raoul Walsh. Anderson was working from a scenario adapted from Remarque's novel by the author C. Gardner Sullivan. Later Laemmle brought on the editor Del Andrews (who had acted as Milestone's mentor in his early Hollywood career) and the playwright George Abbott to work with Anderson and Milestone.

But Milestone, who had strong literary tastes and instincts, was unhappy with what Anderson, a neophyte in the movie business, was turning out. Anderson "came out to Hollywood, as they all do, to grab a little money," Milestone observed with his characteristic candor.[11] He found Anderson's version far too "pedestrian" and "sentimental" for Remarque's hard-hitting story.[12] Milestone and Andrews decided to rent a house on Catalina Island, just offshore from Los Angeles, and assemble the screenwriting team there, so they could work without distractions. For Milestone, the story was always the key to a successful film, as he later told a reporter from the *New York Herald Tribune,* "The story is the most important actor in making a film, and in direction, the use of the camera."[13] Anderson tore up his original script. Milestone told him: "'Get your secretary, go out for a swim, have some fun, and we'll get together tomorrow and decide on a working schedule. You can stay here as long as you wish—there's plenty of room, you can go out on a boat ride, you can do anything you want. Don't rush.' He was delighted with the arrangement."

What Milestone wanted Anderson to do, with his experience as a playwright, was to provide dialogue for the episodes selected to be filmed. "You take the scene, and if you think you can use it, blow the breath of life into it by dialoguing it. Then we'll put the two things together."[14]

Another promising newcomer to Hollywood joined the group in Catalina as dialogue director: George Cukor, hired on the recommendation of David Selznick. Born into a Hungarian Jewish immigrant family in New York, Cukor (1899–1983) started out on Broadway but would eventually become one of the industry's most successful directors (*David Copperfield, Camille, The Women, The Philadelphia Story, A Star Is Born, My Fair Lady*) and one of Milestone's lifelong friends. His work on *All Quiet* was his first serious credit in the business.

In the end, the screenwriting team produced what Andrew Kelly has described as "probably the best script of the early sound period."[15] (The final credit line read, "Screen story by George Abbott, Adaptation by Maxwell Anderson, Dialogue by Maxwell Anderson and George Abbott.")[16] The screenplay addresses all the important themes treated in Remarque's novel: the portrayal of the enemy as a comrade; the brutality of militarism; the horrendous slaughter of trench warfare; the betrayal of the nation's youth by the old men in power; the incompetence of the military command; the suffering of those left behind at home, particularly mothers and wives; the lasting psychic damage inflicted on those who engaged in combat and killing.

Milestone and his team gave the story a brilliant visual interpretation. One of the best examples is the film's opening, a panoramic episode (equipped, as we will see, with brilliant sound design) set on the eve of the war in the town where Paul and his friends live, rather than at the front, as in the novel. This change allowed Milestone to show the frantic nationalism that propels the teacher and others to send the boys off to their almost certain deaths. This scene is later echoed when a desolate Paul returns home on leave and speaks to younger students at his former school, warning them against a romantic view of warfare—a scene absent in the novel. As in the novel, the film's main character and narrator is Paul, whose point of view the camera follows throughout. "Remarque wrote the book in the first person singular," Milestone later told Kevin Brownlow. "So therefore the central character was telling the story. So he actually was like a camera—the camera sees everything but can't look at itself."[17]

Milestone also found a central symbol that helps drive the narrative forward and illustrates the carnage and senselessness of war: boots. Kemmerich, the first member of Paul's group to die, leaves behind a fine pair of boots. These boots are then passed on to other members of the group (first Müller, then Peter, then Albert), who also die in rapid succession. "I hit on the idea of using the boots as they pass from one man to another to get rid of secondary characters, to condense things in the dramatization and to push the picture forward: as one guy wears them and is shot, we go to the boots and come up to another guy, like a montage."[18]

The film's most important departure from the novel is the celebrated ending. In the final chapter, Remarque shows Paul recovering on a brief leave from a gas attack. He is the last of his group of seven classmates to survive. He reflects on his damaged soul and what awaits him after the war: "We will be superfluous even to ourselves, we will grow older, a few will adapt themselves, some others will merely submit, and most will be bewildered;—the years will pass by and in the end we shall fall into ruin."[19] On the novel's final page, without a chapter heading, the narration changes abruptly from first person to third person, in the form of a report, to deliver the news of Paul's death in two short paragraphs that end this way: "He had fallen forward and lay on the earth as though sleeping. Turning him over one saw that he could not have suffered long; his face had an expression of calm, as though almost glad the end had come."[20]

This quiet, undramatic ending did not work on film. "I must have shot six or seven or maybe eight endings," Milestone later remembered. "And none of them worked. I kept throwing them away."[21] He finally found the solution in a conversation with the Czech cinematographer Karl Freund. They were driving in the rain to the Universal studio in Culver City, with the windshield wipers going. For some reason, Freund was repeating in rhythm with the wipers the German word *schmetterling*—"butterfly." He told Milestone that the ending should be "as simple as a butterfly." "That's when the blind spot fell from my eyes. I immediately realized that my mistake was in trying to go for a crescendo and top the whole picture with a final scene."[22]

Milestone also recalled that in the novel, Paul is an avid collector of butterflies, and he decided to use butterflies as a unifying symbol in the film. So he and Freund came up with the idea for the poetic final scene. In the trenches, Paul looks out to no-man's-land and sees a butterfly land "on an empty tin. . . . He can't reach out with an aggressive movement; he's got to reach out with an open palm, in the hope that maybe the butterfly will land in his hand. . . . So he decides to leave his spot and go out of the trench and come around to where he can get the butterfly. While he's moving there we show the first menace, the sniper, taking his time aiming a potshot at Paul. As Paul comes out the sniper fixes him through his B-sights. We'll cut to him again, and finally when Paul's just about to reach the butterfly the guy pulls the trigger and the hand dies. It's going to be my hand; I don't want any actor to do it, I'll do that myself."[23] The sound of a lone harmonica (heard occasionally throughout the film) accompanies the scene, playing a nostalgic tune. Here it intensifies the delicate, tragic pathos of the moment.

And, in fact, the hand we see in that shot is Milestone's. Shooting had already concluded by the time he settled on the ending, so it was also easier and less expensive to use Milestone's hand. After this scene, there is a final shot that returns from earlier in the film, of Paul and the boys leaving the shelter of the truck that has taken them to their first battle. "The truck was the last place that offered comparative security or safety. So as they walk away I had the idea of having each one look back longingly at the last place of safety. Their looking back was almost equivalent to their looking at the audience to inquire of them, 'What the hell are you going to do about it?' I think it worked, and it was a lucid expression of my personal convictions about war."[24]

Indeed, the film's butterfly ending worked so well that people used to tell Remarque what a brilliant idea it was, not knowing that it did not appear in the novel at all. So identified did Lew Ayres, the lead, become with this image that he titled his unpublished autobiography "Reaching for the Butterfly"—even though it wasn't his hand in the shot![25]

A less serious anecdote also circulated about the ending of *All Quiet on the Western Front*. One day during shooting, Carl Laemmle Jr. and

Milestone were chatting on the set. Laemmle commented to Milestone: "You know, Lew, I think we should do something to this picture to make it better 'box office.' What it needs is some sort of a happy ending." Milestone allegedly replied: "Well, we might have the Germans win the war."[26]

In casting the leading roles, Milestone did not necessarily look for big stars. Throughout his career, he was more interested in getting the appropriate performance rather than using glamorous names. And like so many of Milestone's films, *All Quiet* is fundamentally an ensemble piece not dominated by a single actor. For the crucial leading role of Paul Bäumer, numerous candidates were considered, including the matinee idol Douglas Fairbanks Jr. and even Remarque himself. In the end, Milestone chose a relative newcomer, Lew Ayres (1908–1996). By then Ayres had appeared in only a few films, most notably opposite Greta Garbo in her last silent film, *The Kiss.* An intellectual and thoughtful person who became a deeply committed pacifist (he registered as a conscientious objector during World War II and served in the medical corps), Ayres admired Remarque's novel and very much wanted to be involved with Milestone's film. But he almost ruined his chances when he called Milestone (who had been working late nights) very early in the morning on several occasions to press his case.

After looking at some test shots made with Ayres, however, Milestone changed his mind and decided the young actor, twenty years old at the time, was "a hell of a find."[27] Overcoming the objections of Carl Laemmle Jr. and of George Abbott, who considered him too inexperienced, Milestone insisted that Ayres be given the part. He was paid a paltry $2,600 for a role in which he appeared in every scene in the film. It was an inspired choice. Ayres's fresh naïveté onscreen infused the role of Paul with a keen authenticity and sincerity that brought out the novel's central theme of innocence destroyed. Throughout his life, Ayres remained profoundly grateful to Milestone for this huge break. None of his subsequent screen appearances (including the role of Dr. Kildare in nine films) reached the level of intensity and significance he achieved in *All Quiet.*

Louis Wolheim ("the ugliest man in Hollywood") got the important role of the sympathetic and pragmatic Katczinsky ("Kat"), a rough-hewn sergeant and veteran who helps Paul and his friends adapt to military life and provides much of the film's humor. Milestone already knew Wolheim; he had appeared in leading tough-guy roles in *Two Arabian Knights* and

The Racket. After countless screen tests, the remaining roles were given to John Wray (as the sadistic postman turned drill sergeant Himmelstoss), the comic Slim Summerville (as the jokester Tjaden), William Bakewell (as Paul's friend Albert), Ben Alexander (as Kemmerich, the first of the group to die, later featured on television in *Dragnet*) and the silent film comedian Raymond Griffith (in the nearly silent role of the French soldier killed by Paul).

The only important female role in the film is that of Paul's mother. Originally, the comic actress ZaSu Pitts was cast and filmed as Mrs. Bäumer, but at preview screenings in San Bernardino audiences laughed when she came onscreen, having seen her very recently in the musical *Henry.* The producers were so concerned that the scenes were reshot with the lesser-known actress Beryl Mercer. The absence of females was a concern from the outset of the project. After shooting was completed, just several months before the premiere, L. B. Metzger of Universal Film Exchanges in Chicago wrote to Carl Laemmle Jr., reporting on a conversation he had had with the legendary Hollywood columnist Louella Parsons. "The idea on 'Western Front' is this—everyone seems to be a little worried about there not being enough woman angle and heart interest."[28] But Milestone insisted on remaining faithful to the spirit and message of Remarque's text and resisted adding a love interest to a story of male camaraderie (unlike most Hollywood directors who came after him).

The choice of Arthur Edeson as cinematographer also proved to be fortuitous. Already a Hollywood veteran with dozens of silent films (and one sound film, *In Old Arizona*) to his credit, Edeson (1891–1970) brought a tough, realistic, documentary-style approach to the film that was very much in keeping with Milestone's vision. Edeson would go on to become one of the most respected cinematographers in the business, known for his work with James Whale (*Frankenstein,* one year after *All Quiet*) and on such films as *The Maltese Falcon* and *Casablanca.*

In *All Quiet,* Milestone and his collaborators exploited the new possibilities of sound to the utmost. As the first major war movie made with sound, it established a new standard for realism and represents a technical landmark in Hollywood history. At the time, the "sound men" occupied a privileged position in the production process, since the techniques of sound recording were still regarded as something of an "unfathomable mystery," as Milestone later recalled. "At lunch hour, the sound men had their own table. If you happened to pass by, their voices would drop to a whisper so that they wouldn't give away any secrets."[29]

But Milestone also regarded the very novelty of sound to be an advantage, providing the opportunity for creative experimentation. He took the time to learn the basic mechanics of how sound worked from a friend at the Goldwyn Studio. As a result, in *All Quiet,* the sound direction (supervised by David Broekman, who also provided the music and orchestration) is remarkably sophisticated and well integrated, adding immeasurably to the film's emotional effect but never calling undue attention to itself. Sound effects including marching tunes, cheering, singing of patriotic songs, the heavy tread of boots, the screaming and shouts of the soldiers, and of course explosions and gunshots that amplify the realism and sense of being in the midst of combat. Milestone used members of the large German émigré community in Hollywood to sing appropriate German songs. Most of the sound is diegetic, emerging from the narrative, and serves to bring us deeper into the world Paul and his fellow soldiers themselves are hearing, where the unending, deafening sounds of war only increase their feelings of torment, anxiety, helplessness, and desperation.

The only real relief in the soundscape comes from the harmonica, played offscreen by a German man whom Milestone's crew claimed to have found wandering around near the shooting site. Milestone recalled: "He was a one-man orchestra. I hired him as an extra among the soldiers, and whenever I needed marching songs or nostalgic songs about the Fatherland, he unfailingly obliged. He knew all the repertoire."[30]

The sound of gunfire presented special problems. Broekman told Milestone that gunfire usually did not sound authentic because it was recorded indoors. Milestone responded, "So we'll shoot off some live ammunition in the hills at night, record it, cut off the first explosion and just use the reverberation; then you'll have some real sound."[31] With his considerable experience editing documentary footage of World War I in the army, Milestone also insisted that the scenes involving machine-gun fire should accurately reflect what it looked and sounded like:

When a machine gun shoots the man ought to drop with the same rapidity as the bullets leave the machine. And I thought—if I keep that up, as wave after wave comes over, you have six, seven frames of the machine gun shooting and then immediately show the guys dropping, and they drop with the same impersonal unemotional thing as the machine gun spitting bullets—that would be something. That became the central idea. . . . On the film's opening night, some men that were wounded jumped out of their seats and said 'Come on let's get the guys!' and they charged at the screen. That's how close we came to the truth of the thing.[32]

So authentic was the combat footage that scenes from *All Quiet* have since been presented (and accepted!) as documentary material.

Milestone claimed that he filmed *All Quiet* no differently from the way he had filmed his silent movies. Unless the scene required dialogue, the long tracking shots were done with a silent camera. Since cameras made noise that could be picked up by the sound microphones, they were often placed in a soundproof box that severely limited their mobility, but Milestone found ways to get around this problem. A crane was used for overhead close-up shots in the battle scenes. One of the most effective uses of imaginative dialogue/sound/camera direction comes in the sequence when Paul and his buddies spend the night with the French girls at their house. Instead of showing Paul and his girl (Susanne) in bed together, the shot focuses on the shadows around the doorway leading to the bedroom, and we hear their halting, tender conversation, partly in French and partly in English, a strategy that gives the scene a beautiful understated intimacy and lyricism, a brief interlude of happiness amid the horror of suffering.

Although set in Germany and near the French-German border, *All Quiet* was shot at various locations in southern California: the Irvine Ranch in Orange County south of Los Angeles for the trench scenes; the Universal backlot for the German village where Paul lives; the backlot at Pathé studios for the river scene; and Sherwood Forest in the San Fernando Valley for the opening scenes of the boys going to the front. Shooting started on November 11, 1929, exactly eleven years after the signing of the Armistice that ended World War I—now celebrated as Veterans' Day.

For the battle scenes, Milestone had a cement road built that bisected the French and German trenches and the no-man's-land between them, so he could execute traveling shots that showed the real geography of the combat. "In all the war pictures I'd seen in the army and in the stuff that people were shooting for commercial pictures, as soon as the battle starts you don't know who is fighting whom. You lose all sense of geography. I thought if any one kind of picture was entitled to have as many travelling shots as possible, it was a war film. In a war you don't stand around staring—you move. And it worked out."[33]

To camouflage the California background, and to provide the smoke of battle, used tires were burned to create smoke and fog. Amazingly, Milestone employed only seventy-five extras as Frenchmen and seventy-five as Germans. Most were veteran soldiers from local American Legion posts (not from the U.S. Army, as has been erroneously reported). Through artful editing, he created the impression of a much greater number of soldiers, and he boasted that he could have created the same effect with even fewer extras.[34] To ensure authenticity, the German soldiers were dressed in real German uniforms from World War I purchased by Universal, had their hair shaved, and were drilled by German war veterans.

During the intensive editing of the battle scenes, Milestone lived at the Beverly Wilshire Hotel, a car and driver at his disposal. "Travelling to and from the studio I would sleep in that car, something like half an hour each way. I only spent about four hours in bed, and the rest of the time in the cutting room."[35]

For *All Quiet,* and for most of the rest of his films, Milestone very carefully planned out the sequence of shots in advance. This way he wasted less time and less film stock. He made elaborate sketches for most scenes, so he could concentrate when shooting on the acting and not the setups. Also unusual in the film business at the time was Milestone's practice of rehearsing scenes, as in the theater. Because he was shooting with editing already in mind, he used only 20,000 feet of film for the battle scene, and 190,000 feet for the entire movie, slightly less than the producers had anticipated. Owing to the difficulties encountered in shooting the battle scenes, the number of shooting days doubled, from the planned forty-eight to ninety-nine, increasing the budget from $891,000 to over $1.4 million and creating a severe strain on the Laemmles and their "poverty-stricken studio."[36] In the end, however, the extra expense turned out to be an excellent investment, since *All Quiet* went on to be a global box-office smash and one of the most popular and critically acclaimed films ever produced at Universal. Because some of their own theaters were still unequipped for sound, Universal also prepared a different silent version that was shown in France and Australia as well.

An overlooked stylistic feature of *All Quiet* is its close relationship to the aesthetic of montage editing developed in the Soviet Union, especially by the director and theoretician Sergei Eisenstein (1898–1948) in such films as *Strike, Battleship Potemkin,* and *October.* Milestone agreed that "montage is fundamental to cinema," as Eisenstein wrote.[37] When he saw *All Quiet,* Eisenstein was reportedly so impressed that he called it Milestone's "graduation film."[38]

Milestone has often been considered the most "Eisenstein-ian" of all major Hollywood directors. His fondness for montage-style editing, split-screen devices, a hyperrealistic documentary-style approach, and stories focusing on an ensemble rather than on individual characters has been noted by many critics and historians. Like Eisenstein, Milestone was a Jew who had grown up on the periphery of the Russian empire (Eisenstein in Riga, Latvia, and Milestone in Kishinev, Moldavia) during the decades just before the Bolshevik Revolution; both experienced considerable anti-Semitism in their youth. Despite the difference in their social standing (Eisenstein's family belonged to the intelligentsia, whereas Milestone's worked in commerce), both strongly sympathized with the have-nots in society. Both worked extensively in the theater before finding their true calling in the new art form of cinema.

Among others, the opening scene of *All Quiet* shows a strong Eisensteinian influence. Framed by doorways, windows and archways (like some of the crucial scenes in *Battleship Potemkin*), the crowd outside the classroom flows like a river between the buildings on either side of the street. As the teacher rhapsodizes about the romance of war, close-ups of each of the students in Paul's group dissolve into their fantasies (tearful parting with parents, getting girls' attention, receiving honors for bravery) of what awaits them at the front. This technique clearly echoes similar close-ups in *October* and *Strike.* Moreover, Milestone's realistic, newsreel, documentary style in a feature film possesses a strong resemblance to Eisenstein's treatment of similar material.

After an interview with Milestone around the time of the opening of *All Quiet,* William Boehnel wrote in the *New York Telegram:* "Like the Russian directors, Milestone believes that much of a picture's ultimate success lives in the cutting, and his chief complaint against Hollywood is that the producers there pay a director anywhere from $1500 to $4000 a week, entrust him with large sums of money to make films, and then pass the finished product over to some underpaid cutter who is seldom if ever acquainted with either the story or the players."[39]

At the time *All Quiet* was released, Eisenstein's fame was at its height in Hollywood. That very same month, Jesse L. Lasky, vice president of Paramount Studios, extended an invitation to Eisenstein (only three years younger than Milestone) to come work in Los Angeles. Lasky's idea was that Eisenstein "would spend six months in the USA making a film for Paramount, after which it would be open for him to return to Moscow to direct a Sovkino production."[40] There was even naive hope that the relationship would continue beyond that, that Eisenstein would divide his time between Moscow and Hollywood. Such an idea would seem absurd just a few years later, after the Soviet leader, Josef Stalin, asserted full and tyrannical control over the film industry and turned the USSR into a vast prison for artists of all kinds.

On May 24, 1930, the *Film Spectator* commented on Lasky's invitation to Eisenstein in a long, unsigned editorial that praised the superiority of the Russian film industry and suggested that Milestone was the director who could successfully bridge the Russian and Hollywood styles.

> As a class, the Russian motion picture directors are the greatest in the world. . . . The Russian directors are intellectuals; our directors are not. The Russians are technical experts; our directors the box-office experts. . . . If we had known from the start, as the Russians always have known, what constitutes screen art, we never would have put it in. Lewis Milestone, a Russian, knows what screen art is, and he demonstrates it in *All Quiet on the Western Front,* the greatest picture ever made. But if he had remained in Russia he never would have produced a picture that would appeal so grippingly to American audiences.[41]

On American soil Eisenstein was not greeted with universal enthusiasm, however. Numerous anti-Communist politicians attacked him as part of a "Jewish-Bolshevik conspiracy to turn the American cinema into a Communist cesspool."[42] In his highly entertaining autobiography, *Beyond the Stars,* Eisenstein recalls that "America in 1930 was the America of anti-Semitism, of Prohibition: the imperialist America of Hoover, before, two years later, becoming the America of Roosevelt: the America of the New Era and democratic tendencies, which flourished during his second term, and the military alliance with the Soviet Union."[43] On the East Coast, Eisenstein met with Paramount executives, lectured at Harvard and Yale, met Rin Tin Tin at a posh luncheon in Boston, and chatted with D. W. Griffith in the lobby of the Astor Hotel in New York. Douglas Fairbanks took him to a speakeasy.

In the months to come, it became painfully obvious that Eisenstein and Paramount had radically different ideas about filmmaking. None of the projects the director proposed to the studio (most notably, an adaptation of Theodore Dreiser's novel *An American Tragedy*) was filmed, and in October 1930 Eisenstein's contract was canceled. His sojourn in Hollywood failed to produce a single completed film and revealed just how incompatible were the Hollywood and Soviet ways of filmmaking. He returned to Moscow with nothing to show to Stalin and Communist Party officials, and he immediately fell under suspicion and increased ideological scrutiny. He did not complete another film until *Alexander Nevsky*, in 1938. Milestone did not meet Eisenstein during his 1930 American visit (he was in Europe), but they probably met in Moscow during Milestone's trip to the USSR in 1933.

Eisenstein was not alone in his admiration for *All Quiet on the Western Front*. The film's popular, political, and critical reception exceeded all expectations and proved that a "serious" (tragic, really) movie could succeed commercially. As chapter 1 noted, the premiere was one of the most important Hollywood events of the season. It was most certainly the right film at the right time, a powerful indictment of war at a moment when the world seemed to be heading toward another global conflagration. Released at the height of the Depression, just six months after the stock market crashed on Black Tuesday, it was the first feature film produced in Hollywood to portray the real horror of combat, equipped with sound and told from the point of view of the lowliest participants, not the generals or politicians. As the review in *Variety* observed, "Here exhibited is war as it is, butchery."[44] Subsequent events would show that the film also touched sensitive nerves about the role of the military and nationalism throughout the world.

The New York premiere at the Central Theater on April 29, 1930, rivaled the one in Los Angeles for star power and buzz. Among those attending was the starlet Ginger Rogers, who remembered in her memoir rubbing shoulders with Douglas Fairbanks and other celebrities. "Though it was April, ladies wore gorgeous long evening coats and capes trimmed with silver and white fox, ermine, mink, and sable. Diamonds sparkled on throats and around wrists." During the battle scenes the audience fell silent and erupted into "thunderous" applause at the end.[45] The reviews praised the film in rapturous terms, calling it a landmark in cinema history. After three weeks showing five times daily at the Central, *All Quiet* was moved to the much larger Roxy (nicknamed the "Cathedral of Film"), which boasted 6,200 seats. From his collaborator Howard Hughes, Milestone received a breathless telegram.

> Just saw Western Front would have seen it sooner but I have looked at so much film on my picture my eyes were hurting a little and did not want to see any more than I had to stop anyway just wanted to tell you I think it is perfect did not read the book but bet the picture is better stop scene in the shell hole was so good it got me and you know I am usually pretty hard boiled about those things also the scene in the school house where Lew Ayres comes back and tells boys what war is really like was superb and I know you are responsible for it because I saw this boy in a part in one of Greta Garbo pictures and he was not very good stop anyway I am very happy that you have made another click all you need is a story that is suited to you and I sincerely hope you will never consent to make another picture of the type that you know is not up your alley Best regards Howard Hughes.[46]

Lew Ayres believed that it was the way that *All Quiet* upended stereotypes of German soldiers that contributed to its popular success, affirming that war is a catastrophe for both sides, victor and loser. He mused: "The audience had always been told that the men on the other side were horrible people. That they took babies on their bayonets and things like that. And I can remember in my childhood days, there were scenes showing babies on bayonets, in the war films. . . . They were monsters! But *All Quiet on the Western Front* turned that around a little bit, I think, and it's one of the things that people remembered about it."[47]

Censorship boards in some states raised objections about certain scenes. In Pennsylvania, all scenes that included "sexual innuendo and swear words" and the "entire scene of darkened bedroom when voices of Susanne and Paul are heard talking" were cut.[48] Much more strenuous were the criticisms voiced by Major Frank Pease, manager of the United Technical Directors Association. In a wire sent to President Hoover, the secretary of war, heads of national organizations, and prominent editors, Pease ranted that *All Quiet* was "the most brazen propaganda film ever produced in America. It undermines beliefs in the army and in authority. . . . Its continued uncensored exhibition especially before juveniles will go far to raise a race of yellow streaks slackers and disloyalists."[49] But Catholic organizations and the Boy Scouts strongly defended the film's importance. "The picture is bitter medicine, but good for what ails Nations. I hope it runs for a long time."[50]

Compared to the storm it created in Germany, the controversy *All Quiet* provoked in the United States was mild. Even before the official release, the Laemmles expressed concern about the reception of the film's pacifist message in Germany and its unflattering portrayal of the German military. Remarque was already a controversial and unpopular figure in Germany for his pacifist views. At the time, nationalistic sentiment was also on the rise in Germany, as Hitler's Nazi Party continued to gain support and political power, having won 18 percent of the vote in elections in September 1930.

Hoping to avoid conflict, the Laemmles invited Werner Otto von Hentig, the German consul general in San Francisco, to a private screening several weeks before the Los Angeles premiere. Also present was Colonel Jason S. Joy of the Association of Motion Picture Producers and Exhibitors, who filed a report: "On the way to the Studio, Mr. von Hentig stated that he did not like the book, saw no reason for its being written and that he was certain he would not like the picture. The picture ended its showing at three o'clock in the morning, after which Mr. von Hentig and I discussed the picture with the two heads of Universal Studio. While Mr. von Hentig's attitude toward the story was not changed by the picture, he believed that as far as his Government was concerned no official action to reject the picture would be taken."[51]

So concerned were the Laemmles about the lucrative German market, the second largest in Europe, however, that they decided to prepare a different, dubbed version for exhibition in Germany. It toned down the gritty portrayal of life in the trenches and removed some dialogue containing antiwar sentiments (including most of Paul's speech to the classroom when he returns home on leave) and pointed criticism of the Kaiser and German high command. After being screened at the German embassy in the United States, this version was approved for distribution in Germany.

On December 4, 1930, the first public showing took place in the Mozart Hall in Berlin and was received for the most part positively and without incident. But the next day, Joseph Goebbels, Hitler's propaganda and media master, organized an infiltration of the theater by right-wing nationalists and brownshirts who disrupted the screening and released white mice and stink bombs. Goebbels stood up and hotly denounced *All Quiet* as a "Judenfilm," since its producers, the Laemmles, were of Jewish origin—as was its director, Milestone. Several members of the audience were beaten because they were perceived to be Jewish. The screening was halted amid the chaos and violence. Goebbels then led a massive march of his supporters down the neighboring Kurfürstendamm Boulevard.

The representative of the Motion Picture Producers and Distributors of America (MPPDA) sent a cable back to Los Angeles describing what happened. "Under the leadership of a prominent Reichstag deputy Germany Fascist fanatics staged an organized demonstration at ALL QUIET last night, compelling suspension of the performance, resulting in street rioting and a serious collision with the police. The entire press, with the exception of the extreme Right, emphatically denounces the Fascist tactics as unwarranted and disgraceful. After conferring with the authorities Szekeler (Universal's local manager) says the film is to continue under adequate police protection."[52]

Another eyewitness was a young woman who would become perhaps the most important film director of the Nazi regime: Leni Riefenstahl. Her pro-Hitler documentary *Triumph of the Will,* made just a few years after this screening of *All Quiet,* is one of the most notorious propaganda films ever made. She recalled: "Quite suddenly the theatre was ringing with screams so that at first I thought a fire had started. Panic broke out and girls and women were standing on their seats, shrieking. The film was halted, and it was only when I was out on the street again that I learned from the bystanders that a certain Dr. Goebbels, whose name I had never heard before, had caused pandemonium."[53]

Within days, riots provoked by the Nazis and their allies protesting the film's screening spread across Germany. The situation grew so dangerous and uncontrollable that the German Motion Picture Theater Owners passed a resolution refusing to exhibit *All Quiet.* In the Reichstag, the officials who had approved its screening came under attack. On December 11, 1930, the Supreme Film Censorship Board caved in to the intense political pressure and banned the film, arguing that it "showed only the defeat of Germany and the German army and was therefore calculated to injure German prestige."[54] In Germany and elsewhere, the banning of *All Quiet* was seen as an ominous victory for the Nazi Party and a defeat for democracy, "a capitulation before the organized mob, a mob that demonstrated against the world peace as symbolized by this film, a capitulation that is therefore a betrayal of the world's peace."[55] Carl Laemmle even wrote an impassioned defense of his film that was published as a paid advertisement in German newspapers, but to no avail. In the polarized political environment, it had become clear that no further changes to the film would make it palatable to German censors.

In a report filed on December 18, 1930, a certain "United States Government representative in Berlin" sympathized with Universal's position—and its lost potential revenue. "It is, of course extremely unfortunate for the Universal Picture Corporation that this film is a victim of political controversy and that they have not only lost the amount invested in Germany in the film but lost a fine potential business, for the film would have been a tremendous financial success in Germany if it could have run undisturbed."[56]

The intense emotional and political reaction to *All Quiet* in Germany in 1930 proved how powerful the medium of film could be in manipulating public opinion, and it was a tribute both to the uncompromising truthfulness of Milestone's artistic vision and to his faithfulness to Remarque's own intentions. A report from the Foreign Department of the MPPDA concluded that "The trouble over 'All Quiet' had a tremendous effect in Germany. This of course has little to do with the nature of the film itself. It is simply that the film is the thing that precipitated a fundamental internal conflict within Germany . . . films are now in politics for good as far as Germany is concerned."[57]

But the fact that it was *All Quiet,* and not some other film, that exposed this conflict should not be minimized. Its realism and emotional honesty forced audiences to confront extremely uncomfortable truths about themselves, their world, and their shared past. The movies, Milestone was showing—again following Sergei Eisenstein's example—were not just an escapist fantasy, but a tool with which to educate and to reinterpret history.

Years later, in response to a question posed by a participant at a conference held in Aspen, Colorado, on the relationship of government and the arts, Milestone asserted that, yes, he did consider *All Quiet* to be a form of propaganda. His reply could have come from Eisenstein's mouth: "If the director does his job well the audience will not detect propaganda, although propaganda is there as it must be of one kind or another in every picture you make and every story you tell. . . . My wish was to give the audience a ringside seat to war. I believed it was also Remarque's wish. . . . I take no chance of appearing immodest when I boldly say we succeeded."[58]

All Quiet also encountered resistance from censors in other countries besides Germany. In German-speaking Austria, the Nazis had been exerting pressure on the government to ban the film. After initially resisting and allowing screenings to take place with heavy police security and protests, the government acquiesced and halted further showings. German-speaking audiences could see the film across the border in Czechoslovakia, France, the Netherlands, and Switzerland, however. Milestone later proudly remembered that "people would get on buses and cross the border just to get in and see the picture."[59] At various times, *All Quiet* was banned in China, Yugoslavia, Hungary, and Bulgaria. Ironically, it was never shown publicly in the USSR, despite (or perhaps because of) its strong artistic connection to the early avant-garde Soviet cinematic tradition. Sergei Eisenstein believed that a film was successful only when it provoked strong emotional reactions from the audience—and *All Quiet* had certainly done that.

Despite the lost revenue in Germany and some other countries, the ongoing (free) publicity over the film's reception in Germany, widely reported in the American press, created a strong buzz and brought in large audiences at home. It also made Milestone a household name and one of the most sought-after directors in Hollywood. For the third annual Academy Awards, which honored movies shown in the Los Angeles area between August 1, 1929, and July 31, 1930, *All Quiet* received four nominations: for Outstanding Production (now known as Best Picture), Directing, Writing and Cinematography. Strangely, it was not nominated for Sound Recording (a new category at these awards), nor did any of the actors receive nominations, a reflection of the film's focus on ensemble rather than star turns.

At the ceremony at the Ambassador Hotel on November 5, 1930, the film received the two most important awards, for Outstanding Production and Directing. In the Directing category, Milestone's competitors were an impressive group: Clarence Brown (*Anna Christie* and *Romance*), Robert Leonard (*The Divorcee*), Ernst Lubitsch (*Love Parade*) and King Vidor (*Hallelujah*). The award carried more weight and prestige this year, since the entire membership of the Academy (more than four hundred people) had voted, rather than only a small handful of judges, as in the preceding two years.

All Quiet exists in many different versions. Initially, it ran for 145 minutes, very long by Hollywood standards of the time. After the New York premiere, Universal wanted to cut it, and Milestone agreed by allowing the studio to trim "maybe fifteen or twenty minutes. Nothing significant was lost, and no further cuts were made."[60] But in fact in 1934 Universal reissued a new, nine-reel version running about one hundred minutes, nearly one-third shorter than the original.[61] And in 1939, this version was rereleased with several additional features: anti-Nazi voiceover commentary and newsreel footage covering World War I and the rise of Nazism. Critics panned this rerelease as "stupid vandalism," and a shameless attempt to capitalize on rising fear of Nazi Germany.[62] Milestone called this version "a horror" that "was produced by an element that was most anxious to spread the word that 'The Yanks were not coming,' just before they did come. The slogan was of course doomed to failure, as was that version."[63]

In the years since, the film has been rereleased several more times. Reconstructed versions have been produced in Germany, Holland, and the United States. Weirdly, one of the German reconstructions was undertaken with the help of a print from the private collection of the man who had sabotaged the 1930 Berlin screening—Joseph Goebbels. In the 1960s Universal briefly considered producing a colorized version of *All Quiet*, but this project (fortunately) was never pursued.

For the rest of his long career, Milestone came to feel haunted by the enormous success of *All Quiet on the Western Front*. Such success was difficult to repeat. That the filming had taken a severe emotional toll seems clear from his decision to skip the Los Angeles premiere and return to Europe for the first time since coming to America in 1913. During the summer of 1930, he spent some time in Germany, staying at a sanatorium in Dresden "favored by many White Russians." There he observed the increasing militarization of German society, but when he returned to the States, "no one believed me."[64] Having experienced the terrible consequences of anti-Semitism as a child in Kishinev, Milestone was certainly very much aware of the potential dangers of the racist Nazi propaganda directed at his film. Soon he became an outspoken opponent of Hitler's Germany and a member of the Hollywood Anti-Nazi League.

Between May and late summer of 1930, Milestone traveled around Europe. Before sailing on May 30 with his production assistant, Nate Watt, on the liner *Europa* from New York, where *All Quiet* was running to packed houses, he spent some time revisiting the sites of his youth there, when he was a "friendless Russian boy. . . . One can be forgiven, I hope, for getting a kick out of the change in one's fortunes." He also said he planned to see his younger brother, an engineer, in London; to return to "my own country" (Moldavia) "to visit my family"; and to go to Russia, where he intended "to visit Serge Eisenstein and Pudovkin, the leading Soviet directors."[65] It does not appear that he made it to the USSR on this trip, however. His passport shows that he visited England, France, Germany, Austria, Czechoslovakia, Yugoslavia, Spain, Hungary, and Romania.[66]

After the 1917 Bolshevik Revolution in Russia, the province of Moldavia (Bessarabia), formerly part of the Russian empire, became part of the independent kingdom of Romania, including his hometown of Kishinev, where some members of his family still resided. According to the stamps in his passport, he visited Romania in July and August. The Russian stage director Vladimir Nemirovich-Danchenko, who was also in Europe at the time and seeking to connect with Milestone to discuss possible future projects, wrote in a letter to his friend Sergei Bertensson on July 8, 1930, that Milestone "is in hiding, living *incognito.*"[67]

Milestone sailed from Cherbourg to New York on August 14, 1930.[68] From New York he made his way back to California on a ship via the Panama Canal. Back in Los Angeles, he was soon seen about town and became the subject of considerable gossip and speculation in the press. (Would he be directing *A Farewell to Arms*? Was he having a romance with Lew Ayres's sister?) One journalist spotted him lunching with his friend Charlie Chaplin at the Brown Derby.[69]

By now, Milestone had put *All Quiet* behind him and was deep into preparations for his next project, having signed a contract for another picture backed by Howard Hughes's Caddo Company: *The Front Page.*

4

Photoplays

When I got my way, I kept it up.

—Lewis Milestone

When Milestone returned to Los Angeles from Europe and New York in the autumn of 1930, the *Hollywood International Film Reporter* extolled him as nothing less than "the most talked about director in the motion picture industry."[1] The global success of *All Quiet on the Western Front* had turned him into a celebrity and a hot commodity.

Accompanying him on the journey back to California via the Panama Canal were two writers, Bartlett Cormack (author of the play *The Racket*) and Charles Lederer. Together they were working on the screenplay for Milestone's next picture, *The Front Page*. "We had two weeks of uninterrupted concentration. We stopped off in Havana and bought a typewriter." In Cuba they also "witnessed what looked like the beginnings of a full-sized revolution: students demonstrating, etc."[2] At the time, various political action groups were protesting the dictatorial regime of President Gerardo Machado.

The Front Page, by Ben Hecht and Charles MacArthur, was a smash comedy hit of the 1928 Broadway season, one of the most active and productive in American theater history. With the coming of sound films in the next few years, the audience for live theater in New York and other American cities would decline precipitously. At the time, plays about newspapermen enjoyed particular popularity. "Like the hard-boiled detective, the newspaper reporter was an indigenous American character—cynical, wisecracking, without pretension—thus a natural subject for the tough romanticism the theatre was then trading in."[3] Hecht and MacArthur drew on their own extensive experience as journalists in writing *The Front Page,* using reporters and editors they had known as models for the principal characters.

A fast-paced comedy-farce, *The Front Page* takes place in one action-packed day in Chicago. The protagonist, Hildy Johnson, a crack reporter, has decided to give up the newspaper business to settle down with his sweetheart, Peggy Grant, in New York and go into advertising. At his first entrance, Hildy is described as "a vanishing type—the lusty, hoodlumesque half drunken caballero that was the newspaperman of our youth."[4] Hildy's editor, Walter Burns, and his hard-bitten rogues' gallery of cynical reporters gathered in the press room at police headquarters find his decision to abandon the world he loves so much incomprehensible and wrong. "You'll be like a firehorse tied to a milk wagon," his friend Murphy warns.[5]

Two story lines intertwine in *The Front Page:* Hildy's impending marriage to Peggy and his departure from the newspaper business; and the scheduled execution of Earl Williams, an alleged Bolshevik sympathizer, for the accidental shooting of a policeman. When Williams makes a sensational escape from jail (next door to the press room, where he finds shelter) on the day he is supposed to be hanged, Hildy cannot resist the siren call of a big, exclusive, front-page story. Encouraged by his competitive editor, Hildy plunges back into the joyful, chaotic whirl of chasing down leads, nearly forgetting his fiancée and her prim mother in the process. Packed with witty repartee, slapstick physical comedy, lots of slamming doors and urban grit, *The Front Page* entertains as it also pointedly addresses a raft of social problems: police corruption and brutality, graft and influence peddling among politicians, the hypocrisy of Prohibition, yellow journalism, unemployment, and public paranoia about Communism. "Callin' me a Bolshevik. I ain't a Bolshevik. I'm an anarchist," the idealistic, victimized Williams tells Hildy. "It's got nothin' to do with bombs. It's the one philosophy that guarantees every man freedom."[6] Williams is another of the army of the "forgotten men" of the post–World War I period, traumatized by their combat experiences and discarded by the cruel capitalist system. *The Front Page* celebrates working-class values as it skewers those who uphold the establishment.

In an extensive rave review, the *New York Times* drama critic Brooks Atkinson called *The Front Page* "one of the tautest and most unerring melodramas of the day, with a Rabelaisian vernacular unprecedented for its uphill and down-dale blasphemy."[7] It was just the kind of vehicle that would appeal to Milestone, with his already established flair for representing social criticism (*The Racket, The Garden of Eden,* and *The New Klondike*), male bonding (*All Quiet on the Western Front*), and slapstick comedy (*Two Arabian Knights, Seven Sinners*). *The Front Page* has remained popular on the American stage, and it received a highly successful 2017 Broadway revival.

Milestone and Hecht had already met in Florida during the shooting of *The New Klondike* in early 1926, when Hecht (along with Joseph McEvoy) was hired to rewrite the screenplay. They also came from similar backgrounds. Hecht was born in 1893, two years earlier than Milestone, on New York's lower East Side, to Jewish immigrants from Minsk, Russia, in what is today Belarus. (In the 1940s Hecht became very active in the movement to establish Israel as a homeland for displaced Jews.) When Hecht moved to Hollywood in late 1926 to work in the movies, he and Milestone began to move in the same social circles. At the time, Milestone was sharing a house with Hecht's friend David Selznick and his brother Myron, who would become two of the most influential producers in Hollywood. Hecht and Milestone became friends and would work together sporadically on various projects for decades. In great demand as a "script doctor," Hecht even helped with rewrites on Milestone's last film, *Mutiny on the Bounty*. Hecht did not write the screenplay for *The Front Page*, however, because he and MacArthur demanded too much money. Cormack and Lederer were hired instead.

In autumn 1930 Howard Hughes purchased the screen rights to *The Front Page* for the large sum of $125,000, a demonstration of his faith in its box-office appeal.[8] On October 10, 1930, Milestone signed a contract to direct the film for Hughes and his Caddo Company—their third collaboration after *Two Arabian Knights* and *The Racket*. Reflecting Milestone's increased stature, the terms of the contract were notably more favorable for the director. He was to receive 50 percent of "all net profits generated by the picture in perpetuity" and a $30,000 fee to be paid in advance. This profit-sharing agreement was highly unusual and caught the attention of industry insiders, since it signaled that successful directors could now demand more advantageous financial conditions from producers and studios. According to an article in the *Hollywood Reporter* that appeared shortly after news of the contract was made public, "This is believed to be the first time that such a contract ever has been made between a producer and a director."[9] In 1934 Milestone would bring a suit against Caddo and the film's distributor, United Artists, claiming that he had not been provided with accurate profit statements to determine how much he was owed under the profit-sharing arrangement.

The contract also stipulated that Milestone's name was to be advertised "in a prominent and substantial manner in all lithographs and posters and on the main title of the picture, and in all paid publicity and advertising." The contract even specified how Milestone's name should be featured in the credits. "All lithographs and posters should contain an announcement 'A Lewis Milestone Production' . . . the size of the type used for such statement shall be at least as large as that used for the name of the person or company presenting such production. With respect to the picture itself, the main title shall carry a line: 'A Lewis Milestone Production' and immediately following the main title, there shall be an entirely separate title containing the following expression: Directed By LEWIS MILESTONE."[10] This time, Milestone wanted to be sure he received the credit he felt he deserved.

By choosing to follow the dramatic and serious *All Quiet on the Western Front* with a frothy satire, Milestone clearly wanted to demonstrate his versatility. For the leading role of Hildy Johnson, he hoped to cast Clark Gable, but Hughes disagreed, reportedly saying that Gable "will never get any place, this guy. . . . With those ears he looks like a taxi cab with both doors open."[11] Hughes clearly underestimated Gable's raw sex appeal. Instead, the part went to the more conventionally handsome Pat O'Brien, known primarily as a stage actor. Louis Wolheim (veteran of *The Racket* and *All Quiet on the Western Front*) had been scheduled to take the role of Hildy's relentless, tough-talking editor, Walter Burns, but he died unexpectedly of stomach cancer. Adolphe Menjou, an actor previously identified with roles requiring effete sophistication, successfully replaced him, earning one of the film's three Academy Award nominations. In the role of Bensinger, a fussy wannabe poet and germophobe, Edward Everett Horton turned in a memorable, idiosyncratic performance using his quavering, musical voice to great effect. Horton also received the highest salary—$4,000 per week for a total of $21,333.[12]

Once again, as in *All Quiet on the Western Front* and *The Racket,* the ensemble is predominantly male, and, as the critic Michael Sragow has observed, "helped to establish the buddy-movie paradigm of men trying to save a comrade-in-arms from the existential dangers of love and marriage."[13] One of the film's more memorable lines belongs to Walter Burns: "I was in love once with my third wife." Of the three females in the cast, Mae Clarke makes the strongest impression as Molly, the hooker with a heart of gold, who takes pity on Earl Williams.

Milestone felt comfortable with the rough, raw, seedy world of Chicago journalism and politics, perhaps because of his own early experiences of urban poverty and struggle. In his unpublished autobiography, he bragged that he frequented gambling houses and speakeasies during the Prohibition era, and that he was once arrested with a friend near Bakersfield.[14] If anything, the film's screenplay, set design, and shooting style amplify the play's naturalistic grittiness. Most of the action is filmed in the claustrophobic, scantily furnished press room, in addition to a few well-chosen exterior shots. The innovative opening credits, with photos of each actor, roll against the background of an unfolding newspaper. Then a title card appears ("This story is laid in a mythical kingdom"), an ironic disclaimer stressing its nostalgic and romantic (bro-mantic, in fact) aspects. Milestone and his screenwriters also emphasize the brutality of the death by hanging that awaits Earl Williams. The film's expressionistic opening shots show the executioners rehearsing, cutting a rope that allows a sandbag to fall—a scene added in the screenplay.

As he had done in *All Quiet,* Milestone made extensive use of preparatory sketches for the setups before he filmed them. A sketch artist drew "every angle of the piece," Milestone explained later.

> Eventually what we did was this: the assistant director would pick up a day's work—he would take, let's say, ten setups that I had drawn—and he would put them on an easel. The back of the sketches showed the camera position and whatever other information wardrobe and so on might need. It was thoroughly prepared, and then when I finished drawing the whole thing and we had all the sketches, we went out on an empty stage and I laid out all the drawings and examined them to see if I'd repeated any of the shots. When I came upon a repetition I would re-stage it, so that every setup was used only once. We went into production so well prepared that we shot it in record time.[15]

Shooting of *The Front Page* began on January 20, 1931, and ended on February 24. One of those observing was Sergei Bertensson, a Russian who had come to Hollywood in 1926 as the secretary to the famous Russian theater director Vladimir Nemirovich-Danchenko, cofounder with Konstantin Stanislavsky of the Moscow Art Theatre. Nemirovich had been invited to Hollywood by Joseph Schenck, who hoped he would develop some projects for the movies. But Nemirovich failed to understand the way Hollywood operated, and he returned to Russia in 1927. Bertensson remained, however, and eventually became an assistant to Milestone, with whom he eventually worked on four films. At the time *The Front Page* went into production at United Artists studio, Bertensson was employed there and they apparently became acquainted. For him, Milestone's choice of popular material was disappointing after the artistic triumph of *All Quiet:* "What a shame that such a great artist is wasting his talents on such a piece of boulevard trash."[16]

Final process shots were completed on February 26, eleven days over schedule.[17] The workdays were long, beginning at one in the afternoon and lasting until nine at night and often later. After shooting, Milestone would view the day's rushes, sometimes until the early morning hours. On occasion, Hughes visited the set and spoke with the actors and crew. A few scenes were shot at Los Angeles City Hall and at the *Los Angeles Examiner* building. The production cost totaled $557,996.70.[18]

To unwind, Milestone and his crew would take advantage of his friendship with Douglas Fairbanks, who had his own steam room and "ice-filled plunge outside his dressing room on the Goldwyn Studios lot. . . . I had the run of the place; Doug gave me permission to use it. So we'd go and have a steam and a plunge before drinks and dinner. We weren't teetotalers. After dinner, if the gang felt like it, we'd go back to the stage and do a couple of hours' more work. Sometimes we ran the rushes— the daily work—as late as one or two o'clock in the morning: nobody had to work next morning. That's the kind of esprit de corps we had."[19]

The fast pace of the shooting was echoed in the film's quick rhythm, and especially in the rat-a-tat speed of the dialogue, intended to reflect the rapid, ever-changing routine of the newspaper business. Like *All Quiet on the Western Front, The Front Page* creates a remarkably sophisticated world of sound, despite the relatively primitive state of sound technology at the time. Unlike many other early sound films, *The Front Page* allows the actors considerable physical freedom; the microphone does not constrain them. There is no music, but other sounds—ringing telephones, police sirens, fire alarms—abound and provide gritty authenticity. When the film was made, Hollywood sound technology was going through a transition, from sound recorded on disc to sound recorded on film. Eventually, of course, sound on film would prevail, but not all theaters were yet equipped for this system, which was expensive to install. So

United Artists prepared and distributed two different versions of *The Front Page,* one with sound on disc and one with sound on film.

Milestone and his cinematographer, Glen MacWilliams, used clever camera tricks to make the sometimes static action dynamic—restlessly circling the table where the men gamble to pass the time, looking down from above, going to Eisenstein-like close-ups of each character in rapid sequence, accelerating the pace of shots at crucial moments. There are no fade-outs; rather, the action rolls forward without a breath. Characters are frequently shot in lighted window frames surrounded by dramatic darkness. Often the camera travels with the characters, showing the action from their eyes. A notable tracking shot follows Burns as he walks through the city room, past churning presses to the loading dock. At one point, the camera even jumps up and down with the characters. Milestone did not just transfer the play to the screen, he visually reimagined it from inside out. He also added a formalistic stylization to the realism here and there, most notably at the end. After Hildy and his fiancée, Peggy, have finally departed for New York and marriage, not knowing that Burns has planned for them to be detained at a station in Indiana for stealing the watch he has planted on Hildy, the words "The End" appear onscreen—but under a big question mark.

Audiences and critics both embraced the special combination of humor, drama, and social criticism contained in *The Front Page.* It grossed more than $500,000, was widely considered to be one of the best films of 1931, and received three Academy Award nominations, for Best Picture, Best Director, and Best Actor. (Wesley Ruggles's *Cimarron* took the Best Picture award.) In a diary entry of March 27, 1931, Sergei Bertensson, who had initially dismissed *The Front Page* as a piece of "boulevard trash," reported that the film "is breaking all box-office records in New York and has earned in a single day as much as Mary Pickford has in an entire week."[20]

The Front Page also further solidified Milestone's reputation as one of Hollywood's leading and most original directors. In response to different censorship requirements, United Artists prepared three different versions of the film, one for domestic release, one for release in the United Kingdom, and one for general foreign release. They differ in subtle but important ways. The domestic version is the most audacious and pointed, whereas the other two were toned down in terms of language and references, in the assumption that foreign audiences would not understand certain themes and expressions. At the time, in the pre-Code era,

Hollywood directors were considerably less constrained by censorship concerns regarding the use of off-color language and sexual innuendo. (The 2017 Criterion Blu-Ray restoration of *The Front Page* is the closest to Milestone's original vision.)

Two other versions of Hecht and MacArthur's play were filmed in later years. In *His Girl Friday* (1940) the director Howard Hawks had Charles Lederer rewrite the part of Hildy for a woman, and he cast Rosalind Russell in what became one of her most famous and successful roles, opposite Cary Grant as Walter Burns. Largely on the strength of their appearance in *The Odd Couple,* Billy Wilder chose Walter Matthau and Jack Lemmon to play Burns and Hildy in his superfluous 1974 remake of *The Front Page.*

With another solid success to his credit, Milestone took some time to consider various options. He continued to be drawn to "Russia projects," and he read widely in classic and contemporary Russian literature, consulting with members of Hollywood's large Russian émigré community. One of the authors who captured his interest was Vladimir Nabokov, at the time living in Berlin and publishing stories in Russian under the pseudonym of Vladimir Sirin. His story "The Potato Elf" made an especially strong impression on the director. According to Sergei Bertensson, who became a close artistic adviser during this period, Milestone even wanted to bring Nabokov to Hollywood, but that idea did not come to fruition until many years later.[21]

By late 1931 rumors were circulating that Milestone would be appointed as production head at United Artists. News had reached Bertensson that Milestone also wanted to appoint him as an assistant. Unemployed in the midst of the Depression, nearly penniless and almost stateless as a Russian émigré, Bertensson decided to travel to Europe to meet with Milestone, who was spending time there between projects. They met in Paris. Bertensson's extensive description in his diary of the time they spent together provides a fascinating glimpse into the milieu of Russian émigré theater and film people in which Milestone was moving at the time—and shows his love for food, drink, and entertaining company. The following scene began in Milestone's hotel:

December 11, 1931. [Milestone] greeted me very warmly. He said that yes, in fact he had been appointed as chief director at United Artists and proposed that we work together. He spoke about his plans to collaborate not with "stars," but simply to make good pictures for which we would find suitable actors. He had me talk on the phone with Tourjansky[22] and Fedya Chaliapin,[23] who both wanted to see me. I invited Fedya to come see me the following morning, and Tourjansky and I agreed to go have dinner together. Millie yelled into the telephone to him: 'We have to feed Bertenson.' Together we went to the Russian restaurant 'Moscow Hermitage.' There we had vodka, caviar, wonderful Russian hors d'oeuvres, and listened to the singing of Vertinsky,[24] who later joined us, and we sat until 4 A.M.

December 16, 1931. . . . I have been spending all my time with Millie. . . . and most of it in restaurants. Once again lunch at the Hermitage, with Fedya Chaliapin, then at "Casanova" in the evening, where we were joined by Mosjoukine[25] and his wife. The next day we had supper until the early hours of the morning at the "House of Artists" owned by Muratov.[26] He is from Kishinev, like Milestone, so the evening turned into a celebration in honor of Millie. . . . I returned home at 5 A.M. in horror that I was leading such a life.

I have been strolling several times with Millie along the Champs Elysées and the boulevards. Once we sat for a long time in some café, drinking port wine, and I told him a great deal about the Imperial theaters, about my former work in Russia, and the theatrical personalities I had met. Millie listened to all this with great interest.

December 17, 1931. Early in the morning I went to the station to see Millie off; he is leaving for America. At the station we met Douglas Fairbanks, who asked me, so when are you going back?[27]

In Berlin, Bertensson paid a visit at Milestone's request to Vladimir Nabokov to inquire if he had interest in writing for the movies. "He [Nabokov] got very excited about this idea. He said that he actually adores the cinema and watches films with great interest." Nabokov even gave Bertensson a manuscript copy of his forthcoming novel, *Camera Obscura*, which Bertensson judged to be unsuitable for the American film audience, despite the fact that the main character meets his love interest at the cinema.[28] (Nabokov later changed the novel's title to *Laughter in the Dark*, and it was made into a film under this title in 1969 by the director Tony Richardson.)

After returning to America from Europe, Milestone remained in New York until early April 1932, preparing the script for his next film, *Rain*. Bertensson was with him, acting as assistant and literary adviser. "The entire month of March my work continued just as intensively as in February," wrote Bertensson in his diary on April 5, 1932.

> Working for Milestone—or Millie, as we call him—is easy and pleasant. Unfortunately he is so busy that it is difficult to meet with him for a serious discussion of our literary program and consideration of the large volume of material that I have prepared for him.

> On April 3 we finally left for Hollywood. Millie's entourage consisted of eight people (including three servants), so they gave us a separate car on the train, and we traveled straight to Los Angeles in it, without changing in Chicago. We have lots of wine and we are having a very merry journey, so we hardly notice the time passing. Millie has invited me to travel with him in the same compartment, so we have been able to talk over a lot of things.[29]

Soon after they returned to Los Angeles, Milestone began shooting *Rain*. The film, his first in his new capacity at United Artists, marked Milestone's return to serious drama. An adaptation of a short story of the same title by the British author Somerset Maugham, it was Milestone's first melodramatic feature revolving around a central female character.

An inveterate traveler of the Pacific and South Seas, Maugham wrote what became his most famous story about several characters he had observed in Hawaii and on a ship sailing to Pago Pago, Samoa. Sadie Thompson (Maugham kept her real name in the story), a prostitute traveling to Samoa from Iwelei, the red-light district of Honolulu, especially captured the author's interest. She annoyed the other passengers (including Maugham) by playing her gramophone loudly at all hours of day and night, and by entertaining various gentlemen in her cabin. This behavior continued when the passengers were forced to lodge in the same hotel in Pago Pago for some days because of a quarantine inspection. Sadie's impudence and flagrant sexuality particularly bothered a medical missionary and his wife who were already shocked by the "depraved" customs of the island's native population.

Out of this raw material Maugham fashioned a compelling tale of sexual repression, religious fanaticism, and class antagonism set against a background of incessant rain in an exotic South Seas setting. In the story, Sadie
and four other passengers from the delayed ship (a missionary and his wife,
and a doctor and his wife) must share quarters in a small rooming house on
Pago Pago during the rainy season. The missionary couple (Mr. and Mrs.
Davidson, from uptight Boston) find living in such close quarters with a
"harlot" nearly unbearable. Davidson becomes obsessed with Sadie's sinful
nature and after intense (even obsessive) effort succeeds in converting her
to repentance and religion. She stops playing her beloved gramophone and
neglects her appearance. Now apparently transformed, she agrees to return
to San Francisco to face the criminal charges and "penitentiary" she is trying to flee. But on the eve of her scheduled departure, Davidson succumbs
to his own demons and has sexual relations with Sadie. In the morning he
is found dead on the beach by one of the natives, his throat cut by his own
hand, having committed suicide out of guilt and shame.

When the doctor and his wife (Dr. and Mrs. MacPhail) return from
identifying the body, Sadie has reverted to her former sluttish appearance
and manners. Her gramophone is blaring its former sexy ragtime. "She
was no longer the cowed drudge of the last days. She was dressed in all her
finery, in her white dress, with the high shiny boots over which her fat legs
bulged in their cotton stockings; her hair was elaborately arranged; and she
wore that enormous hat covered with gaudy flowers. Her face was painted,
her eyebrows were boldly black, and her lips were scarlet. She held herself
erect. She was the flaunting queen that they had known at first."[30] The out-
raged Dr. MacPhail demands an explanation for her impudence. She turns
on him with a contemptuous gaze and spits out these famous lines:

> "You men! You filthy, filthy pigs! You're all the same, all of you.
>   Pigs! Pigs!"
> Dr. MacPhail gasped. He understood.[31]

The dramatic possibilities (sin, sex, South Seas) of Maugham's story,
published in 1921 as part of the collection *The Trembling of a Leaf,* soon
caught the attention of two playwrights, John Colton and Clemence
Randolph. Their dramatized version, *Rain,* opened on Broadway on
November 7, 1922, starring Jeanne Eagels as Sadie. While generally faithful to Maugham's original, the play added a subplot involving an upright

American marine, Sergeant O'Hara, stationed on the island, who takes a fancy to Sadie and takes her off to Australia at the end, providing a happy ending and some relief from the brutal tension. Largely on the strength of Eagel's performance, *Rain* was a smash hit that ran for 648 performances. The play went on to become a fixture in stock companies across the country.

Movie rights to the play were sold for $150,000. (All together, Maugham made more than one million dollars on royalties from "Rain.") Three film adaptations eventually appeared: *Sadie Thompson* in 1928, a silent version starring Gloria Swanson; Milestone's *Rain* in 1932; and *Miss Sadie Thompson* with Rita Hayworth and José Ferrer in 1953. The story even spawned a short-lived 1944 musical, *Sadie Thompson,* with a score by the Russian American composer Vernon Duke.

Milestone had serious reservations about undertaking the project, since he believed Eagels had become so strongly identified with the role of Sadie. "I was afraid from the very start that the zeitgeist was not right for this kind of a piece." But despite his recent successes, Milestone claimed to need money: "I was not in a position to choose very carefully."[32] In the end he succeeded in creating a powerful, psychologically probing, and evocative film that conveys both the psychological conflicts and the exotic setting with force and visual originality.

Milestone's most daunting challenge was to cast the role of Sadie. His producers insisted on a box-office attraction—Joan Crawford was the eventual choice. Having already appeared in numerous silent films, and one of the most popular leading ladies of the moment, she also appeared in 1932 in *Grand Hotel* as a meek secretary. (At the time, Crawford was married to Milestone's friend Douglas Fairbanks Jr., although their marriage was breaking up while she was filming *Rain*.) Because Crawford was under contract to MGM, she had to be "borrowed" to make the film for United Artists. According to Milestone, this led to some problems during filming because Crawford felt she had been "demoted by going in with some independent company. . . . At MGM they babied performers; they'd renovate their dressing rooms, anything to make them happy, and suddenly Joan Crawford was working with a crew that was not trained to wait on her hand and foot. But it wasn't her fault; it was what she had been conditioned to expect as her due."[33]

Playing opposite her as the Reverend Davidson was Walter Huston, a serious Broadway actor beginning his long career in the movies. Beulah

Bondi took the role of the shrewish and puritanical Mrs. Davidson. Two newcomers, Matt Moore and Kendall Lee (more about her later), were Dr. and Mrs. MacPhail.

Maxwell Anderson, creator of the scenario for *All Quiet on the Western Front,* adapted the play for the screen. Perhaps his most significant addition to the Maugham story was a scene in which the hotel proprietor and homespun philosopher Trader Horn, played by Guy Kibbee, ruminates on the writings of the philosopher Friedrich Nietzsche, particularly *Thus Spake Zarathustra.* This rather awkward intellectual interpolation seems intended as an explanation of Davidson's behavior and his inability to avoid the same end that awaits us all: death.

Rain was made quickly: shooting began on May 19, 1932, and ended on June 22, only ten days later than scheduled, at a total budget of $636,668. Milestone received $104,250 for his work.[34] Most of the film was shot on Catalina Island off the coast from Los Angeles, where a South Seas tropical environment could be created with reasonable accuracy. "I built a whole set there, constructing it in such a way that wherever you looked you saw the ocean."[35] He also took great care in creating the persistent dominant image of rain, seen by one of Maugham's biographers as a symbol for "Davidson's self-righteous pursuit of Sadie Thompson. As in Noah's flood, rain entraps the characters and punishes them for both carnal and spiritual sin."[36] The film's opening shots poetically re-create the start of a tropical rainstorm as a prelude to the action, as Milestone later told an interviewer.

We started with clouds gathering. Then you heard faint thunder. That was followed by a closeup of the first raindrop hitting a leaf. I followed it as it rolled down and hit the dust and became a globule; that was done in slow motion. Then came the second drop . . . then four drops . . . they kept multiplying. We kept increasing the quantity and intensity of drops. When the leaf began to be bombarded with drops we panned down to a rainbarrel beneath the roof guttering. The water begins to come out of the roof guttering first as a trickle, then faster and faster until the barrel starts to fill up. Then you saw enormous drops hitting the water surface of the barrel. By the time they were really bombarding it pretty heavily, we widened the angle by pulling the camera back and disclosed the whole vista of the street. This was the introduction of the rain.[37]

Milestone's skillful use of music in the opening minutes—first a lush orchestral theme, then a marching song sung by the Marines trudging through the ubiquitous mud, then ragtime music at Sadie's first appearance—helps create an immediate sense of the oppressive atmosphere and psychological dynamics. Alfred Newman, at the dawn of an illustrious career as a Hollywood composer and arranger, acted as musical director.

Always insecure about her intellectual abilities and humble origins, Crawford struggled with the role of Sadie and apparently with Milestone's directing style. Years later, in her autobiography, the star admitted, "I was haunted by my inferiority to famous Sadie Thompsons of the past, Jeanne Eagels, who created the part on the stage, and Gloria Swanson, who appeared in the early silent-film version. I hadn't seen them, but they were constantly held up to me by my co-workers. Mr. Joe Schenck thought I was worried unnecessarily, he told me to listen to my director, but Lewis Milestone frightened me. I wasn't wise enough or talented enough about acting to understand how brilliant a man this was or how talented a director. He had worked out blueprints for every scene, precisely what I was to do and how to do it; but to me, no actress worthy of the name could be a puppet in anyone's hands. I was no Method actress, I was an emotional one—in *Rain,* far too emotional. All you have to do is check the excellent pictures Mr. Milestone has made to see who was right. I was wrong."[38]

At the time, Milestone had the deserved reputation (from *Two Arabian Knights, All Quiet on the Western Front,* and *The Front Page*) of being a "man's director" who did not enjoy directing women. Crawford also disliked the actor (William Gargan) chosen to play her romantic interest, Sergeant O'Hara, and tried to get Schenck to replace him with her real-life love interest, Clark Gable, but to no avail. Nor did it help Crawford's mood that she fell ill during the shooting, discovered she was pregnant (and uncertain who the father was), and had an abortion (allegedly not her first).[39] She also found Huston arrogant and unappealing, and she even joked sarcastically that she wished he had committed suicide in real life.[39] Milestone later admitted that he had difficulty directing stars like Crawford. "That means turning into a kind of dressmaker, standing in line until the star has finished with her hairdresser, her manager, all the rest of the entourage. It means arguing about whether or not she will play this scene with her back to the camera. In the end she will do it; but that all takes it out of you."[40]

For all that, Crawford's performance in *Rain* is a memorable one, and it shows her ability to portray the lives of lower-class women (like the later Mildred Pierce) forced to make their way in a harsh man's world on strength of will and brash personality. Milestone and his cinematographer (Oliver Marsh) made the most of Crawford's strong features, especially her huge eyes. Her first entrance onto the screen is masterfully composed in a series of montage shots (reminiscent of Eisenstein) that present her bracelets, her white patent leather shoes, and then finally her face framed by a cigarette and a too-fancy feathered hat—accompanied by loud ragtime music that becomes her leitmotif. This same series of visual and sonic images returns in the film's final minutes, after her seduction by the Reverend Davidson. Released not long before the Production Code Administration censorship guidelines came into full effect, in 1934, *Rain* treats Sadie's sexuality and the world of prostitution with a frankness that would soon disappear from Hollywood feature films. Even so, censors did demand that the character of Davidson be changed from an ordained minister to an evangelist.[41]

For many of Crawford's fans, her portrayal of the slutty Sadie went too far. "Sadie *was* a whore, with no redeeming qualities—pretty much like Dietrich's Lola-Lola in *The Blue Angel*—and upsetting her beloved camp-followers distressed Joan far more than some acid-tongued critic ever could. When they wrote to her telling her how *Rain* had been a big mistake, she made a public apology to them."[42] Milestone, not used to working with Hollywood divas and always critical of Hollywood's star system, also felt that her performance fell short, that it was too much a caricature. Years later he confided to an interviewer that "Crawford wasn't up to it, and the picture didn't get off the ground—although there were a few things in it I liked."[43] Most of the reviews panned the picture. W. H. Mooring wrote a review so scathing for *Film Weekly* that the editor refused to run it.[44]

With time, however, *Rain* has come to be appreciated as a film ahead of its time, and it has found a new audience. When the film was screened as part of a Joan Crawford retrospective in 1977, the *Los Angeles Times* critic Kevin Thomas wrote, "Drenched in steamy tropical atmosphere and charged with the electricity of a conflict between flesh and spirit, 'Rain' is enormously vital and entertaining."[45]

Milestone brings the tawdry story alive with restless, circling camera work and a sensual, tactile, almost ethnographic or documentary re-creation of the island setting. Besides the meticulous representation of the effects of the inescapable rain, the mise-en-scène foregrounds the role of the natives and their culture in upsetting Davidson and leading him astray from his rigid puritanical convictions. In the opening minutes, we see and hear the nearly naked native men singing as they pull in their fishing nets—an image repeated at the very end when they haul in Davidson's dead body. Throughout, we hear the drums of the natives in the background, reminding the visitors of the repulsive but fascinating "primitive" rituals going on around the island. In the climactic scene just before Davidson's seduction of Sadie, on the balcony outside Sadie's room, he begins to move gradually in rhythm to the drums as they rise to a crescendo, until, finally overcome by his sexual desire, he enters her room. One of Milestone's most impressive achievements in *Rain* is to convey the interaction of the characters with their exotic environment and to show how their behavior changes under stress—one of the director's lifelong preoccupations.

The film's deliberate pace and careful creation of atmosphere are among the film's strongest features, but Milestone came to feel after shooting that perhaps it was too slow.

> I thought they were ready for a dramatic form, that now we could present a three-act play on the screen. But I was wrong. People will not listen to narrative dialogue. They will not accept the kind of exposition you use on the stage. I started the picture slowly, too slowly, I'm afraid. You can't start a picture slowly. You must show things happening. When you say "This is the way missionaries did things on our islands fifteen years ago," people lean back and go to sleep. You can occasionally slip in a line and say, "Do you remember—?" and they will say, "Oh, yes, I saw that happen." So my next picture will be seventy-five per cent silent. It is the kind of story that lends itself to that treatment.[46]

In the course of the filming, Milestone's own life changed as well. He began a romance with Kendall Lee, cast in the small (mostly nonspeaking) role of Mrs. MacPhail, that eventually led to their marriage. At the time, Lee was thirty-two years old—and a married woman. In *Rain*, Lee's performance as the wife of Dr. MacPhail consists mostly in sitting or standing near her husband, expressing sympathy with his predicament as he attempts to act as a mediator between Sadie and the Davidsons. An attractive if unremarkable actress, her most important previous experience in the movie business had been to appear in a minor role along with the stars Constance Bennett and Basil Rathbone in the 1930 feature *Sin Takes a Holiday*. In the 1920s Kendall had been a "very well-known ballroom dancer" in New York.[47]

Exactly how quickly their relationship progressed after they met while working together on *Rain* is not exactly clear, but by autumn 1933 Milestone was sending Lee a series of affectionate telegrams from Europe, like this one from London on October 22: "Leaving for Paris today will stay at Kittys till sailing Wednesday I love you. Milly."[48] In April 1934 Lee obtained a divorce in Reno from her husband, Jules Glaenzer, described in an article in the *Sunday Mirror* of May 13, 1934, as a "jewel expert and vice-president of Cartiers, Inc. of New York." According to this report, Glaenzer and Lee had married in 1925 and separated some time in 1933. Lee received a divorce on the grounds of "cruelty."[49]

Kendall Lee was the daughter of Mrs. Richard Kendall Lee, a well-known member of New York society. It was reported that "her association with Milestone began when she went to the Coast and procured a small part in the film, 'Rain.' Last July he followed her to Paris, where it was believed she would secure her divorce." Apparently, however, she did not receive this divorce in Paris and went to Reno instead.[50] Because of Milestone's work and travel obligations, he and Lee did not marry until July 1935, when they eloped in Tucson, Arizona.[51]

In a letter to Milestone written years later, in 1947, after their work together on *Arch of Triumph*, Ingrid Bergman shared her impressions of Kendall's first husband, whom she had encountered socially in New York. "Give Kendall my love. I have met her ex-husband a couple of times. He is funny and can tell stories, too. But yours are funnier! So she did the right thing."[52]

Kendall Lee boasted a fine pedigree: she was a Lee of Virginia, a distant descendent of the Confederate commander in chief, Robert E. Lee. Milestone's friend Norman Lloyd described her as "a beautiful lady" who became "one of the great hostesses of Hollywood."[53] Her family owned a large estate in Virginia that Kendall and Milestone frequently visited in later years. Kendall Lee's sister, Frances, was the second wife of the famous American realist painter, muralist, and political figure Rockwell Kent (1882–1971). Kendall, and later her husband Milestone, were frequent guests at Asgaard Farm, the estate and dairy farm the Kents had purchased in the Adirondacks in 1927, in remote Au Sable Forks, New York.

Like Milestone, Rockwell Kent was drawn to socialism early in life, and he fell under the suspicion of the U.S. government for his views. Kent was called twice to testify before the House Un-American Activities Committee, in 1939 and in 1953, and his passport was even briefly revoked in the early 1950s. In his later years he traveled frequently to the USSR, donated numerous paintings to Soviet museums, and received the International Lenin Peace Prize in 1967.

For years, Milestone had been one of Hollywood's most eligible bachelors and had been linked in gossip columns with various women, including Lew Ayres's sister, Agnes. His marriage to Kendall Lee, who abandoned her own career and devoted herself to the role of Milestone's wife, was by all accounts a happy one that lasted until Lee's death, in 1978. They had no children, but they became well-known for their elegant parties. Kendall Lee encouraged Milestone's love of the good life—fine wine, excellent cigarettes, good food, luxurious accommodations, and hobnobbing with high society in New York and Hollywood.

Norman Lloyd (who knew Milestone better than almost anyone) believes that the director's fondness for the high life he shared with Kendall (who was used to and expected this sort of existence) was one of the reasons his career faltered in later years.[54] That Milestone chose for his life partner an apparently discreet, understated, and sophisticated woman from elite New York society rather than a sexy, glamorous Hollywood starlet like so many of his director peers seems to indicate that he desired a stable and decorous home life. The drama would go into his movies, not his personal life.

Milestone continued his collaboration with Joseph Schenck and United Artists for his next project, a curious Depression-era musical entitled *Hallelujah, I'm a Bum*. From the start, the project was intended as a vehicle for Al Jolson, who had burst onto the Hollywood scene in 1927 with his energetic and soulful performance in the title role of *The Jazz Singer*, the "first talking picture," produced by the enterprising Warner Bros. As a triple threat (singer, dancer, actor), Jolson was versatile, but his range was rather narrow. Although he was already under contract with Warner Bros. to make three more films, in 1928 Jolson and his friend Schenck signed a contract on a brown paper lunch bag (the "banana bag" contract) for him to star in four films for United Artists for a total fee of $2 million, an enormous sum at the time.[55] But first Jolson appeared in five Warner Bros. features: *The Singing Fool* (1928), *Say It with Songs*

(1929, his first all-talking picture), *Show Girl in Hollywood* (1930, including newsreel footage of Jolson performing), *Mammy* (1930, directed by Michael Curtiz) and *Big Boy* (1930, directed by Alan Crosland, director of *The Jazz Singer*). Footage of Jolson also appeared in *New York Nights* (1929), the Schenck-Milestone project that Milestone attempted later to disown.

Schenck invited Ben Hecht to find a story for a new Jolson feature that was originally to have been directed by Harry d'Abbadie d'Arrast. D'Arrast and Hecht came up with a fable about homeless people living happily in Central Park that was based in part on Floyd Dell's 1926 short story "Hallelujah, I'm a Bum." S. N. Behrman adapted Hecht's story into a screenplay. But after only one day of shooting, d'Arrast told Schenck he couldn't work with Jolson, and he was replaced by Chester Erskin, who completed a version (originally called "Happy Go Lucky") that was previewed in September 1932 to such a disastrous reception that Milestone (now finished with editing *Rain*) was brought on to remake the entire film.

The original songs (by Irving Caesar) were replaced with new ones by the formidable team of Richard Rodgers and Lorenz Hart, fresh off the success of their 1932 film collaboration on *Love Me Tonight*, with its hit song, "Isn't It Romantic?" For this project, they tried a new musical style of "rhythmic dialogue," which sounds something like rap music. Because of Jolson's other commitments, the production schedule was very rushed; as Herbert Goldman writes, "The script had to be rewritten, the songs and rhythmic dialogue learned, and the film entirely reshot—all within three weeks." Shooting took place in the ironically upscale environs of the Riviera Country Club in Pacific Palisades.

In a letter to his wife, Rodgers described a typical day of filming in late October 1932:

> Today was one of those mad ones that made me satisfied that you were away. It started with writing, manuscripts to be done, conferences about rehearsals, orchestrations, and everything else. I had half an hour for dinner, alone, at the Derby, and then back to a rehearsal. Jolson wouldn't work because he wanted to go to the fights. I agreed to go with him if he'd promise to work with me later. So to the fights we went (terrible ones) and then to his apartment where I rehearsed him for an hour. Then to meet the

boys at Milestone's house to hear the final dialogue scenes, then home. It's two a.m., and I'm pooped.[56]

Milestone and Jolson (1886–1950) came from very similar backgrounds. Both were Jewish immigrants to the United States from the fringes of the tsarist Russian empire: Milestone from Kishinev in Bessarabia, and Jolson (his real first name was Asa) from Kaunas in Lithuania. Both were familiar with poverty and struggle, so they could easily identify with the down-and-out characters of *Hallelujah,* unemployed inhabitants of Central Park. (Milestone even claimed to have spent a few nights sleeping there in his early days in New York.) Jolson plays the role of Bumper, a wily and resourceful operator who claims to prefer unemployment and becomes the charismatic de facto leader of the park's remarkably cheerful homeless population, accompanied by his ever-smiling black sidekick, Acorn (Edgar Connor, in an embarrassing Stepin Fetchit stereotype). Bumper has a knack for charming people, even those in power. One of his friends is the mayor of New York (played by Frank Morgan before his *Wizard of Oz* fame), whom he once saved from a brick thrown in his direction.

The plot turns on the familiar ingredients of mistaken identity and class distinction, like the plots of so many classic comic films of the 1930s (*My Man Godfrey, City Lights*). After the mayor and his girlfriend, June (Madge Evans), have a falling-out because he wrongly suspects her of continuing her relationship with a former suitor, she wanders despairingly into Central Park and jumps into a pond in a suicide attempt. Bumper saves her, only to discover that she is suffering from amnesia as a result of the psychological shock. He takes her into the fold of the Central Park homeless and they initiate a romance. Bumper and Acorn even briefly take jobs in a bank in a doomed attempt to "go straight" in the awful world of capitalism so they can pay her rent. In the end the mayor and June are happily reunited through a rather improbable chance meeting, and Bumper happily returns to his previous unencumbered Arcadian existence in Central Park.

At the time *Hallelujah* was filmed, American attitudes toward Communism and capitalism were in a state of flux. The Depression had led many Americans to question whether capitalism really was the best economic and social system; membership in the American Communist Party soared. Behrman's screenplay reflects this uncertainty. Several characters express sympathy for socialist ideas. The gainfully employed trash collector Egghead (Harry Langdon) criticizes the park squatters with these awkwardly rhyming lines:

I accuse you all of wasting your time,
While I slave away for the City.
You're parasites all! You're Brothers in Crime!
When the revolution comes you won't sit pretty!

Exactly which revolution Egghead has in mind is not clear, however, since the homeless are part of the proletariat who, according to Marxist thinking, will be the ones to stage the revolution. Later Egghead criticizes June for "dressing like a capitalist," to which Bumper responds: "Some of my best friends are capitalists." During the sequence showing Bumper and Acorn working in a bank, the bank employees disdain average customers (refusing to cash a five-dollar check while striking deals with corrupt fat cats); Acorn's work consists (rather improbably) in counting soiled towels in a bank. And even though the mayor accepts bribes and shirks his duties, he is a devoted friend to Bumper and popular with his constituents. In a key scene, the mayor lays the cornerstone for a new public school. Arriving two hours late, he is greeted by a chorus of children fervently singing "My Country 'Tis of Thee," shot in a rapid montage style as a series of facial close-ups reminiscent of the schoolroom scene in *All Quiet*. Here American patriotism reigns.

As Joseph Millichap writes, the "ambiguous handling of the social problems" undermines the artistic integrity of *Hallelujah*.[57] The film wants the audience to find the predicament of the Central Park homeless humorous, but poverty and unemployment were no laughing matter in early 1933, when the film was released. For the most part, the reviews were damning, and even Al Jolson's name did not bring in the crowds. Of the songs Rodgers produced for *Hallelujah*, the only one that enjoyed a life beyond the film was "You Are Too Beautiful," sung by Bumper to June during their brief (and not very believable) romance. In style the film employs many of the same techniques Milestone had used in his earlier films: montage sequences (especially of faces), diagonal wipes, a restlessly moving camera.

United Artists had spent $1,250,000 making the film—and lost most of it. The failure of *Hallelujah, I'm a Bum* also brought an end to Jolson's film career. Although he was under contract with Schenck for three more films, they decided mutually to terminate the agreement. As Pearl Sieben writes, "Al was angry and shaken. It was his first flop in more than twenty years."[58]

Even so, some judge it to be Jolson's best film, as the *New Yorker* writer Penelope Gilliatt observed forty years after the premiere, in 1973: "Although the released film was not well-received in 1933, film critics now consider it the finest and most interesting of Jolson's movies. Jolson comes off well as an actor in this effort, and it is fascinating to see him both without his blackface persona and without a backstage plot in which he is playing a variation on himself."[59] Milestone also spoke very little about the film in future years, as if he would have been just as happy to forget about what turned out to be (despite the impressive talents involved) an embarrassing step backward (or sideways) in his creative evolution.

5

Up and Down

In Hollywood one can't do what one wants. And that goes for more places than Hollywood.

—Lewis Milestone

After shooting *Rain* and *Hallelujah, I'm a Bum* in rapid succession in late 1932 and early 1933, Milestone turned his attention to a project much closer to his heart: a film about Russia. Even though he had lived in America for twenty years, many of Milestone's closest friends and artistic associates (including his personal assistant, Sergei Bertensson), were Russian, and he continued to read widely and deeply in Russian literature. Over the coming years, Milestone doggedly pursued several projects based on works of Russian literature, although none was realized. Among others, he prepared plans or drafts of screenplays for films based on Fyodor Dostoyevsky's novels *The Eternal Husband* and *Crime and Punishment;* Leo Tolstoy's *Resurrection;* and Nikolai Gogol's Ukrainian epic *Taras Bulba* (eventually filmed in 1962 starring the unlikely duo of Yul Brynner and Tony Curtis, but not by Milestone).[1]

Perhaps Milestone's most interesting unrealized Russia project, however, was his attempt to bring to the screen an adaptation of a 1923 novel by the Soviet writer Ilya Ehrenburg, *The Life and Downfall of Nikolai Kurbov* (*Zhizn' i gibel' Nikolaia Kurbova*). Milestone spent nearly a year on this project, retitled *Red Square,* in 1933–34, and he even produced a complete screenplay coauthored with Laurence Stallings (1894–1968), who wrote the screenplay for the classic silent World War I film *The Big Parade,* as well as the play *What Price Glory?,* among many others.

The story of his aborted collaboration with Ilya Ehrenburg tells us a great deal not only about Milestone's working methods, but also about the difficulties Hollywood studios faced in attempting to bring stories about life in the new USSR to the screen. Milestone signed a contract for the film version of *Red Square* with Columbia on April 4, 1933, but in early 1934 the studio canceled the production.[2] What exactly happened during the ten-month period between the signing of the contract and its cancellation is not entirely clear, but the project began with high hopes. In an extensive article published in the *New York Sun* on May 24, 1933, Milestone told the writer Eileen Creelman about his plans for the movie.[3] He had signed a three-picture deal with Columbia, the first of them to be his "Russia picture," and was sailing to Europe with Laurence Stallings and Columbia's producer Harry Cohn to work on it. Columbia had promised Milestone complete control over his projects.

"This first picture will be the type of story from which all Hollywood has shied away, although they would all like to tackle it," wrote Creelman. "It is a tale of modern Russia with as its central figure a chief of the Cheka." (The Cheka was the early Soviet secret police, later the KGB). "Russian pictures, as Mr. Milestone remarks, have told of peasants, of czars, of factories, of planted fields. They have not told of the Cheka. And American pictures, except for a few prettified romances of the revolution, have not touched upon life under the Soviet."[4]

"'The story is an involved one,' said Mr. Milestone, 'but I think it will make a good picture, the sort of picture I want to make, with a modern Russia background but taking sides neither for nor against the Soviet. It is simply a slice out of Russian life with no propaganda.'" Milestone added that he did not want to cast big stars. "I am primarily interested in the story. There are two kinds of pictures, star pictures and story pictures. *All Quiet on the Western Front* was a story picture. There were no big names in it. I think if your story is powerful enough, you do better without a star. You do not have to tailor a story to fit a personality."[5]

Milestone and Stallings stayed abroad for about six months. First they worked on the script for ten weeks in London. But dissatisfied with the result, they decided they needed to go to the USSR, to Leningrad and Moscow, to research local color and detail.[6] According to the stamps on Milestone's passport, it seems that he traveled from New York to France, then from France to England, where he and Stallings boarded a ship to Leningrad, arriving there on September 14, 1933, and staying for about two weeks in the USSR, including a visit to Moscow. Milestone arrived back in London on October 2, 1933.[7]

As Stallings told a writer for the *Los Angeles Times,* "When we got there we found that our script wasn't worth 10 cents." So in Moscow they sought out Ilya Ehrenburg himself to help them, hired the artist Nathan Altman to provide sketches for designs, "and, what was most important, they absorbed all the atmosphere there was to be absorbed. . . . 'Now,' Milestone jubilated, 'we hope to be the first Americans to give a true view of what is really going on over there. And take it from me, it must be seen to be believed. Look here.'" "Every kind of theater flourishes in Russia. There is no box office to worry about," Milestone explained. "The artists feel that they are all broke together, in a manner of speaking, so they all pull together for the common good. Some one gets the idea of doing 'Hamlet' on a wire; someone else says, 'Let's try it.' And they do. It is all very much in a festive spirit, from the workers' theater up onto the Moscow Art."

No Communist, Milestone was able to appreciate the humor of one conception almost universally held by the Russians. "They really believe," he declared, "that all Hollywood-made films are 'propaganda' made under direct instruction from the American government! What else is one to think, they shrug, when people are shown to be so happy and prosperous under a regime which is 'capitalistic,' 'imperialistic,' certainly not Communistic? It is to laugh."[8]

In his memoirs, *People, Years, Life* (*Liudi, gody, zhizn'*), published during the early 1960s, Ehrenburg provides his own account of his friendship and attempted collaboration with Milestone on *Red Square*. The two men had a great deal in common. Milestone was only four years younger than Ehrenburg. Both were Jews born in Ukraine. Ehrenburg did not emigrate to the West, as Milestone did, but he spent much of his adult life living in Europe as a correspondent for Soviet newspapers.

> In 1933 I met the American film-director Lewis Milestone and we soon became friends. He is a very stout and very kindly man. . . . He loved everything Russian, retained the colourful southern modes of speech and was happy when offered a small glass of vodka and some pickled herring. When he came for a few weeks to the Soviet Union he was at once on the best of terms with our film-directors and kept saying: "I'm no Lewis Milestone, I'm Lenya Milstein from Kishinev."
>
> He decided to make a film out of my novel *The Life and Death of Nikolay Kurbov*. I tried to dissuade him: I did not care for this old book and besides, it would have been ridiculous in 1933 to

show an idealistic Communist aghast at the sweeping tide of NEP [New Economic Policy]. Milestone pressed me to write a scenario in any case, suggesting that I alter the story and describe the construction works and the Five Year Plan: "Let the Americans see what the Russians are capable of achieving."

I had great doubts about my ability to do the job. I am no playwright and I was not sure I could produce a decent scenario, while a rehash of several books combined seemed to me silly. But I liked Milestone and agreed to try and write the script with his collaboration.

He invited me to the small English seaside place where he was engaged on a difficult task—slimming. He weighed almost sixteen stone, and every year starved himself for three weeks, losing some three stone; after that he would naturally start stuffing with a vengeance and very soon look as he had done before. To do his fasting he would choose a comfortable hotel where the cooking was so bad that he did not envy the people who lunched and dined.

He lay supine and slimmed while I sat at his side, ate indifferent food and wrote. Milestone had a wonderful feeling for the rhythm of a picture and would say: "Here we must have a break. . . . Maybe it starts to rain? Or a little old woman with a shopping bag comes out of the house?"

I have not kept the script: I remember it vaguely; I think it represented a mixture of Hollywood and the Revolution, of some of Milestone's bright inspirations and film routine, a melodrama seasoned with the irony of two adults.

We managed to fill a fat writing-pad. Milestone had grown thinner, his suit hung on him in folds, and at long last we left for Paris. In Montparnasse Milestone met the artist Nathan Altman and asked him to prepare sketches for the sets and costumes.

Milestone's pessimism was justified. Harry Cohn, the president of Columbia, said after reading the scenario: "Too much social stuff and not enough sex. This is no time for throwing money down the drain."

Milestone was naturally upset: he had wasted almost a whole year, but he managed to make Columbia pay both Altman and me.[9]

Ehrenburg's novel *The Life and Downfall of Nikolai Kurbov* is set in the years before and after the 1917 Bolshevik Revolution. Its hero, Nikolai Kurbov, a prostitute's son, grows up in a wealthy home where he is employed as a tutor and views firsthand the decadent and corrupt behavior of the upper classes under tsarist rule. Eventually he joins the Bolshevik movement and is arrested and sent to Siberia, but he escapes. Nikolai greets the Bolshevik Revolution enthusiastically and even joins the Cheka. His idealism is tested when he sees the unsavory conduct of many of his colleagues and the materialism growing during the NEP period, when Lenin and the new Communist leadership instituted limited capitalism in hopes of restoring the ruined Russian economy. An underground rightwing group sends an attractive young woman to seduce and murder him. After meeting him, however, her resolve fails. She gives the intended murder weapon to Nikolai. Meanwhile, Nikolai has become even more despondent over the betrayal of the revolution by leaders such as Trotsky. A meeting with Soviet leaders at the Kremlin brings him to the decision that life is not worth living. After another sexual encounter with his intended assassin, Nikolai shoots himself with her gun.

Because of its harsh portrayal of both ends of the political spectrum in Russia, Ehrenburg's novel found little favor either in Soviet Russia or in émigré circles abroad. In preparing to adapt it for the screen, Milestone undertook serious research on the postrevolutionary period. Besides the trip he made to the USSR in 1933, he consulted numerous primary and secondary historical sources.[10]

The screenplay opens with a scene in a casino where Russian aristocrats are gambling recklessly as they eat and drink to excess. One of them callously sells his girlfriend (Masha) to cover his debts, leading her into prostitution. Nine years pass, and Masha has borne a son named Nikolai Kourbov, who becomes involved in revolutionary activity. As a tutor to the children of a wealthy family, Kourbov observes firsthand the decadence of the aristocracy. Eventually he loses his position and goes to work for the Communist Party. Soon imprisoned for revolutionary activity, Kourbov is sent to work in a Siberian mine.

When World War I breaks out, he agitates for the Bolsheviks at the front. The soldiers begin to mutiny against their officers, and political prisoners are released. Kourbov has become a Red Army commander.

Abruptly, the scene shifts to Paris three years later, where Kourbov's former aristocratic employers are living the sad life of emigrants, and then to Soviet Russia, where things are not going much better. Kourbov is now a high-ranking official in the secret police. When his long-lost father resurfaces, Kourbov has him shot. The screenplay has a happier ending than Ehrenburg's novel. Kourbov overcomes the desire to commit suicide and finds new purpose in working to build the new Soviet society, joining the crew at a vast construction project in Siberia.

Why Columbia and Harry Cohn chose not to make Milestone's *Red Square* after so much preparatory work had been done remains a mystery. The studio's decision to cancel the project deeply upset Milestone, as he made clear in a letter to Columbia dated February 19, 1934.

> Both prior to and since the execution of the contract between us, which is dated April 24, 1933, you definitely committed yourselves to making and assigned to me the direction of a photoplay to be based upon the book entitled "Life and Death of Nicholas Kourbov" and to which you gave the working title "Red Square."
>
> During the period of almost ten months which has elapsed since the execution of that contract, I have been engaged practically continuously (except for a very brief interval during which I was engaged in rendering other services for you), in accordance with your directions, in rendering my exclusive services to you in connection with the preparation of said photoplay.
>
> At the end of the period aforesaid and after a complete dialogue shooting script of the photoplay had been prepared under your supervision and in accordance with your instructions, you blandly announced your intention of not making the picture. . . .
>
> I hereby notify you that I shall hold you responsible not alone for the damages which you have already caused me but in addition thereto for the damages which you are continuing to cause me by holding me inactive during the continuance of your refusal to permit me to make "Red Square."[11]

It was not unusual in Hollywood, of course, for projects to be abandoned. It happened all the time. But it seems likely that the recent change in Soviet-American relations had something to do with the decision.

On November 17, 1933, just as Milestone and Stallings were heading home to Hollywood, diplomatic relations between the USSR and the United States were finally established by the newly installed Roosevelt administration, sixteen years after the Bolshevik Revolution. This no doubt made studio heads, always acutely aware of the political situation and the resulting implications for box-office success, uncertain about how the USSR and its people should be portrayed in a Hollywood feature.

Not coincidentally, another major film dealing with life in Soviet Russia also in the planning stages in 1933, Frank Capra's *Soviet,* never made it to the production stage, despite substantial preparatory work by the screenwriter Jules Furthman. By this time, too, Sergei Eisenstein had been shown the door by Paramount after failing to complete a feature. And in 1931 the celebrated Soviet novelist and screenwriter Boris Pilnyak, invited to Hollywood at the invitation of MGM's wonder boy producer Irving Thalberg, had returned home to the USSR in frustration after he and the studio were unable to agree on an appropriate scenario. Pilnyak was executed in the late 1930s in the Stalinist purges of artists and intellectuals, in part because his earlier ties to the American film industry came to be viewed as dangerously anti-Soviet.[12]

Milestone's experience with *Red Square* was another instance of Hollywood's anxiety about collaborating with Soviet film people—or even shooting films about the USSR. Afraid of landing on the wrong side of rapidly shifting American political and popular opinion regarding Communism and the USSR, and driven by their innate capitalist inclinations, risk-averse studio bosses repeatedly backed away from the dicey proposition of representing contemporary Russia onscreen. But this would not prevent Milestone from continuing to try.

Milestone's failure to bring *Red Square* to the screen after nearly a year of intense effort left him at loose ends. His relationship with Kendall Lee also remained in limbo. In April 1934, two years after they had met during the filming of *Rain,* she obtained a divorce from her previous husband in Reno. But their lives still kept Kendall on the East Coast and Milestone in California for long periods. On June 16, 1934, he sent her a melancholy letter on stationery of the Beverly-Wilshire Apartment Hotel in Beverly Hills, bemoaning their separation.

> Sweet Darling—
> I have always loved you—I love you now, and I always will—
> But somehow, I feel I'm fighting a losing fight. I feel that since
> Reno you are even farther away from me than you were before—

Darling why do I always learn about your plans from people who couldn't be as close to you as I am—It was not from you that I heard that you were going east after Reno—and it's not from you that I learn that you expect to spend most of the summer on the east coast. You once told me that you couldn't fit into my life that you thought I didn't need you. How do I fit into yours and when will you need me?

I'm lonesome

I miss you

God damn it!

I love you

Still under contract for three pictures at Columbia Studios, Milestone now proposed to its mercurial head, Harry Cohn, a much less serious project, *The Captain Hates the Sea*. Milestone saw this rather derivative romantic drama/comedy as a perfect vehicle for John Gilbert (1897–1936), one of the biggest male stars of the silent era (his performance in *The Big Parade* is particularly memorable), whose career had sputtered since the advent of sound. It didn't help, of course, that Gilbert's heavy drinking had undermined his health and reliability on the set. As a Russian well-acquainted with drinkers (both problem and otherwise), Milestone felt deep sympathy for Gilbert's situation, and he persuaded Cohn to give him another chance.

"I know Jack very well," Milestone reportedly told Cohn. "I'm convinced he can come through with a performance. . . . It's a gamble, but a good gamble. Everybody in town is kicking Jack, now that he's down. Here's a chance to prove them wrong."[13] At Milestone's urging and with his careful assistance, the veteran Gilbert even agreed to take a humiliating screen test, and he succeeded in overcoming Cohn's resistance. "If you keep your nose clean on this picture, I'll see that you get work. I'll go to bat for you with every producer in town," Cohn told Gilbert.[14] The actor was signed to a five-year contract, but in fact *The Captain Hates the Sea* would be the last film he made before his death in January 1936, aged thirty-eight. Later, Milestone called Gilbert a "victim of sound, although there was nothing basically wrong with his voice. The only time his voice went up was when he was over-excited. If he was sure of what he was going to say, and you gave him time to say it, his voice would be absolutely normal. Off-screen he never screeched."[15]

Often compared to Edmund Goulding's 1932 feature *Grand Hotel,*
The Captain Hates the Sea also turns on the social, financial, and sexual
entanglements of a group of hotel guests—but on a cruise ship sailing
from Los Angeles to New York via the Panama Canal. Its cast, however, is
less impressive than *Grand Hotel*'s, which boasted the talents and drawing
power of such glamorous stars as Greta Garbo and Joan Crawford. Besides
Gilbert, Milestone's actors included Victor McLaglen (who would win an
Oscar the following year for *The Informer*), Wynne Gibson, Alison
Skipworth, the Romanian-born Garbo wannabe Tala Birell—and even
the Three Stooges in their Columbia feature debut as the clutzy shipboard
musical combo. The Russian-born character actor Akim Tamiroff appears
in an entertaining cameo role as a Central American revolutionary
returning to face death; this marked the beginning of a long artistic collaboration with Milestone. Wallace Smith adapted his own popular novel
for the screenplay, featuring the mostly comic capers of a gruff captain
who hates sailing, his lazy steward, and the various passengers—an unsavory crowd of gangsters, alcoholics, and women with shady reputations,
intentions, and pseudonyms—all, in the captain's words, "trying to run
away from themselves."

In an unfortunate art-imitates-life twist, Gilbert played Steve Bramley,
an alcoholic writer trying (unsuccessfully) to get sober and begin a new
book. As the shooting progressed, and despite his promises to Milestone
and Cohn, Gilbert's own drinking not only did not stop, but worsened.
The ship where the film was shot in Los Angeles Harbor "became a floating bar."[16] Gilbert managed to stay dry for one week, but he was soon joining the other cast members in heavy drinking sessions that consistently
delayed production. So fragile was Gilbert's health after years of alcohol
abuse that he suffered recurring bleeding ulcers, and sometimes halluci-
nations and fever, following each drinking bout, which caused him to
miss work or show up late. Shooting dragged on through the summer of
1934, and Cohn was increasingly concerned about the ballooning budget.
(The good-natured offscreen clowning of the Three Stooges, who would
push each other off the ship for fun, did not help matters.) According to
Hollywood legend, Cohn sent Milestone a cable: "Hurry up. The cost is
staggering." The director replied with dry humor, "So is the cast."[17]

The shooting occupied all Milestone's time and energy, as he described
in a letter dated July 18, 1934, to Kendall, who was back east in
Southampton, on Long Island. "Sorry darling but my work is harder than

Siberian salt mines finishing tomorrow will call you the next day will arrange the time by wire."[18]

In his direction, Milestone repeatedly returned to a few comic bits. A meek older passenger reminds the exasperated captain of his hated father, whose beard was always about to fall into his soup (and finally does in one of the film's final scenes). Alison Skipworth plays a Molly Brown–type character, a loud and lusty widow on the prowl for young male companionship. As a general from a corrupt regime, Tamiroff philosophizes (in a heavy Spanish accent) about his colorful life: "I have been in many revolutions—ten or eleven—and I have learned that a revolution is never so dangerous as when it is successful." The flimsy plot turns on some stolen bonds hidden in a chair, and it is mainly an excuse for broad verbal and physical humor. But the proceedings lack the wit and fast pace of Milestone's silent comedies, *Garden of Eden* and *Two Arabian Knights.* The often pedestrian dialogue gets in the way of the dramatic action and comedy.

The Captain Hates the Sea was released in late October 1934, just as the censorship guidelines of the Production Code were coming into full force. The film's numerous situations of sexual promiscuity, adultery, and lewd language seem a last gasp of the freewheeling pre-Code Hollywood cinema.

Whether it was the result of the production problems caused by Gilbert's drinking, the weak screenplay, or Milestone's lack of passion for the project, *The Captain Hates the Sea* fared poorly with the critics and at the box office. The *New York Times* praised Milestone as "a fine director," but judged the film "generally meaningless" and "dull."[19] Harry Cohn didn't much care for it, either. This was the last film Milestone ever made for Columbia Studios, although under the terms of his 1933 contract he had been scheduled to shoot two more. Stricken by a heart attack in 1935 while working on his next film with Marlene Dietrich, *Desire,* John Gilbert never returned to the screen. Gary Cooper replaced him.

In 1935 two important changes took place in Milestone's life. Leaving Columbia, he moved to Paramount Studios, where he received a lucrative contract and shot his next four pictures. And in July he and Kendall Lee were finally married in Tucson, Arizona. In May he and Kendall had spent some time together in California. After she left to return to New York, he wrote her a cheerful note from the Arrowhead Springs Hotel in the resort of Arrowhead Springs, in the mountains east of Los Angeles, that reveals him in an optimistic frame of mind.

> At the risk of boring you dear duchess I must again tell you that I love you and am in love with you and that I must have been nuts to have let you leave here and yet I'm glad you went because everything seems to be working out swell for us. . . .
> Have been up here a week and we are staying on. Haven't had a drink and am on a diet since we've been up here. Playing tennis and taking all sorts of steam baths. Never felt better in my life and never loved you more—write, wire or talk.
> Milly
> Love from the gang[20]

At Paramount, Milestone worked under the newly appointed production head, Ernst Lubitsch. They had known each other since the silent days. Even Milestone later dismissed his first two Paramount features as "insignificant musicals" produced in Paramount's assembly-line atmosphere.[21] The first, *Paris in Spring,* was based on a play by Dwight Taylor with a Noel Coward–esque story line involving two couples who break up and then reunite after the four partners incite jealousy in each other. Lubitsch made several films with similar story lines, but with a lighter and more vibrant touch. Harry Revel's music made less of an impression than the set re-creating Paris designed by Hans Dreier and Ernst Fegté.

Paramount had signed the young English actress Ida Lupino in 1933, hoping she would become another Jean Harlow. *Paris in Spring* was her fourth feature for Paramount, and the first of two she made with Milestone there. Much to her chagrin, Lupino received third billing, behind Mary Ellis and Tullio Carminati. Despite some inventive camera work, Milestone's treatment fell flat with critics and audiences, who clearly expected more from the director of *All Quiet* and *The Front Page.* One review noted a lack of "sparkle" and doubted "that such a vehicle is Director Milestone's métier." Another described the film as "pleasant, if slow-moving entertainment."[22]

No doubt because of his experience in shooting the onboard comedy *The Captain Hates the Sea,* Paramount next assigned Milestone to make a screen version of the hit Broadway musical *Anything Goes,* also set on an ocean liner. In real life, Milestone was an accomplished sailor, who liked to take friends (including Marlene Dietrich) out on his yacht around Catalina Island, as we know from some home movies that recorded the fun.

With music and lyrics by Cole Porter, *Anything Goes* had a strong run of 420 performances on Broadway after its opening in late 1934, at a time when Broadway was suffering from the economic effects of the Depression. The legendary team of Howard Lindsay and Russel Crouse (they would later collaborate on *The Sound of Music*) wrote the book, an antic tale of masquerading gangsters, stowaways, and colorful gamblers engaging in high-spirited hijinks and an exchange of romantic partners as they sail from New York to London. Ethel Merman burst into stardom in the role of Reno Sweeney, an evangelist turned nightclub singer, thus cementing her image as a "softhearted tough girl."[23] The show also marked the beginning of a long collaboration and friendship between Merman and Porter, despite their seemingly antithetical social origins and styles. Merman got many of the best songs, which were destined to become popular standards, including the title song, "Anything Goes," and two duets with William Gaxton in the role of her sidekick, Billy Crocker: "I Get a Kick Out of You" and "You're the Top." Merman's vivacious personality and brassy vocal style proved perfect assets for Porter's witty, bawdy lyrics and catchy tunes.

Paramount purchased the rights to film *Anything Goes* for the sizable sum of $100,000. From the start, the film was intended to showcase Bing Crosby, who received top billing and $100,000 for the role of Billy Crocker—more than the $97,500 that Milestone was eventually paid for directing, and much more than Merman's $30,333 and the paltry sum of $9,875 given to Ida Lupino for playing the part of Crocker's love interest, the innocent heiress Hope Harcourt. Originally budgeted at $902,000, the film's cost rose to $1,103,500 because of production delays. Shooting began on September 4, 1935, and ended on November 9, nineteen days behind schedule.[24]

By this time, the Production Code Administration, headed by Will Hays and his grim associate, Joseph Breen, a Catholic journalist, had come to exert enormous censorship power in Hollywood. All scripts had to be submitted for PCA approval. Every word and nuance were scrutinized for offensive language or sexual innuendo. Breen demanded extensive changes in the racy and irreverent screenplay for *Anything Goes*, prepared by the original team of Lindsay and Crouse. The Hays Office even raised objections to the film's suggestive title—not to mention the fact that the "plot involved a gangster who impersonates a priest while toting a violin case with a machine gun."[25] In the end, the film retained only four songs from the original musical, and changes were made to the lyrics of those as well. The naughty title song, "Anything Goes," was heard only during the opening credits—and only its first verse. Naturally, the PCA also demanded the reference to "sniffing cocaine" in the song "I Get a Kick Out of You" be excised; it was replaced with "whiffing perfume from Spain."

Crosby wanted new songs added, supplied by Richard Whiting, Hoagy Carmichael, Leo Robin, Edward Heyman, and Friedrich Hollaender. None, with the possible exception of Carmichael's "Moonburn," crooned by Crosby, rose to the level of Porter's frothy creations. Leo Robin's embarrassing and racist faux-Chinese number, "Shanghai-dee-ho," became the over-the-top finale, created by "more than 500 actors, dancers, cameramen, grips and handymen,"[26] and Merman resplendent "in a silver frock and a headdress made of peacock feathers," surrounded by dancing Chinese slave girls.[27] For Milestone, who had said repeatedly that he didn't like working with stars, and who had been used to controlling all aspects of production, working on *Anything Goes* must have been a difficult and even painful experience. Here Paramount's executives were calling the shots, and Milestone merely followed orders. He had little opportunity to make the film his own, working like a cog in the industrial machine of the studio system at its height.

That Milestone was less than entirely enthusiastic about the project seems clear from a reprimand he received from a Paramount executive, Henry Herzbrun (copied to Ernst Lubitsch), dated September 26, 1935, about his working habits:

> Dear Millie:
>
> It has been called to my attention that you reported late on your set this morning, and that when you did report you proceeded to read your script, and at the time of this writing, which is 11 o'clock, not a shot has been taken. . . .
>
> I shall appreciate it if you will do everything in your power to speed up your production so that you do not fall further and further behind. I am certain that the quality of the production will not suffer in the slightest degree by closer application.[28]

Crosby also caused headaches for the producers. On one occasion, they had to chase him out to Santa Anita Race Track and Bel-Air Country Club to get him to come to work when he had supposedly called in sick.[29]

Paramount went to considerable lengths to publicize *Anything Goes* before its New York premiere on January 24, 1936. "It's Leap Year, Girls; So Trot Out Your Stuff," Merman proclaimed in a studio press release. An animated lifeboat display was to be set up in theater lobbies, and theater owners were encouraged to dress their ushers in nautical outfits. "The girls should be trained to salute smartly, and to respond to patrons with a nautical 'Aye, aye, sir!'" Sports fans were to be reached "by offering a 'Bing Crosby Trophy' for the freestyle event at an important local swimming meet. This particular angle is suggested because the free-style event is the one in which literally 'anything goes,' as far as style is concerned, and it's a logical tie-up with the title." Crosby did a promotion of Dodge automobiles timed to coincide with the film's release. The extensive press book prepared by Paramount advised: "It's not often that a title is so beautifully adapted to merchandise tie-ups as 'Anything Goes.' And because it's one of the biggest pictures of the year, every exhibitor will want to take advantage of it to line up as much cooperative space as possible."

Much ink was spilled in describing the technical innovations employed in the shooting, but Milestone's name goes without mention in any of the promotional materials. *Anything Goes* belonged to Paramount, not to the director.

Mainly because of Crosby's strong box-office appeal, the film received mostly positive reviews and did good business. *Time* called it "rapid, hilarious and competently directed by Lewis Milestone."[30] For Merman, making *Anything Goes* was a generally positive experience, although she writes in her autobiography that "for me it lacked zing."[31] She also found Hollywood early-to-bed and dull compared to New York: "But what a dead life it is out there. There's just nothing to do."[32]

6

"The Goose Hangs High"

You ask why I'm for oppressed people? Because I got a background of oppression myself.
    —*Gary Cooper as O'Hara in The General Died at Dawn*

After the unsatisfying task of completing *Anything Goes,* Milestone went for "about ten or twelve weeks without being given a picture."[1] So he complained to his old friend Lubitsch, asking for a new assignment. While they were talking, Milestone noticed "a thick manuscript on his desk bearing an intriguing title (which I read upside down): *The General Died at Dawn.* Lubitsch dismissed it as junk, a pulp serial, but eventually allowed me to take it away and read it, in case it might yield a usable idea."[2]

What appealed to Milestone about the story was its setting: contemporary China. At the time, a savage civil war raged there between Communist and Nationalist forces. War had already been the subject of several of Milestone's most successful films, and the topic continued to attract him for its dramatic and psychological possibilities. China's exotic setting had inspired numerous Hollywood features, most notably Josef von Sternberg's fanciful *Shanghai Express* (1932), starring Marlene Dietrich as Shanghai Lily, "the notorious white flower of China." Pearl Buck's 1931 best-selling novel *The Good Earth* also proved that Chinese subjects could be profitable.

From the beginning, Milestone had a writer in mind—Clifford Odets—who could turn Charles G. Booth's unpublished novel into a screenplay that would revolve around a stark contrast between its two main characters, one representing American democracy and the other Chinese authoritarianism and militarism. "That's the focal point—then we can use whatever incidents out of the manuscript we want, provided we get a writer who understands the political setup."[3]

Although they were not acquainted at the time, Milestone chose the playwright Odets (1906–63) for the job because he had recently seen his two hit plays, *Awake and Sing!* and *Waiting for Lefty*, both staged on Broadway in 1935, and was "very impressed."[4] Milestone and Odets came from similarly humble backgrounds and shared strong left-wing political convictions, including a distaste for the evils of capitalism and a belief in the power of the little guy. But Odets took his ideological commitment even further, becoming a Communist Party member in 1934–35. In later years, both men would come under the scrutiny of the U.S. Congress during the period of the Hollywood blacklist in the late 1940s and early 1950s. (Odets, unlike Milestone, was actually summoned to testify before the House Un-American Activities Committee, in 1952.)

Milestone's choice of Odets at the height of his theater career as a playwright was a bold one, since he had never worked in Hollywood before. Odets arrived in Los Angeles in early 1936, hoping to earn some quick money to support his real passion: writing stage plays. Shortly after he arrived, he was invited to a party by his actor friend Franchot Tone. There he rubbed shoulders for the first time with Hollywood celebrities such as George Gershwin and Joan Crawford. Across the room he saw someone he did not recognize, "the distinguished face of a man of gentle mien, with the sharply defined and intelligent features of a 'head on a Russian coin.' The man moved toward him and in a faintly Russian-Jewish accent asked, 'Mr. Odets, are you here to work or are you here to take bows?' With that he moved away again. Odets, attracted by this obviously cultivated and worldly man addressed by others as 'Millie,' immediately set about discovering his identity."[5]

Later that same evening, Milestone asked Odets if he would be interested in working on the screenplay of what became *The General Died at Dawn*.

Milestone went about introducing Odets to Hollywood in a gentle and encouraging manner, taking him under his wing. When he offered the struggling playwright $10,000 for ten weeks' work, Milestone remembered, "It was like putting steak before a starving man." In the end, Odets would earn $27,500, an enormous sum for him at the time. Milestone also arranged for Odets to live in a comfortable house in Beverly Hills "complete with Filipino houseboy," introduced him to maître d's "at the best restaurants," and provided a studio car and driver. Odets became very fond of Milestone and Kendall, who even served as best man and "best woman" at Odets's marriage to actress Louise Rainer in early 1937.[6]

In the winter of 1936, Milestone took Odets to his favorite hideaway at Arrowhead Springs to work undisturbed. But as Milestone wrote for *Stage* magazine, "It rained continually," and several earthquakes completely unnerved the New York City native Odets. "We packed our bags and went back to Hollywood. Odets took a room on the ninth floor of a hotel, but the idea of a possible earthquake so bothered him that a few days later he moved to the ground floor."[7]

Such problems paled next to the obstacles their script confronted from Joseph Breen and the PCA. Paramount had already encountered severe objections from the Chinese government regarding its previous "China picture," *Shanghai Express,* which led to the temporary banning of all Paramount films in China. In a letter to a Paramount executive, Breen advised, "We recommend and urge strongly that before putting this picture into production, you secure the services of a competent authority to advise you with regard to the possible reaction of the Chinese Government to this particular story. We think . . . that the Chinese will seriously resent the implication that foreign interests are at work to cheat and to grind down the Chinese workman. Because of this and a number of other details, we do hope, for your own sakes, that you will get competent advice from the Chinese angle before you begin to shoot."[8]

Milestone described the difficult back-and-forth with the PCA as "a free-for-all in which any one from the Chinese consulate had the right to write a scene, and anyone from the censorship board had a right to suggest new lines and situations." It was even proposed that the final shot of the romantic leads, Gary Cooper (as O'Hara) and Madeleine Carroll (as Judy Perrie), "take place before the Chinese flag while the Chinese national anthem was being played in the background." One Chinese official who saw the script complained that "the people in your story make love like very low people."[9]

Breen and the PCA also insisted that Milestone and Odets remove numerous comments they considered too harmful or risqué for American audiences. They warned that Judy's "body must be fully covered at all times," and insisted that O'Hara's comment "You got me by the well-known short hairs" be removed. Although Prohibition had recently been repealed (on December 5, 1933), Breen advised Paramount "that you ought to *cut to an absolute minimum* all scenes of drinking, even where these are necessary. We wish to remind you again of the action of the Board of Directors of this Association in directing the Production Code

Administration to refuse to approve pictures containing excessive or unnecessary drinking. Where the drinking is necessary for the proper telling of your story, there can be no reasonable objection, but where it is not absolutely necessary, it should not be shown. Please ask Mr. Milestone to keep this in mind in shooting his picture."[10]

The PCA's demands were so extensive and numerous that Milestone joked that "it took as long to incorporate the censors' revisions as it did to write the original script. But finally the captains and the kings departed, the censors nodded approval, the whistle blew, and the shooting was on."[11]

In letters to Kendall, Milestone described the high-pressure atmosphere in which he and his crew were working. During the shooting, she was on the East Coast, staying either at the Savoy Plaza Hotel in New York City or with her sister, Frances, and her husband, Rockwell Kent, at their estate in Au Sable Forks, New York.

> June 11, 1936 Received your letter the minute after I wired you I am being called to shoot a scene this very second so just let me say I love you and run. . . .
>
> June 23, 1936 Hello baby please don't be angry with me but I have really been working like a dog went on location Saturday morning and finished it twenty six hours later am back without a stop I shall finish shooting in about a week and then hi ho the picture looks very good I think I have got something this time so again please forgive me. . . .
>
> July 10, 1936 Today is my first day in the cutting room with Clifford [Odets] yesterday and he got so excited at the scene that he kissed me. Please forgive me. . . .[12]

In its final version, the film's attitude toward the conflict between the Nationalists (officially supported by the U.S. government) and the Communist insurgents is intentionally vague and confusing. The relationship among three characters propels the drama. O'Hara (he doesn't get a first name), the hero of the piece, is a swashbuckling American soldier of fortune. He has arrived in China with money to supply weapons to the democratic (actually, Communist) forces fighting against the evil warlord and sadist Yang (apparently a Nationalist). "What's better work for an American than helping fight for democracy?" he declares.

The sultry leading lady, Judy Perrie, the beautiful daughter of a cynical and tired old China hand willing to do business with Yang, has no political convictions and is torn between her love for O'Hara and sense of duty to her father. Much of the action takes place on the romantic setting of a train (as in *Shanghai Express*) or on a meticulous reconstruction of Yang's ornate junk, complete with torture chambers below deck. (In fact, the scenes on board the ship were shot in a "huge tank on the Paramount lot, large enough to float a sea-going tug.")[13] O'Hara's cash (kept in a money belt) falls into Yang's hands, but after extended complications and interference by seemingly countless minor characters on both sides of the conflict, Yang is killed, along with Judy's father. Justice prevails, and the lovers face the future together in a striking final profile shot.

By the time he appeared as O'Hara, the versatile Gary Cooper had amassed an impressive list of screen credits in both comedies and dramas stretching back more than a decade. Just before starting shooting on *The General Died at Dawn*, Cooper appeared as the lead in Frank Capra's *Mr. Deeds Goes to Town*, which brought him his first Oscar nomination, as Best Actor in a Leading Role. Tall, handsome, and sexy, he brought to the role of O'Hara (a former boxer) a natural physicality and reticence in tune with the film's noir atmosphere. Milestone also took care to give him nice clothes and to show him removing them to display his muscled chest on numerous occasions. As in his later classic appearance as the upright town sheriff in *High Noon*, Cooper personified the American values of honesty, courage, and modesty. "To my jaundiced eye you're a social disease," he tells that "four-star rat" Yang with the forthright candor of a reformer. O'Hara also got a pet monkey named Sam (he liked animals, too) that jumps out of his raincoat pocket at their first appearance onscreen.

As O'Hara's nemesis, Yang, Milestone cast the Russian-born character actor Akim Tamiroff, who had appeared briefly in *The Captain Hates the Sea* as a Spanish-speaking revolutionary. Here he is Chinese. It was not easy (and, of course, not at all politically correct) to provide Tamiroff with the necessary Asian features, as Milestone later recalled. "To achieve his 'Chinese' appearance, I at first instructed the makeup man to superimpose a Chinese-shaped eyelid on him, using the liquid rubber employed by dentists. They tortured the poor guy and blistered his eyelids, all to no avail: he still looked like Tamiroff. Finally I suggested that they bring in a real Chinese, make a facsimile or cast of his eyelid and then apply it to

Tamiroff, using the same principle as in key-cutting. They tried it, and of course it worked; as a result I almost became an honorary member of the makeup men's union."[14]

Milestone also had Tamiroff occasionally spout what sound like Chinese phrases, although for the most part he converses in an almost laughable approximation of English spoken by a Chinese native, with a sprinkling of malapropisms and missing verbs: "You big bother on me," "You make decide." Viewed today, his portrayal of Yang as a bloodthirsty warlord seems less evil than campy caricature, but it is extremely entertaining nonetheless. Hollywood insiders obviously appreciated Tamiroff's acting; he was nominated for his first Oscar, for Best Supporting Actor, for his work in *The General Died at Dawn*.

Of Tamiroff's performance as Yang, Milestone joked that "he was so suited for the part, that I had no other choice in the matter. Sometimes we have to break our own rules. This was one of the times I had to. As it turned out, I had to use every precaution that Tamiroff didn't steal the picture from the stars."[15] In creating Yang's character, Odets drew from speeches delivered by Adolf Hitler, seeking to give a convincing portrayal of a ruthless tyrant.[16]

Playing opposite (or between) Cooper and Tamiroff was the English actress Madeleine Carroll (1906–1987). She had made a big impression in Alfred Hitchcock's *39 Steps* in 1935, as the first of his trademark "icy blondes." Paramount signed her up soon after. As the prematurely world-weary Judy Perrie, she gets some of Odets's most stiffly poetic lines: "Maybe someday there'll be a law to abolish the blues, something like an amendment to the constitution," "I've got a good solid chunk of anguish in me," "I could kill myself for next to nothing." After initially double-crossing O'Hara, she sides with him against her despicable, immoral, and sickly father. Sporting an odd Continental accent that sounds like an imitation of Marlene Dietrich or Greta Garbo, Carroll does lots of statuesque posing and inspires immense passion in O'Hara, who declares in a moment of doubt, "This is the girl I loved with vitamins A, B and C."

The Irish actor Dudley Digges played in the supporting role of Wu, although several other small roles were given to ethnic Chinese actors. In a press release, Paramount reported that since "three other studios were shooting Chinese pictures, a special party had to be sent into the San Joaquin Valley to wheedle Chinese farmers away from their plows and into pictures before the full quota was reached" for the crowd scenes and

Yang's sailors.[17] Another Hollywood Russian émigré, Leonid Kinskey, later cast as the bartender in *Casablanca,* made the most of the cameo role of the steamship agent.

The General Died at Dawn opens with a brilliant, highly atmospheric credit sequence. Tracking across bustling Shanghai Harbor, the camera stops on one of the junks' sails, where the main title appears. The titles continue as the camera tracks across other sails, to the accompaniment of Werner Janssen's evocative orchestral score, with Orientalist flavor. The music, said Janssen, is "an integral element—not just an accompaniment tacked on as an afterthought. Each of the leading characters is associated in my mind and consequently in my score with a theme, a melody whose color suggests the quality of the character. Sometimes when two characters are seen together on the screen, two melodies will be heard interwoven in what musicians call counterpoint. The melodies are varied with the vicissitudes of the characters."

The novelist and critic Graham Greene praised the film's opening sequences as "as good as anything to be seen on the screen in London: the dead Chinese village with the kites circling down towards the corpses, the long pale grasses shivering aside as the troops trample through, the General with the scarred face riding along the road in the slick American car." But he had reservations about what followed. "After that it becomes a melodrama, though a melodrama of more than usual skill."[18]

Other arresting visual images abound: a dissolve from a white porcelain doorknob to a billiard ball; the mirror in the train compartment that first reflects Judy's face and then O'Hara's; a shot (in Hitchcock style) taken from below as the lid of a chest opens containing what we know is a corpse. But what most impressed critics and audiences is a five-way split-screen representation of the numerous characters pushing the convoluted plot along: four diagonal shots arranged at the corners of a diamond-shaped shot in the center, separated by borders that look like bamboo. Expressionistic lighting conveys a sense of mistrust and unease, a reflection of the constantly shifting identities and loyalties.

As the film progresses, however, the plot becomes unduly complex and improbable. Nor does Odets's heavy, often stilted literary diction help matters. As a playwright, he was used to giving his characters long editorial speeches that can work onstage but not onscreen. After he is beaten by Yang's men, O'Hara declares with an eloquence that seems ill-suited to his action-man character: "I feel like a bag of broken glass." But Odets did give us a line destined to become a Hollywood cliché when O'Hara says to Judy toward the end: "We could've made wonderful music together."

Although unhappy with the finished product, Odets continued to believe that "the movies are the most potent means of conveying to the public the drama of world problems."[19] He remained active as a writer in Hollywood for the next few decades. He and Milestone would collaborate on several more projects in the late 1930s, but none was produced. In June 1936 Odets wrote to a friend just before returning to New York after his first Hollywood sojourn: "Milestone and I got on very well. He is a nice fellow, albeit a little dulled by California, as all talented people are."[20]

Imperfect though it may be, *The General Died at Dawn* was a noble and innovative attempt to bring a story of political conflict, corruption, and economic oppression to the screen. Critics generally admired the film's artistic ambition. A few years later, Milestone would revisit some of these same social themes with considerably greater success in his masterpiece *Of Mice and Men*.

More than three years passed after the release of *The General Died at Dawn* before Milestone completed his next feature. Now in his early forties, at what should have been the height of his career, the director once again became entangled in studio politics and lawsuits. But this had become a familiar pattern for Milestone as he struggled to make what he considered to be "serious" films (*Red Square*, for example) in a studio environment that valued efficiency, entertainment, and stars above all else. In an interview given at the time of the New York premiere of *The General Died at Dawn*, he expressed his skepticism about what makes a star. "Your guess is as good as mine. It's something indefinable that comes in through the lens and microphone, and can just as well be based on the lack of ability as on ability. It may be just luck that whatever a person has gets over." Milestone, the interviewer suggested, "has always endeavored to give audiences something they didn't expect, an artistically set and mounted film, a new face, a new name, or any number of things which might make them sit up and take notice and realize they were getting something extra for their money."[21]

In an eloquent essay titled "The Reign of the Director" published in *New Theatre* in early 1937, Milestone mused on the declining power of directors in a Hollywood increasingly driven by studios and producers. Directors were the "kings" in early Hollywood, he writes—gigantic figures like D. W. Griffith and Erich von Stroheim. But when Irving Thalberg (at MGM) and other producers like him came on the scene in the early 1930s, they gained the power to fire even the most well-known directors. "Those men knew only one way of working—the way of a director: select the story, have a hand in the writing of the story, cast it, cut it, etc. Deprived of that method, they couldn't function. They were forced to go and they went." And once out of favor with influential producers, he continued, "a come-back for a top-notch director is practically impossible. The reason is simple. To make a great picture a director needs the producer's absolute trust and confidence and a great deal of money, money to buy material, cast, etc. Once fallen into disfavor he gets none of those things, yet, because he had a great name once, the producer expects him to deliver a picture up to his old standard."

Milestone ended the essay with a question about his own future: "What am I now? You'll have to wait until the next storm to get the answer."

What followed was a succession of frustrating projects aborted at various stages of completion. First, in the fall of 1936, Milestone began work on a film version of a 1935 autobiography (*Personal History*) by Vincent Sheean, about his adventures as a journalist reporting from the Far East and Europe in the 1920s. The influential Walter Wanger, who had been working at Paramount but like Milestone was a "prominent and omnipresent critic of Hollywood escapism,"[22] was to produce. In the summer of 1936, however, Wanger left Paramount for United Artists, where he would supervise seventeen high-quality pictures (including *Stagecoach*) over the next four years. According to Wanger's biographer, Milestone "failed to adapt a shootable script" of Sheean's book, and the project was abandoned—for the time being.[23]

A few months later, in February 1937, Wanger (who had apparently been paying Milestone a salary) came up with another idea: a film about the Spanish Civil War. Since it erupted in summer 1936, the conflict in Spain between Franco's fascist forces and the Loyalists (including Communists) had attracted international attention and outrage. Numerous American and European intellectuals (including Ernest Hemingway and George Orwell) had gone to Spain to fight on the side of the anti-Franco armies. In Hollywood, too, prominent film industry people had taken sides, including Milestone, who along with other left-wing friends worked to raise funds for the Loyalists. Wanger shared Milestone's antifascist sentiments, which no doubt was a factor in why he chose him—along with

Clifford Odets—to develop a screenplay that dealt directly with the events in Spain.

For this purpose, Odets and Milestone prepared a script they called "The River Is Blue," based on a novel by Ilya Ehrenburg that had been made into a silent film by C. W. Pabst in 1927 as *The Loves of Jeanne Ney.* They altered the original story set in Crimea during the Russian Civil War following the 1917 Revolution to one about Spaniards in Paris "trying to decide whether to return home." Wanger then brought a group of actors— Odets's close friends and associates—from New York's Group Theatre to Hollywood for screen tests, along with their intellectual leader, Harold Clurman. At this point, the PCA warned Odets and Milestone that they could not "identify any of the combatants with either faction of the Spanish Civil War."[24] Wanger and Milestone also disagreed about casting. Odets wrote in a letter back home that the film was being postponed "perhaps forever . . . unless they can get big stars to make it box office."[25]

The Group Theatre actors and Clurman went back to New York, and Wanger and Milestone parted ways. Subsequently, Wanger approached the screenwriter John Howard Lawson with the intention of reviving the project. What Odets had prepared was discarded, and Wanger did succeed in bringing his Spanish Civil War project to the screen in 1938 as *Blockade,* directed by William Dieterle and starring Madeleine Carroll.[26]

Milestone's work for Wanger on Sheean's book had a similarly unfortunate fate. In 1940 Wanger borrowed Alfred Hitchcock from David O. Selznick. Initially they were going to collaborate on a film based on what Milestone had begun, later revised by another writer. But Hitchcock found the material unusable, and he had his own screenwriter, Charles Bennett, create an entirely new story, keeping only the character of the journalist abroad. It appeared in 1940 as *Foreign Correspondent,* a huge success that received six Academy Award nominations, including one for Best Picture.

Also, in winter 1937, Milestone nearly ended up as the director of Samuel Goldwyn's film *Dead End,* based on a hit play by Sidney Kingsley. William Wyler had been selected as the director and started shooting, working with the screenwriter Lillian Hellman. One day Goldwyn, who could not abide dirt, visited the set and vigorously objected to its naturalistic rendering of a garbage-strewn New York street. When Wyler refused to remove the trash, Goldwyn impulsively fired him. But Hellman threatened to quit, too, if Wyler went. She recalled: "The next day Goldwyn called me up and said, 'We've got Lewis Milestone.' I said, Well, you keep Lewis Milestone. You don't get me.' Two days later we got Wyler back."[27]

Later in 1937 Milestone signed a contract for a film to be developed from a novel by Eric Hatch, *Road Show,* about a traveling carnival. Shooting began, but after ten weeks, the film's producer, Hal Roach, pulled the plug on the project, claiming that Milestone was turning what was intended as a comedy vehicle into a serious drama and that it would cost the studio $420,661 to "scrap what had been done and to remake the film."[28] According to Ed Sullivan, who was then working for Roach, when Milestone, "never too diplomatic," was removed from the project, he "stomped into the office of studio boss Milton Bren and proceeded to tell him off." Bren then "told off Milestone" and fired him.[29]

Just as he had done in the past, Milestone responded aggressively to this breach of contract, filing a suit for $90,000 in damages. A judge upheld Milestone's right to sue, and Roach decided to resolve the case out of court. The producer agreed to provide partial financing for a project dear to Milestone's heart, a film adaptation of John Steinbeck's novella *Of Mice and Men.* Roach also agreed to give Milestone 18 percent of the film's gross—a decision that proved highly advantageous to the director since the movie became one of the most critically and commercially successful films of Milestone's career. "I got more out of that picture than I ever got in salary—and I used to get some pretty high salaries."[30]

In the three months before Hal Roach Studios and United Artists were scheduled to begin shooting *Of Mice and Men,* Milestone tossed off a slight melancholy drama for Paramount, *The Night of Nights.* Eager to make a film after several frustrating years, he took advantage of the fact that a cast and crew (including the actor Pat O'Brien from *The Front Page*) had been idled by scheduling problems. Working just one step ahead of the daily shooting, Milestone and the writer Donald Ogden Stewart collaborated on a tale of an aging alcoholic actor (played by O'Brien) confronting his earlier mistreatment of his wife and daughter. The story grew out of an incident Milestone had once witnessed at a New York lunch club in the Prohibition era: a fistfight between two of his friends, the actors Walter Catlett and Louis Calhern. This scene became the opening sequence, and the most interesting part of the film. The screenplay turned the two men into a producer and a star actor working in the same play. In the final, highly melodramatic scene, the actor dies a happy man in the dressing room of his daughter, now starring in the same drama in which he had triumphed eighteen years before. *The Night of Nights* attracted little attention and lukewarm reviews, leaving some Hollywood insiders to wonder what had happened to Milestone's promising and original talent.

Around this same time, in the spring of 1938, Milestone underwent a minor medical procedure. "Operation successful but am afraid will live," he wrote with his characteristic ironic humor to his wife, Kendall, who was staying, as she often did, in New York while he toiled in Los Angeles.[31] At the time, Milestone and his wife did not have a house of their own, so he sometimes stayed in her absence with friends such as his fellow Russian émigré director Anatole Litvak, whom he affectionately called "Tola."

In a letter to Kendall written when he was waiting for final approval of the deal for *Of Mice and Men*, Milestone confessed to "having adventures galore" with Litvak. "Last night I couldn't find Tola's place at the beach so we spent the night at Ira Gershwin's—that's open all night as you know. Will have news for you in another day or so—I hope all good. . . . My address is nineteen one three naught Roosevelt Highway Malibu Beach care of Litvak."[32]

By mid-February 1939, the contract for *Of Mice and Men* was finalized. "The goose hangs high," Milestone wrote to Kendall, using one of those folksy Russian expressions he liked to employ.[33]

When Milestone acquired the screen rights to *Of Mice and Men* from George Kaufman and Sam Harris, the director and producer of the stage version, John Steinbeck was assured by the documentary filmmaker Pare Lorentz (acclaimed director of *The Plow That Broke the Plains*) that he "could not have found a better person" to adapt his novella. Milestone was "a man of high intelligence and artistic integrity."[34]

Once the news got out that Milestone was preparing to film Steinbeck's novel, hopes ran high in the film community that he had finally found an appropriate project. As Thornton Delehanty wrote in the *New York Herald Tribune*: "Milestone . . . will not touch a subject in which he is not passionately interested. The fact that his standards are severe and his tastes uncompromising explains his comparative inactivity in recent years. It also explains the peephole activity now going on about 'Of Mice and Men.' At the tennis club, where film people sip tea between sets, you will hear it discussed. And those who claim to know what's what will tell those who don't that the picture will assuredly be good, that it stands a chance of being great."[35]

As for Steinbeck, by early 1939 he was already well known as the author of several well-received works of fiction, including *Of Mice and Men* and *The Red Pony*, both published in 1937, and both to be filmed by Milestone. *Of Mice and Men,* a compassionate portrait of disability and the lives of migrant workers in Depression-era central California, had surprised its publishers by becoming a best seller. Its popularity led the Broadway producer George S. Kaufman to persuade Steinbeck to create a stage version of the novella, which opened in New York on November 23, 1937, and had a respectable run of 207 performances before going on a cross-country tour. Less than two years later, *The Grapes of Wrath* was published, raising Steinbeck to the status of one of the leading American writers of the twentieth century, a position solidified by the award of the Nobel Prize in 1962.

The novel *Of Mice and Men,* like *The Grapes of Wrath* after it, was received by many critics as a propagandistic tract or even a "proletarian saga" with obvious Communist sympathies.[36] Appearing in the mid-1930s, when American enthusiasm for Communism was at its height in the wake of the Great Depression, the novel projected a loathing for middle-class materialism and harsh criticism for monopoly capitalism. The myth of the American dream of owning one's own property shared by George and Lennie is shown to be a sham, a goal unobtainable for the common laborer. Migrant farm workers (the proletariat) like the protagonists, George and Lennie, are marginalized and exploited by heartless owners and corporations out to maximize their personal gain and profit. The critic Sylvia Cook has analyzed the presence of Communist Party influences in Steinbeck's work and concludes that although he never embraced Marxism or Communism as an ideology, and avoided political involvement, he did share many of the same concerns as socialist realist writers.[37]

The ten-year collaboration of Steinbeck and Milestone (on *Of Mice and Men* and *The Red Pony*) was one of the most harmonious and successful between a writer and a director in Hollywood history. Steinbeck felt that he was respected by Milestone, an experience very different from that of many other important American authors lured to Hollywood (William Faulkner and F. Scott Fitzgerald come to mind). Further, Milestone and Steinbeck both believed that literature and film should not only entertain but also educate. In their respective fields, both artists most often chose subjects that focused on the underdog, on those left behind by capitalism, on injustice and economic inequality. "Like so many writers of this era," writes Jay Parini of Steinbeck, "he considered it part of a writer's responsibility to bear witness, to address a social crisis with the hope of effecting some kind of change."[38] The same could be said of Milestone. This shared belief in the power (necessity, even) of literature and film to convey an ideological message also brings both artists close to one of the basic tenets of Soviet socialist realism.

So it hardly seems surprising that both Steinbeck and Milestone repeatedly fell under suspicion for their alleged links to Communism. In 1939, just before publication of *The Grapes of Wrath,* Steinbeck became the target of a campaign to portray him as a "dangerous revolutionary," and he learned that he was being investigated by the FBI.[39] Although Steinbeck had serious reservations about Communism and never considered joining the Communist Party, he did remain deeply interested in the USSR for his entire career. In 1948 he spent two months with the photographer Robert Capa touring the USSR, an experience on which he reported with a mixture of objectivity and naïveté in *A Russian Journal.* In 1963 he was sent as a goodwill ambassador to the USSR in the heyday of Cold War cultural exchange. And Steinbeck was one of the most published and popular American writers in the USSR, in no small part because his novels could easily be seen as delivering an indictment of the abuses of the capitalist system. Milestone and Steinbeck possessed a shared ideological vision and mutual respect that greatly facilitated their work on both *Of Mice and Men* and *The Red Pony.*

Despite the popularity of Steinbeck's novel and the Broadway staging, Milestone did not find it easy to find backers for a screen version. Many film industry people believed the story too depressing and profane to appeal to a mass audience. Hal Roach's reluctant backing did not provide a large budget. "We produced *Of Mice and Men* for $220,000 direct charges. You couldn't make a Z-grade picture for that money, even back then," the director recalled.[40] *Life* magazine later called it "the most economical Grade A movie to come out of Hollywood in a decade."[41]

The veteran screenwriter Eugene Solow and Milestone first developed the concept of the film over a meal at 21 in New York. Once they got the go-ahead from Sam Harris and Steinbeck, they were granted two months to "get financial backing, have John Steinbeck okay the script and be ready to shoot."[42] They began work at Rockwell Kent's house in Au Sable Forks in upstate New York, then continued in a New York hotel. In

New York they ran into Anatole Litvak, who offered to lend them his beach house in California. There "they lived in their pajamas for two weeks, never leaving the house."[43]

Steinbeck joined them in Los Angeles in June 1939. By this time, *The Grapes of Wrath* had been published and was already in production as a film to be directed by John Ford. "Steinbeck is one of those rare novelists who actually had a happy relation to Hollywood," Gore Vidal said. "His work adapted well, and it was treated with respect. He was lucky in the people who worked with his books, too. They knew what they were doing."[44]

At the end of June, Milestone took a break to enjoy one of his favorite pastimes, sailing. This time, he was a guest for the weekend on the boat of Frank Morgan, who had just finished shooting *The Wizard of Oz,* in which he took several roles, including that of the title Wizard.[45]

In July, Milestone, Solow, and Steinbeck met at Steinbeck's ranch near Los Gatos to polish the script. While there, Steinbeck entertained them by driving them "around the fruit country, to the settlements and ranches where he had gathered his own material."[46] After hearing Solow read their adaptation, Steinbeck, according to an interview with Milestone, responded with just a few changes: "He was going through the dialogue changing the punctuation, and then he would change an 'if,' 'but,' 'and,' and whatnot, and before my very eyes the whole thing was being changed and became Steinbeck's writing."[47]

A more serious obstacle than Steinbeck's approval of the script was that of the Production Code Administration, headed by Joseph Breen. In its initial review of the *Of Mice and Men* screenplay, the PCA raised numerous objections, especially to the obscene and vulgar language and the portrayal of the mentally challenged character Lennie. In a memo and a letter to Milestone, Breen and his colleague Will Hays doubted whether the project could be approved.

> The script, in its present version, is not acceptable under the pro-
> visions of the Production Code. It is, likewise, enormously dan-
> gerous, in spots, from the standpoint of political censorship, both
> in this country and abroad. . . . Care must be exercised to prevent
> either dialogue or action suggesting that Lennie is a sex pervert
> as well as an imbecile. His feeble-mindedness is strongly empha-
> sized in the play but there are occasional details which might lead
> a portion of the audience to assume that his playing with the

dead mouse, his killing of the puppy and stroking of its body, and his stroking of the girl's hair prior to strangling her to death, gave him some degree of sexual satisfaction.

Breen was also concerned that after George shoots Lennie in the final scene, he should be shown to be in the custody of law enforcement officials.[48]

"We didn't devitalize the characters for cinematic purposes, nor did we dilute the pathos and drama of their situations," Milestone explained to Lewis Gannett.

We added depth to the characters of Curley and Mae. Especially Mae, who we thought required some clarification for motion picture audiences. We made her more sympathetic than she appeared in the play. . . . The screen can't put itself in the position of condoning "mercy killings," so we altered the finale somewhat. In the book George goes scot free after shooting to death his pal Lennie to save him from a posse. We show him giving himself up to the sheriff. We leave it up to the public to furnish a sequel concerning whether George is punished by the law. Steinbeck approved all of the changes.[49]

Milestone, Solow, and Steinbeck did remove the offensive language and made the modifications requested by the PCA. Numerous critics noticed these changes in their reviews of the film, like this one writing in the movie trade magazine *Variety:* "In transferring the story to the screen, scripter Eugene Solow eliminated the strong language and forthright profanity of the book and play. Despite this requirement for the Hays whitewash squad, Solow and Milestone retain all of the virility of the piece in its original form."[50] Steinbeck resented the changes made to accommodate the censors, but he appreciated the care with which Milestone approached the material, as he wrote in a letter to Milestone that was reprinted in *Variety* as part of an advertisement ("The Picture Hollywood Said 'Couldn't be Made'") with a photo of Milestone and Steinbeck together.

Dear Milly,

I just saw the picture, "Of Mice and Men." I have a problem in telling you what I think of it. The picture industry has wilted the language like the Surrealist Dali's watches. There are no good stiff adjectives left. Suppose I try to rebuild English from the bottom and say that it is a very good and very moving picture and that I am proud to be associated with it.

John Steinbeck[51]

In a letter to his agent, Elizabeth Otis, Steinbeck wrote that he thought the film was "a beautiful job. Here Milestone has done a curious lyrical thing. It hangs together and is underplayed. You will like it."[52] Milestone and Steinbeck apparently got along well personally, since they remained friends for years afterward. In 1944 Milestone wrote to Kendall that he was providing support to Steinbeck as he waited for his wife to give birth: "Spent last night holding Steinbeck's hand and won a five dollar bet from him. It was a boy."[53]

In their screen adaptation, Milestone, Solow, and Steinbeck considerably amplified the role of the only female character, the wife of Curley, the quarrelsome and bullying son of the ranch owner. (Like so many of Milestone's films, this one also revolves around the relationship between men laboring or waging war under pressure.) In the novel, she does not even merit a name, but in the film she becomes Mae (played by Betty Field), a neglected and emotionally abused wife trapped in an unhappy marriage by economic necessity.

Her only economic asset is her sex appeal, which she uses in order not to become invisible to her husband and father-in-law and the men who surround her. One of the film's most powerful scenes occurs at dinner time in the dining room of the main house, where Mae is surrounded at the table by the disgusting eating noises of the men at the table, consumed by their animalistic hunger. The masterful sound direction (as in Milestone's *All Quiet on the Western Front*), conveying Mae's rising desperation as the lone female in a world dominated by men who ignore and belittle her, was recognized with an Oscar nomination for Best Sound Recording. We come to see Mae, like Lennie and George, as the victim of a cruel system that rewards only the wealthy and entitled. Significantly, Milestone also played up her backstory of a neglected childhood and her longing to become a movie star as an escape from the gritty reality of her existence.

In preparing for the role, Betty Field "went shopping in the downtown Los Angeles department stores—the kind of shops she imagined

Mae would patronize. Finally she paraded before Director Lewis Milestone in the cheap, pathetically vulgar trappings she had selected. Milestone was impressed. He was even more impressed when Betty said the whole outfit cost eleven dollars and thirty-five cents. Thirty cents of that had gone for carfare."[54]

In casting the film, Milestone and Solow decided against using any actors who had appeared in the Broadway version, saying they wanted a "fresh approach."[55] They "had decided to use only actors who would fit the part. They weren't going after name actors. First, they couldn't afford it and secondly, they wanted people who would be Lennie and George, not mere Hollywood imitations of them."[56] Allegedly, the gangster star James Cagney wanted to play George; Spencer Tracy and John Garfield also expressed interest. After testing twenty actors for the role of George, Milestone and Solow agreed on Burgess Meredith, at the time better known for his theater work on Broadway, *Winterset* being his only previous film credit. According to the columnist Irving Hoffman, Meredith almost didn't get the role "because he refused to submit to a long-term contract with Hal Roach. But one night when he thought the deal was cold, he visited a few pubs with John Steinbeck and explained his difficulties. The following morning Steinbeck called at Roach's studio and threatened to call off the picture if Meredith weren't hired on his own terms."[57]

The central and difficult role of the mentally disabled Lennie fell to a relative unknown, Lon Chaney Jr. Chaney, the son of legendary silent film actor Lon Chaney (*The Hunchback of Notre Dame*, *The Phantom of the Opera*), had appeared in the West Coast production of the stage version of *Of Mice and Men* in early 1939, replacing Broderick Crawford, who'd played the role in the New York production. Eager to break out beyond the tiny parts he had been playing in movies, Chaney one day visited Milestone's office and asked for a test. At first reading Lennie's lines with actresses trying out for the part of Mae, he so impressed Milestone that he was hired over twenty-five others considered. Physically and vocally Chaney certainly had the right look for the big, ambling, slow-witted, and clumsy George, and he came eventually to be identified more with this role than with any other in his long career (including *The Wolf Man* and its many sequels). At first lacking in confidence, and wary of being compared to his father, Chaney was encouraged when the electricians and crew "burst into spontaneous applause in appreciation for what they had witnessed" on the set.[58] Chaney found the vulnerable and "slow" Lennie "the biggest, most lovable man that ever happened," and he brought to the role a deep pathos, sympathy, and compassion that Milestone shared for Steinbeck's downtrodden characters.[59]

Among the minor characters, Leigh Whipper's heartbreaking portrayal of Crooks, the elderly and disabled African American farmhand who bonds with Lennie over the discrimination and humiliation they both endure as social outcasts from the other men, is an unusually candid and raw representation of racism in Hollywood films of this era. Whipper was the only cast member who had appeared in the original Broadway production.

The extended cast also included numerous animals: the puppy that Lennie accidentally suffocates; the stallion that Curly rides so proudly; the cattle in the fields; and the old dog that the bunkhouse manager, Candy, adores but others despise. A publicity brochure commented: "Chickens, dogs, and horses wandered over the set, but it was a pair of mules that caused the most trouble because of their snorting and braying. Rex, the 17-year old dog who appears, . . . got silk-glove treatment during his stay on the Roach lot. He had a stand-in and was never worked for more than one hour at a time."[60] Lon Chaney Jr. developed such an attachment to the puppy he worked with that he took him home at the end of shooting.

To find a suitable shooting location, Milestone sent a scout to search California for a ranch with the right look. In the end, however, he decided to build a new one on a corner of a vast property owned by William Randolph Hearst, Agoura Ranch, forty miles north of Hollywood. According to a studio publicity brochure, "The buildings were so sturdy and so well equipped, the picture-makers left them intact, hoping some worthy rancher would turn up from the west and take over. . . . They did it in eight days, erecting nine buildings, sinking a well, building stockades, populating the place with farm animals." The final scene on the Salinas River was filmed in the studio, using more than three thousand gallons of water and eight truckloads of sand. "Producer director Lewis Milestone wanted authenticity and he got it."[61]

In preparing for the shooting, Milestone had his art director, Nicolai Remisoff, sketch out most of the scenes beforehand, a technique he had been using since the silent era. This eliminated delays on the set, so precious time would not be wasted. *Of Mice and Men* was shot in only thirty-nine days—very quickly for a major feature with a large cast. A publicity brochure described this process in detail:

The most striking aspect of the production, to ringsider and casual onlooker alike, was the facility and speed of the shooting. There were no frantic huddles before every new scene, no repeated rehearsals, no fumblings for "mood." The reason lay in a series of 500 sketches, delineating the characters, background, camera positions and even dialog for each scene in the picture.

The initial step in the technique consists of rehearsing each scene with the bit players, extras and stand-ins. With the raw materials of background and people, Milestone then works out the action, camera positions and lighting and pictorial effects. Then his art director, Nicolai Remisoff, preserves the information in the form of sketches.

Such methodical preparation, Milestone points out, does not hinder creative direction or dampen spontaneity on the part of the actors.

"I have found that with this system of preliminary rehearsals and sketch reminders, a short-cut through the mechanics of production is afforded. The director is then free to devote all his attention to the cast, to the development of characterization, to that important phase known as 'business.'"[62]

Remisoff was working with Milestone for the first time. Like Milestone, he had emigrated from Russia, fleeing in 1918 with his family to Paris, where he began his career in the theater, designing sets for the popular Russian cabaret show *Chauve-Souris*. In 1923 Remisoff arrived in the United States, and he continued his theatrical career in New York and Chicago before moving to Hollywood in 1937. When asked about his relationship to Russia around the time he was working on *Of Mice and Men,* Remisoff replied, "Russia? I don't think I go back any more. They have their way of doing things, a very interesting way, too; but I have my way of doing things, and I think I do it by myself."[63] Before designing the production of the film, Remisoff and Milestone met together with Steinbeck.

When Steinbeck explained that the subject of his novel was quintessentially American, Remisoff objected. "'Your story,' he said, 'is about peasants, and peasants are fundamentally alike in Russia, the United States, Mexico, anywhere in the world. They all face the problems of soil, crops and weather. They live much alone, think simple thoughts.' The session wound up with each swearing the other talked his same language."[64]

That one of the most iconic American films ever made, with its Western frontier setting and atmosphere, was directed and designed by two Russian émigrés—and scored by the Brooklyn-born son of Russian immigrants—speaks not only to the universality of Steinbeck's message, but to the cosmopolitan nature of the Hollywood film industry, shaped and run by immigrants from all over the world. Remisoff and Milestone went on to collaborate on five more films over the next twenty years: *My Life with Caroline, No Minor Vices, The Red Pony, Pork Chop Hill,* and *Ocean's 11.*

Milestone's brilliant choice of the composer Aaron Copland to write the score for *Of Mice and Men* confirms his keen appreciation of music and its importance in creating a dramatic atmosphere. At the time, Copland was still relatively unknown and had written only one score, for the short film *Quiet City,* which Milestone had seen. "I liked the music very much, so I talked to Al Newman, who was then the music director at the Goldwyn Studio," Milestone recalled. "If you can get him, grab him," was Newman's sage advice.[65]

Just five years younger than Milestone, a Russian Jew from Kishinev, Copland was the son of Jewish immigrants from Lithuania who had settled in Brooklyn. The score for *Of Mice and Men* added immeasurably to the film's emotional effect, and it launched Copland's very successful career as a movie composer. His understated style, drawing on the intonations of American folk songs and hymns, perfectly suited the subject. Perhaps the best example is the music Copland wrote for the scene of the threshing in *Of Mice and Men,* which amplifies the theme of glorification of farm labor, remarkably similar to scenes of agricultural productivity in Soviet films of the time.

Copland's fellow American composer and critic Virgil Thomson declared that the score for *Of Mice and Men* established Copland as the creator of "the most distinguished populist musical style yet created in America."[66] On the strength of his music for *Of Mice and Men,* Copland would go on to score *Our Town* the next year. He also provided the scores for two more Milestone films: *North Star* and *The Red Pony.*

By early October, *Of Mice and Men* was completed. On October 6, 1939, Milestone wrote to Kendall, who was in New York: "Today at 5 p.m. I finished the picture now darling I can trade your car for a new buick for $480 difference leather upholstery and colored dark green or same as your old car wire your choice and it shall be done love Milly."[67]

Of Mice and Men scored a significant box-office and critical success, and it is still regarded as one of the best film adaptations of a novel ever made in Hollywood. The premiere at the Four Star Theater in Los Angeles on December 22, 1939, was a glamorous, star-studded affair. Among those attending were Paulette Goddard (who arrived with Milestone), Charlie Chaplin, Frank Capra (then serving as president of the Academy of Motion Picture Arts and Sciences), George Burns and Gracie Allen, Ernst Lubitsch, the screenwriter Dalton Trumbo (he would later join Milestone on the blacklist), King Vidor, the Russian-born character actor Mischa Auer, Rudy Vallee, Jack Benny, Sam Goldwyn, Anatole Litvak, and Ira Gershwin. "Even though the holidays are upon us, thousands of fans gathered in front of the Four Star Theater to witness the parade of the celebrities marching in to see the picture," Milestone wrote to Kendall.[68]

The reviews were almost universally positive. Richard Griffith wrote that "'Of Mice and Men' rescues Lewis Milestone's career from a 10-year decline, restores him to the front rank of brilliant directors. . . . It does more than that, really, for there is no one in Hollywood who has equaled Milestone's achievement here, unless it is John Ford. The talents of both men are renewed by contact with such vital material and they emerge as new and unique figures."[69] *Variety* praised Milestone for producing a "superlative job of motion picture making. It rates among the tops of the year for direction; its strong, positive virtues springing from deep understanding of the human values and the exceptional dramatic opportunities as well as thorough competence in the craftsmanship. Numerous of the keynoting scenes have not been bettered for screen technique in any picture. But chiefly it impresses for the terrific emotional reactions it honestly begets."[70]

Of Mice and Men faced some stiff competition at the box office: the blockbuster *Gone with the Wind* had opened just one week earlier. In an article in *The Tatler,* James Agate compared the two, preferring *Of Mice and Men.* "This is a tragedy of the subhuman, and there is a far greater pathos and a far deeper integrity of emotion in Mr. John Steinbeck's little picture than in the whole of Miss Mitchell's unconscionably big canvas. . . . I admire this film enormously. . . . There is a magnificent musical score which is at once intensely modern and entirely right."[71] The *New Yorker* credited Milestone with improving on the stage production. "There's a pace to this film, a direct, unflagging force, which wasn't always the case with the play. . . . The action is swift and telling from the start. It is all the more to the director's credit that this is true since there was easy temptation here to hold the camera for vistas of Western landscape—mountains, ranches, and the like."[72]

Hollywood insiders declared that Milestone had returned to top form. In the *Hollywood Reporter*, W. R. Wilkerson wrote, in his "Tradeviews" column, that "'Millie' Milestone is not one of those individuals who 'play safe' and follow the leader or are content with formula. Almost every effort he has exerted in this business has been in the direction of 'something different,' and this effort has jammed him up at times in both his work and negotiations for that work. But always, in a Milestone picture, an audience was shown an effort that was not guided by formula and always a picture that pointed towards the unusual."[73]

Congratulatory telegrams arrived at Milestone's new residence at 1156 San Ysidro in Beverly Hills from numerous old friends, including Mary Pickford, one of the founders of United Artists, the film's distributor and coproducer.

Feb. 18 [1940]

DEAR MILLIE SAW OF MICE AND MEN AT THE ROXY TO A PACKED AND THRILLED HOUSE CONGRATULATIONS ON THE PIECE OF WORKMANSHIP AM PROUD IT IS A UNITED ARTISTS RELEASE KINDEST PERSONAL REGARDS MARY PICKFORD[74]

Box office proved strong. In San Diego, the opening weekend proceeds rose to 180 percent of average, the best three days the theater had seen in months. In Philadelphia, the third day beat the second day by more than $300. In Cincinnati, the third day "soared $1500 over the opening day." In Los Angeles, reported *Variety* breathlessly, four weeks after opening the "end of the engagement nowhere in sight as crowds continue to storm box-office."[75]

Such robust success was even more surprising considering that *Of Mice and Men* opened in late 1939, the year generally considered to be the most artistically impressive in Hollywood history to date—"the very apex of the Golden Age of Cinema."[76] Although most American industries and workers were still recovering from the Depression, the major film studios were thriving. In 1939 the number of movie theaters in America exceeded the number of banks. Each week, more than 50 million Americans went to the movies. More than four hundred new features were produced that year, in an assembly-line process that ran smoothly and efficiently on the strength of the studios' absolute control over all aspects of their business. Actors, writers, distributors, and exhibitors were all under the strict control of the studio bosses, who were running what amounted to an "illegal cartel."[77]

The films released in 1939 include some of the most enduring and important classics Hollywood ever produced. Bette Davis gave one of her most memorable performances as a terminally ill patient in *Dark Victory*. Vivien Leigh, Clark Gable, and Olivia de Havilland teamed up for one of the highest-grossing films in history, the massive Civil War epic *Gone with the Wind*, filmed in splendid color. Jimmy Stewart took on government in *Mr. Smith Goes to Washington*. As a humorless Soviet commissar, Greta Garbo came to love hats and capitalism in Ernst Lubitsch's romantic political satire *Ninotchka*. *Stagecoach* set the standard for celluloid Westerns. And of course *The Wizard of Oz* revolutionized moviemaking with its combination of black-and-white, color, music, fantasy, metaphor—and the child star Judy Garland.

That *Of Mice and Men* was one of the ten films nominated for the Best Picture Oscar for 1939 was in itself a major victory considering the competition: *Gone with the Wind*; *Dark Victory*; *Goodbye, Mr. Chips*; *Love Affair*; *Mr. Smith Goes to Washington*; *Ninotchka*; *Stagecoach*, *The Wizard of Oz*, and *Wuthering Heights*. Bob Hope hosted the Academy Awards ceremony on February 29, 1940, at the Coconut Grove in the Ambassador Hotel, the first to be filmed. As expected, David Selznick's *Gone with the Wind* dominated the proceedings, winning a record eight Oscars. *Of Mice and Men* received four nominations—for Best Picture, Best Sound Recording, Best Scoring, and Best Original Score—but did not win in any category. Its uncompromising, scruffy realism and unflattering portrayal of the injustices of the American economic system were perhaps too threatening to the Academy voters, protectors of the film industry's status quo and vendors of escapist entertainment.

For Milestone, however, *Of Mice and Men* was a personal triumph and marked an important turning point in his career. After several years of drifting and unfinished projects, he had reestablished himself among Hollywood's artistic leaders. He had also succeeded in producing a serious, non-escapist film that carried a potent message and did not compromise his political and creative ideals. *Of Mice and Men* brought Milestone welcome financial security and renewed bargaining power for future projects. "It was an enormous success," he said later, "and after television came in they wore the sprocket holes off the picture—it was never off the screen. It was not only a profitable film but a prestigious one as well." *Of Mice and Men* continued to generate royalties for many years—in the twelfth year after its release Steinbeck was still receiving $25,000.[78]

By the time of the film's release in late 1939, the international situation had taken a drastic turn for the worse. After the signing of the non-aggression pact between the USSR and Nazi Germany in summer 1939, war broke out in Europe. Nazi forces crushed Poland, and the United Kingdom declared war on Germany. At the time of the Oscars ceremony in February 1940, German armies were threatening France and other countries in Western Europe. For the moment, the United States was staying out of the fighting, but the ominous events threw a dark shadow even over distant Hollywood, where so many refugees from Nazi Germany had found shelter.

7

The Home Front

Everyone in the film industry—writers, directors, actors—has to compromise: you're faced with the alternative of staying out and telling everybody what a big hero you are.

—*Lewis Milestone*

Encouraged by the success of *Of Mice and Men,* Milestone started working on obtaining financing for another Steinbeck adaptation, *The Red Pony.* In early 1940 he and Steinbeck were already meeting to discuss the project. Milestone took a room in a boardinghouse in Monterey, near Steinbeck's home, while they labored over the script. For various reasons, however, including the American entry into World War II, the project stalled and shooting would not begin until 1948.

But Milestone was not idle for long. He signed a new contract with RKO Studios and made two rather slight comedies there over the next two years—*Lucky Partners* and *My Life with Caroline*—both starring Ronald Colman (1891–1958). Colman, a debonair, British-born romantic lead best known for his portrayal of the British diplomat Robert Conway in the 1937 Frank Capra film *Lost Horizon,* had formed a production company with his business partner, William Hawks (brother of the director Howard). They needed a project. Milestone and Colman were also friends and neighbors in the Summit Drive neighborhood of Beverly Hills.

Although better known today for his serious dramatic films, in fact nearly half of Milestone's movies could be called comedies. As he liked to point out, he started as a director of comedies. "Comedies, in fact, aren't easy at all, but to the viewer it seems as if everybody's having a lot of fun."[1] Milestone complained that he never got respect for his comedic work. "The critics always expected something weighty from me, so whenever I did a comedy—like these two [with Colman]—they'd usually say,

'Milestone takes a holiday!' These two films had to be made to keep Ronnie's production company active. It was just Go, and we had to find stories at pretty short notice."[2] Milestone admitted that he accepted these two projects because he wanted to stay in the business, and he hoped they might lead to better opportunities.

This pragmatic, even cynical, attitude clashed with statements Milestone had made earlier in his career about his passion for making films with a message, and it reflected his gradual (if reluctant) accommodation to the realities of the Hollywood industry. As a married man with a stylish wife and a taste for an expensive lifestyle, Milestone also had to pay the bills.

For *Lucky Partners,* Milestone had the playwright John Van Druten and Allan Scott adapt a story, "*Bonne Chance,*" by Sacha Guitry. The far-fetched plot (in some ways similar to *His Girl Friday,* released the same year) revolves around the relationship between a Greenwich Village bookstore clerk (Ginger Rogers) and a pseudo-artist (Colman). They impulsively decide to share a lottery ticket. When they win, they agree to take a "platonic" honeymoon to Niagara Falls, masquerading as brother and sister, before her real scheduled wedding to a boring fellow (played by Jack Carson as a quintessentially American guy) from Poughkeepsie. (In *His Girl Friday,* Rosalind Russell's boring fiancé comes from Albany, a bit farther up the Hudson.) In the end, of course, after train trips, repeated frantic slamming of doors, and a slapstick courtroom scene, Rogers and Colman find true love with each other.

Milestone liked working with Colman. "If you took the trouble to wait until you got through that first layer of defense, he was warm and friendly. A couple of times he invited me and a few other people to have a drink with him after the shooting. He had a wonderful sense of humor which he would project on the screen."[3] But there was little real onscreen (or offscreen) chemistry between Rogers and Colman, and much of the humor seems forced. The material did not inspire Milestone, who fell back for the most part on standard clichés. For the music, Milestone for the first time employed a fellow Russian émigré, Dmitri Tiomkin, who would go on to become among the most successful composers in Hollywood history.

Lucky Partners was made quickly, in spring and early summer of 1940. When released in August, it earned mostly favorable reviews. The *Hollywood Reporter* opined that "the story has been given every advantage of sound, intelligent direction by Lewis Milestone, who definitely proves with this effort that a good director can do a good job with any kind of a picture—either light or heavy—providing always he has the proper materials. In this case Milestone had the ingredients, all of which mixed properly."[4] A review in the *New York Post* praised the director's editing: "While his more serious pictures are made by their sensibility and sincerity; his comedies are made by the artful pacing of the dialogue, and the swift cutting. As a matter of fact, Mr. Milestone uses cutting as a prime structural element."[5]

Despite the polite critical reception, in the words of Ronald Colman's biographer Lawrence J. Quirk, this slight project was "distinctly an also-ran."[6]

In autumn 1940 Milestone spent a month in New York with Kendall and began work on the second RKO project with Ronald Colman, *My Life with Caroline*. It was a cosmopolitan project, cooked up from a French story, starring three Britishers and one Mexican, and designed and directed by Russian émigrés.

Once again, John Van Druten prepared the screenplay, along with Arnold Belgard, an adaption of a play by Louis Verneuil and Georges Berr. A frothy confection of little substance, it stars Colman as Anthony Mason, a rich New York publisher, living for long periods apart from his Palm Beach home and flirtatious wife, Caroline (the English actress Anna Lee, in her Hollywood film debut). Caroline dallies with two would-be suitors (Reginald Gardner and Gilbert Roland) in various fashionable resorts, as her rotund father Bliss (the character actor Charles Winninger) provides humorous commentary. Not at all surprisingly, Colman's suave husband brings Caroline to her senses, and order is restored after many rather tedious antics. A farce of this kind relies on witty repartee, timing, and chemistry between the actors—the sort of ingredients found in the romantic comedies of Ernst Lubitsch and Preston Sturges. Most are sorely lacking here. The opening shot is promising: Colman faces the camera to confide with misogynistic pleasure about the trials of marriage to a flighty female.

Nicolai Remisoff supplied the stylish sets, one of the film's more successful features. Milestone told Remisoff that for the Masons' upscale Palm Beach house, he wanted a staircase that appeared to float without support. "To Milestone's way of thinking, settings must match the sophistication of the story." And so Remisoff complied, creating "the first free-standing stairway in movie history."[7]

For most critics, *My Life with Caroline,* which opened in New York on August 1, 1941, seemed labored and trivial. Bosley Crowther's assessment in the *New York Times* stated the case vividly. "Things have come to a pretty pass certainly when Ronald Colman, that old debonair dog, has to work to hold on to his lady as laboriously as he does here. Let's call *My Life with Caroline* time ill spent and draw the curtain quietly thereon."[8]

One of the film's problems was Anna Lee's performance. She was half the age of Ronald Colman, who turned fifty in 1941, and her youth contrasted drastically with his maturity. During the filming, she amused the crew with her clumsiness. "The poor girl," Milestone told Colman's daughter, rather uncharitably and with a certain sexism, "if there was nothing in her way she would nevertheless find something to stumble over."[9]

Colman allegedly considered *My Life with Caroline* one of the worst films he ever made.[10] But this did not prevent him and Milestone from developing an affectionate offscreen friendship. As neighbors in Beverly Hills (Milestone's house was located behind Colman's), they met socially. At the time, the Russian virtuoso pianist Vladimir Horowitz was renting a house nearby that belonged to Marion Davies. Horowitz, then at the zenith of his fame and celebrity in America, was sharing the house with Milestone's cousin, the violinist Nathan Milstein, so naturally Milestone went to visit. On one occasion, Milestone asked Horowitz why he had two concert pianos. "Rachmaninoff plays this one," Horowitz replied. (The Russian composer Sergei Rachmaninoff was then frequently in Los Angeles, and he would move there permanently himself shortly afterward, in early 1942, joining a large group of émigré Russian musicians and composers, including Igor Stravinsky.) When Milestone told Colman about this talented household, the actor begged to be invited along with his wife, Benita, to one of their musical evenings, as he later told their daughter.

"What nobody reckoned on was that Charlie Chaplin would also be there. When Charlie came in, all those great musicians sat at his feet, and he spent the whole evening telling them anecdotes. Mostly about his own life. They were so fascinated there was not one note of music played."[11]

In 1941 the Nazi assault on the USSR that began in June, the Japanese attack on the U.S. Navy at Pearl Harbor on December 7, and the entry of the United States into World War II the following day dramatically changed Milestone's life and the subsequent course of his career. In the decade that had passed since the release of *All Quiet on the Western Front,* in 1931, Milestone had turned away from the subject of war, with the exception of *The General Died at Dawn.* Beginning in 1942, however, war in its various aspects became Milestone's favored subject. Nine—half—of the eighteen films he made between 1942 and 1962 deal with either World War II or the Korean War.

At a time when Milestone was searching—not always successfully—for appropriate projects, as his recent disappointing experience with *Lucky Partners* and *My Life with Caroline* seems to indicate, war as a subject came to his rescue. As a committed political progressive and pacifist, with a strong personal interest in what was happening under Nazi and Soviet totalitarianism, he found renewed purpose in creating films dealing with stories of resistance, bravery, and teamwork. Some of these films, it is true, veer into the realm of propaganda—but propaganda for a noble cause. Nearing fifty, Milestone was too old to enlist as a soldier but uniquely qualified to contribute to the Allied cause through his art.

His first contribution was to a short documentary, *Our Russian Front,* about the Nazi assault on the Soviet Union. The Dutch documentary filmmaker Joris Ivens (1898–1989) launched this project in a desire to support the embattled USSR, for which he had great sympathy, having spent several years working with Soviet filmmakers in the mid-1930s in Russia. In late summer 1941, Ivens obtained backing from the Russian War Relief organization and Artkino, distributor of Soviet films in the United States under the auspices of the Soviet embassy, to make a compilation film for American audiences.[12] From the beginning, then, *Our Russian Front* was a work of pro-Soviet propaganda controlled indirectly by the Soviet government. Ivens was personally inspired by the heroic teamwork of Soviet cameramen, who had immediately set about documenting what was happening at the front and behind the lines.

On the East Coast, Ivens quickly began assembling footage and hired the writer Ben Maddow (working under the pseudonym Dave Wolff) to produce a script. They had help from the American filmmaker and scholar Jay Leyda (he had studied with Sergei Eisenstein in the USSR) and the director Joseph Losey. Ivens viewed 15,000 feet of newsreel and short subject material, choosing 7,000 feet "from a dramatic rather than pictorial viewpoint, on the basis of their emotional quality."[13]

With a preliminary cut ready, Ivens flew to Los Angeles "to find some famous Hollywood director willing to symbolically add the finishing touches so that his name could be used in the publicity."[14] He met with William Wyler, Milestone, and Anatole Litvak. None liked the script or what had been done so far. But Milestone agreed to take on the film. With the help of the Hollywood chapter of the Russian War Relief, 20th Century Fox provided studio facilities. Of the three candidates, Milestone had the most relevant experience, since he had edited combat footage of World War I during his army days, had created one of Hollywood's most successful antiwar films (*All Quiet on the Western Front*), and still had strong contacts with family and friends in the USSR.

"They all dismissed it saying, 'We won't be doing them any favors; we'll only be exposing their weakness against this enormous might,'" Milestone explained later. "So I talked to Joris about the thing and said, 'Therein lies the tale. I think it's very good to show what efforts they've made.'"[15] Milestone, a master editor, then took "full charge." In the end, the film, which runs about thirty-seven minutes, was credited as "Produced by Lewis Milestone and Joris Ivens." Milestone brought on the Hollywood writer Elliot Paul to adapt Maddow's original commentary, and the distinguished actor Walter Huston "recorded the narration in one night at the Fox studios."[16]

Artkino, Ivens, and Milestone initially disagreed with Litvak over the content. At the time, of course, the United States was still technically neutral, so any mention of outright American support for the Soviet war effort could not be included. Litvak found the text "obvious and propagandistic" and resisted—until December 7, 1941, when the Japanese attacked Pearl Harbor. Overnight, the United States and the USSR became allies, and the image of the Soviet Union changed drastically in the eyes of the American government and citizens. *Our Russian Front* was quickly completed and released to tremendous acclaim in February 1942. At the Rialto Theatre on Times Square, the film "broke all box office records," screening for more than twenty hours a day.[17]

Our Russian Front attempted to show that Russians and Americans were mostly alike, and that the struggle against the Nazis on Soviet soil was also a struggle waged by and for Americans. At the outset, a quotation from Franklin D. Roosevelt appears on screen: "We are fighting on the same side with the Russian people who have seen the Nazi hordes swarm up to the very gates of Moscow and who with almost superhuman will and courage have forced the invaders back into retreat." Later, the American businessman Averell Harriman (at the time the chairman of the board of the Union Pacific Railroad) is seen making a visit to Soviet leaders to assess the combat situation for FDR and declaring: "Hitler's friends cannot be our friends."

Throughout, the people of the USSR are referred to exclusively as "Russians," even though about half of the country's citizens did not belong to the Russian ethnic majority. There is almost no mention of the word *Soviet,* nor any mention of Communism—the sworn and bitter ideological enemy of American capitalism since the 1917 Bolshevik Revolution. Naturally, the fact that Stalin had signed a nonaggression pact with Hitler in 1939, causing outrage in the United States and Europe, is also forgotten here. The brutal Soviet leader Josef Stalin (now transformed into kindly "Uncle Joe") makes a brief appearance, while we hear excerpts from his famous speech to the Soviet people after the Nazi invasion in English voice-over: "In this we shall not find ourselves alone." Most of the footage stresses not the military or political elite, but instead the efforts of "ordinary" people—soldiers on the way to the front; women taking over jobs in factories and agriculture to replace men called up for combat ("The girls do not cry—they work instead"); children sheltered from the violence behind the lines. Russia's industrial might receives lavish praise. Toward the end, Milestone used footage of an interview with a young lieutenant who had survived being shot down in his plane, now chatting cozily with his proud mother at home.

The composer Dmitri Tiomkin assembled the score, mostly excerpts from Dmitri Shostakovich's Fifth Symphony and Russian folk songs. "The biggest and only real problem centered around recording the musical score. Having no budget to speak of, it was impossible to obtain an orchestra, so Mr. Tiomkin did the next best thing: he collected a batch of records containing Russian symphonic music, Red Army songs and folk tunes. With score pad and pencil Mr. Tiomkin sat down to listen and note while the victrola worked overtime. Thus was the score made."[18]

Tiomkin made highly effective use of passages from Shostakovich's heroic and tragic Fifth Symphony. Its heartbreaking adagio movement accompanies scenes of young women donating blood carefully packed in sterile containers to be sent to the front, while the triumphant music of the finale celebrates the Soviet military response.

This and numerous other episodes in *Our Russian Front* served as models for Milestone a year later when he came to make his ambitious feature film about the Nazi attack on a Ukrainian village, *The North Star.*

But first Milestone turned to another front in the war: Norway. The recent success of *Of Mice and Men* led Warner Bros. to reengage the director for a new picture, *Edge of Darkness,* his first there since his silent film *The Cave Man* in 1926. His collaborator on the screenplay was Robert Rossen. They would develop a close personal and professional relationship on *Edge of Darkness* and two more films (*A Walk in the Sun, The Strange Love of Martha Ivers*). The two men shared Jewish Russian heritage: Rossen's parents had emigrated from Russia to New York, where they settled on the East Side close to the Jewish ghetto. An active member of the Communist Party and chairman of the strongly left-leaning Hollywood Writers Mobilization, Rossen (1908–66) eventually went on to become a distinguished director himself (*All the King's Men, The Hustler*). Rossen's biographer Alan Casty has called him "the most accomplished and significant filmmaker who was a longtime active member of the Communist Party."[19] His Marxist convictions would eventually cause serious damage to his career and legacy.

Initially, Rossen and Milestone were intending to make a film of Herman Melville's *Moby-Dick,* but they abandoned that project. For *Edge of Darkness,* his tenth filmed screenplay for Warner Bros., Rossen adapted William Woods's novel about the Norwegian resistance to the Nazis. Nazi forces had occupied Norway since April 1940.

The action takes place in October 1942 in a small Norwegian fishing village. As the film opens, a German patrol plane discovers that virtually all the inhabitants of the town (both German and Norwegian) are lying dead in the streets. An extended flashback that chronicles events leading up to the massacre follows. The townspeople are divided among those who resist the Nazi occupation (either actively or secretly), those who support it, and those who try to remain neutral and uninvolved. The local fisherman and labor organizer Gunnar, played by Errol Flynn, leads the resistance forces. His romantic interest is Karen (Ann Sheridan), daughter of the local doctor (Walter Huston) and his wife (Ruth Gordon). Karen's uncle and brother, however, willingly collaborate with the Nazis out of economic self-interest. Other important characters in the large cast include the local teacher (Morris Carnovsky) and preacher (Richard Fraser), dispensers of moral and philosophical guidance. Not surprisingly, the occupying Germans are evil caricatures, with a few exceptions.

At first practicing passive resistance, the villagers eventually rise up, led by the heroic Flynn, spurred to action when a German soldier rapes his fiancée, Karen. (Milestone deftly films this sequence by showing the movement of her legs as she is tripped and assaulted.) Fortified by the singing of the hymn "A Mighty Fortress Is Our God," the townspeople decide to accept a British offer of weapons. Franz Waxman's score reworks this hymn and the Norwegian national anthem. Predictably, Waxman also employs citations from Richard Wagner's music (the funeral march from *Siegfried* for the final sequence) as background for the Germans.

A bloody battle begins between the nearly defenseless Norwegians and the heavily armed Germans. Karen's brother, the former collaborator, gains courage and warns his fellow citizens that the Germans are hiding in the forest, only to be shot and redeemed as a martyr to the resistance. The few who survive the slaughter go on (in an epilogue) to continue the struggle, including (of course) the hero, Gunnar, Karen, and her father.

Milestone and Rossen brought considerable moral complexity to the narrative, showing how various characters (especially the pastor and teacher) change their nonviolent views and how easy it is to slip into a posture of collaboration. Their script celebrates the power of ordinary people to resist and even overthrow oppression when united for mutual interest in community and comradeship. One of Rossen's favorite themes, it was a foundation of Communist doctrine.

Milestone never joined the Communist Party, but "he was a regular and faithful presence in left-wing Hollywood circles." Perhaps because of their shared political ideals, Rossen and Milestone worked well together. "There was just no separation between us at all," Rossen said. "We agreed 100 percent on the approach to that film." Rossen, found in Milestone "a friend and sympathetic mentor, passing on his store of lore and craft of directing movies to the younger man, who was preparing for his own debut as a director in 1947."[20]

Edge of Darkness ends with a strong external political message. FDR's voice proclaims: "If there is anyone who still wonders why this war is being fought, let him look to Norway. If there is anyone who has any delusions that war could have been averted, let him look to Norway. And if there is anyone who has doubt of the democratic will to win, again I say, let him look to Norway."

Rossen came up with an unusual idea for enlivening the dialogue. Since he didn't know anything about Norway or how Norwegians spoke, he decided to use the Jewish conversational idiom that he knew very well. So, according to Milestone, he "wrote all the dialogue as if he were writing it for Jewish actors. That was his great contribution. I thought it was very logical. Nobody else knew about it; it was our secret. And since nobody else knew anything about Norwegians when the film came out, they ate it up."[21] This was always a problem in Hollywood movies: how should English-speaking actors talk when cast as characters who should be speaking a foreign language?

To replicate the Norwegian location, Milestone chose to film on the California coast around Carmel and Monterey, whose lush vegetation bears little resemblance to Norway, and where persistent fog delayed the production. Shooting finally wound up at the Warner Bros. studio in Burbank. The obvious use of models of ships and planes, and of painted studio flats of mountain landscapes, at times undermines the sense of realism. As in *All Quiet on the Western Front,* Milestone achieved authenticity (and obscured the background) with clouds of smoke in the combat scenes.

At the time Errol Flynn was cast for the leading role of the dashing and rugged fisherman–turned–warrior Gunnar, he was in the headlines almost more for his womanizing and legal problems than for his work in the movies. While *Edge of Darkness* was being filmed, he was charged with raping a young woman named Betty Hansen. This was not the first time rape and other criminal charges had been made against the handsome and promiscuous star, who often chose inappropriate companions and found himself in compromising situations. Flynn was acquitted just before shooting concluded, but Jack Warner feared that the bad publicity would hurt at the box office. Milestone dismissed Flynn's extracurricular reputation, and the two men got along well, as he recalled in a later interview.

> Flynn kept underrating himself. If you wanted to embarrass him, all you had to do was to tell him how great he was in a scene he'd just finished playing: he'd blush like a young girl and, muttering "I'm no actor," would go away somewhere and sit down.
>
> Maybe not enough people knew Flynn well. I not only admired him as an actor, I liked him very much as a person. I knew him as a perfect host, a marvelous connoisseur of good food and wine, and as a beautifully behaved guest in my home. His faults harmed no one except himself.[22]

Flynn also worked well with his friend and costar Ann Sheridan, also his costar in the 1939 Western *Dodge City.* Milestone's willingness to overlook Flynn's bad behavior was at the time unfortunately typical of male-dominated Hollywood long before the #MeToo era.

When it opened in April 1943, as the tide of the war on the Eastern Front seemed to be turning in favor of the Allies, *Edge of Darkness* received highly favorable reviews—more for its political message than for its artistic merits. Even non–film publications praised it. A notice in *Family Circle* noted its strong community values: "The dynamic montages of battle, the terrible cumulative effect of clashing armies (even though on one side there are but civilians, the common people goaded beyond endurance into spontaneous revolt)—for these things 'Edge of Darkness' must be given a place beside the great mob films of all time, not excepting the early Russian silents. And what a music score!"[23]

Viewed today, *Edge of Darkness* seems excessively melodramatic and tendentious, but its moral complexity and strong cast raise it above the level of three other features released around the same time that dealt with the Nazi occupation of Norway (*The Avengers, Commandos Strike at Dawn, The Moon Is Down*). It cannot compare, of course, to another film about resistance to Nazi occupation—Michael Curtiz's *Casablanca*, whose heroine, Ilsa Lund (Ingrid Bergman), is a most memorable Norwegian refugee.

After *Edge of Darkness*, Milestone ended his relationship with Warner Bros. He would return there only years later, for *Ocean's 11*. "I can't be a front office man," he allegedly told the fearsome Jack Warner. "Every time you suggest that I do a picture I'm going to judge it on its merits. I'm going to be a lot of trouble to you because I won't accept anything that you just shove under my nose."[24] Within a few years, this rigid studio system, which treated actors, directors, and writers as property to be managed at will, would begin to weaken. Throughout his career, Milestone was a pioneer in challenging the power of the studios to control creative talent, not always with much success.

Edge of Darkness had attracted the attention of another mogul, Sam Goldwyn. He engaged Milestone to direct *The North Star*, set in Soviet Ukraine on the eve of the Nazi invasion. Despite considerable promise and an impressive creative team, it would prove to be one of Milestone's most frustrating and disappointing projects.

In the years before the United States and the USSR became allies in the war against Nazi Germany in late 1941, the major Hollywood studios had treated the Soviet Union and its citizens mainly as material for jokes.

This attitude perhaps most successfully informs *Ninotchka* (MGM, 1939), released just a few months after Hitler and Stalin signed their nonaggression pact and the Nazis invaded Poland. A send-up of Communist ideology directed with biting irreverence by Ernst Lubitsch and starring a deadpan Greta Garbo as a humorless Soviet commissar who finds love and happiness in Paris with a confirmed capitalist playboy, *Ninotchka* encouraged American audiences to view the people of the USSR as unfortunate prisoners of a perversely antihuman and silly system.

And yet just two years later, after the Nazi invasion of the USSR and the Japanese attack on Pearl Harbor, Hollywood's portrayal of the USSR underwent a complete transformation. Suddenly it was no longer appropriate to belittle and ridicule the Soviet people or even Communism. The U.S. government decided that German fascism was far worse and represented, at least in the short run, a much graver threat to the American way of life. By late 1941 representatives of the Roosevelt administration and the Office of War Information were approaching the heads of the major Hollywood studios, urging them to make films that would help the American public better understand Russia and its people. The studio chiefs were willing to comply, and over the next few years, until the end of the war in 1945, pro-Soviet feature films were produced by most of the leading studios. It also helped that many prominent Hollywood producers, such as Sam Goldwyn, were Jews born in Eastern Europe whose abhorrence of Nazi policies of anti-Semitism led them to embrace the Soviet Union as the lesser of two evils.

From Warner Bros. came *Mission to Moscow,* based on the controversial memoirs of the former American ambassador to the USSR, Joseph Davies, released in April 1943 and directed by Michael Curtiz. Also released in 1943 was *Three Russian Girls,* starring the Russian American actress Anna Sten (United Artists). From RKO came two major pro-Soviet features: *The North Star,* released in November 1943, and *Days of Glory,* starring Gregory Peck in his first major screen role, released in June 1944. From MGM came the musical extravaganza *Song of Russia,* directed by Gregory Ratoff, released in June 1944.

Besides these Hollywood features, several pro-Soviet documentaries using Hollywood behind-the-camera talent were produced and widely distributed with the help of the U.S. military and affiliated organizations. Most important were *Our Russian Front* (1942) and *The Battle of Russia* (1943), directed by Anatole Litvak and Frank Capra as part of the *Why*

We Fight series produced by the U.S. Army Signal Corps. The feature films borrow heavily from these documentaries for talent and material, including newsreel footage, and in fact frequently veer over the line separating feature from documentary. As André Bazin writes in "On *Why We Fight*: History, Documentation, and the Newsreel": "War, with its harvest of dead bodies, its immense destruction, its countless migrations, its concentration camps, and its atomic bombs, leaves far behind the creative art that aims at reconstituting it."[25]

Since they had been asked by President Roosevelt to make Russians as sympathetic as possible, Hollywood producers and their studio personnel heavily stressed "universal" values and the aspects of Russian culture that were the most familiar and nonthreatening. This required minimizing the diversity of the Soviet Union and presenting Russian nationalism as dominant and triumphant. This meant, for example, in *Mission to Moscow,* presenting (as former U.S. Ambassador to the USSR Joseph Davies did in the book on which the film is based) Stalin as a completely rational and dignified statesman, and the terrible Soviet purge trials of the late 1930s as justified and necessary.

This also meant, in the fictionalized features, omitting almost any reference to Soviet ideology or political life. One looks in vain for any visual evidence of Soviet power (such as the hammer and sickle or prominent portraits of Lenin) in *The North Star, Days of Glory,* or *Song of Russia.* None of the characters discusses the Soviet system or the ideals of Communism. Even more, Christian ritual is shown to be tolerated and practiced.

The Soviet-American love-in that began in Hollywood in 1941 was very short-lived. Almost immediately after the end of World War II, anti-Soviet and anti-Communist sentiment grew and rapidly intensified in the United States, culminating in the era of McCarthyism that dominated the American political and cultural scene from 1949 to 1959. During this period, the House Un-American Activities Committee and its related committees in the U.S. Congress summoned many prominent cultural figures to Washington to testify about their own alleged involved with the Communist Party. The pro-Soviet films made at such great expense and with such great fanfare during World War II suddenly became a terrible embarrassment for the studios and all the creative personnel involved with them.

Indeed, these films were one of the main factors that led to the campaign against alleged Communist influence in American culture and education during the postwar years. Numerous producers, directors, actors, screenwriters, and even composers who had worked on the pro-Soviet wartime Hollywood features would be called up for questioning by the House Un-American Activities Committee, including Jack Warner, Louis B. Mayer, the actor Robert Taylor, the screenwriter Lillian Hellman, and the composer Aaron Copland. Milestone would not be spared—as a member of the so-called Hollywood Nineteen, the first group of "unfriendly" witnesses summoned in September 1947 to testify before HUAC for their alleged—and sometimes real—involvement with the Communist Party.[26] Only eleven of these nineteen were actually called to testify, however— and Milestone would not be among them.

Revisionist historians like Kenneth Lloyd Billingsley have also suggested that the not insignificant group of Communist Party members and sympathizers present in Hollywood before the war (which included a number of people born in the Russian or Soviet empire) happily contributed to the creation of pro-Soviet films, only to be caught a few years later in the anti-Communist backlash.[27] As the scholars Clayton R. Koppes and Gregory D. Black write, "For a time the interests of communists in the film colony converged with the mainstream, but this was temporary, coincidental and not of their making."[28]

Besides Milestone, other members of Hollywood's large Russian-speaking community participated in the making of Hollywood's pro-Soviet wartime films. The veteran character actor Vladimir Sokoloff (1889–1962) played both Mikhail Kalinin in *Mission to Moscow* and Meschkov (head of the local music school) in *Song of Russia*. Gregory Ratoff (1897–1960), who in real life served in the tsar's army before leaving Soviet Russia, directed *Song of Russia*, a few years before his memorable appearance as the wise-cracking impresario Max Fabian in *All About Eve*. *Song of Russia*'s cast includes Michael Chekhov (1891–1955) and Feodor Chaliapin Jr. That these Russian-born actors had fled Bolshevik Russia for the freedom of American capitalism and the warmer climate of southern California— and had no apparent desire to return—did not prevent directors from casting them as characters embodying Soviet patriotism.

Significantly, however, Russian American actors were given only minor character roles, whereas the leading roles in the feature films were given to red-blooded Americans. The casting of Americans in the major Russian roles helped promote the propaganda point that Soviets were just like Americans—here, in fact, they actually were Americans!

Hollywood's manner of dealing with the issue of language similarly served to minimize perceptions of cultural difference between Russians and Americans. In the war documentaries, an authoritative American voice interprets the visual images—the Soviet soldiers or citizens never actually have the opportunity to speak for themselves. In the feature films, virtually no Russian words are heard, even though the action takes place almost exclusively in Russian-speaking territory.

The Soviet or Russian characters speak fine English to minimize the perception of their "otherness," but the German characters (especially in *Days of Glory*), on the other hand, speak either German or heavily accented English to emphasize their "other-ness." In *The North Star*, Erich von Stroheim lays his German accent on heavily in his role as the perverted doctor bleeding Russian children, but Walter Huston as the heroic Russian village doctor is allowed to speak in easy American English.

In attempting to make Soviet citizens as nonforeign as possible, linguistic and territorial distinctions were minimized. *The Battle of Russia* deals with combat in Ukraine and the Caucasus as well as within the Russian Soviet Republic, but it makes no attempt to distinguish between the regions or their cultures.

A similar geographic, linguistic, and ethnic confusion afflicted the making of Milestone's feature *The North Star*. Much of the problem lay in the clash of egos involved in its creation: the studio head Samuel Goldwyn, the writer Lillian Hellman, and Milestone. As author of the screenplay (her only produced original movie script), Hellman (1906–84) was the principal creative force. By this time, she was a playwright famous for *The Children's Hour*, *The Little Foxes*, and the anti-Nazi hit *Watch on the Rhine*. No stranger to Hollywood, she had worked as a script reader for MGM, and in 1935 she signed a long-term contract with Goldwyn. Between 1936 and 1943, she adapted her own plays *The Children's Hour* (as *These Three*), *The Little Foxes*, and *Watch on the Rhine* (with the help of Dashiell Hammett) very successfully to the screen. A member of the Communist Party between 1938 and 1940, Hellman had also long been interested in Russia and the USSR. She went to Moscow in 1937 for a theater festival, later described in her memoir *An Unfinished Woman*. She returned to the USSR in 1944 and in 1967.

So when Samuel Goldwyn was discreetly approached by a representative of the Roosevelt administration and the Office of War Information in late 1941 with the suggestion that the studio make a film to help the

American public better understand Russia and its people, America's new wartime partner, he naturally thought immediately of Hellman. At first, Hellman wanted to do a documentary with William Wyler, who had directed the films *These Three* and *The Little Foxes*. But they had a terrible argument with Goldwyn over salaries, which ended with Hellman shouting one of her famous quips: "Sam, your problem is that you think you're a country . . . and that all the people around you are supposed to risk their lives for you!"[29]

Wyler ended up enlisting in the military and abandoned the project. But Hellman and Goldwyn decided to proceed, and Hellman wrote a scenario for what she was calling a "semi-documentary." That was done by summer 1942, when Russia's military fortunes were at their lowest ebb, and American public opinion toward the USSR had swung in a positive direction.

Although Hellman later charged that Goldwyn ruined her concept, and "phonied" up the film, her published screenplay is fairly close to the characters and story line of the completed film: a portrait of life in a "typical" Soviet village (North Star) just before and after the Nazi invasion on June 21–22, 1941. The action opens on graduation day at the local high school and focuses on the graduating students and their families, whose peaceful, apparently prosperous lives (and budding romances) are about to be tragically disrupted. After the attack, the characters respond with various acts of superhuman courage, some surviving with terrible wounds and others perishing in the effort. Meanwhile, evil German officers—led by the bloodthirsty and sadistic surgeon Dr. Otto von Harden, played by Erich von Stroheim as though he had wandered in from a horror film—take over the town and start harvesting blood from the children. (In fact, German occupying forces were known to indulge in this practice.) The heroic Russians receive moral strength from the elderly Doctor Kurin (Walter Huston), who overcomes his pacifist nature and finally shoots Harden, which leads to the expulsion of the German forces from the town.

For the details of life on a Soviet collective farm, Hellman relied heavily on a visit she had made to a collective farm near Moscow in 1937. But there was one big problem that she and her collaborators overlooked. The film is set in Ukraine, near Moldova, not in Russia. And yet the title page of the screenplay bears the pretentious subtitle "A Motion Picture about Some Russian People." Ukrainians are not Russians. They speak a different language and have a significantly different religious, cultural, and political history—as well as different music. The screenplay and film ignore such subtleties.

Even more, Ukrainians, especially under Stalin, were extremely anti-Russian and anti-Soviet. Collectivization was forced on Ukrainian peasants in the 1930s and resulted in terrible loss of life and property. Many Ukrainian peasants burned their own property rather than give it up to the Soviet state. When Hitler's forces entered Ukraine in June 1941, a significant portion of the population—especially in western Ukraine, where this film is set—actually greeted the Nazi army with open arms, since they saw them as bringing their land back into the Austro-German orbit in which it had originally been, and as saviors from Stalin's brutality.

Lillian Hellman saw or knew none of this, however, from her supposedly exhaustive research, which was confined to reading genteel nineteenth-century Russian novels, official falsified *Pravda* accounts of the triumphs of the Soviet economy, and cocktail lounge conversations in Moscow hotels with foreign journalists and official government spokesmen. Milestone later fumed that "Hellman knew nothing about Russia—especially the villages." For Hellman, the film was an opportunity to provide a positive portrayal of the Russian people, "who had been presented to two generations of Americans as passive slaves." Even so, she admitted "I'm just no good at writing about people and places I don't know about."[30]

After Wyler's departure for the front, Goldwyn chose Milestone to continue work on the project. Like many directors, Milestone found working with Goldwyn difficult. "I just didn't like working with him, didn't feel in accord with him at all; he was too adamant, too dictatorial and you had to go his way, because he'd never change his mind about anything. Besides, I was outnumbered: there were too many of 'them' and not enough of me."[31] Milestone told the *New York Times* that he hoped the film would "show that war is a hell of a mess. But it will also show that fighting, dying, struggling and sacrificing in defense of one's homeland against a cruel and ruthless invader are much better than accepting slavery. Better to die on your feet than spend the rest of your life on your knees."[32]

In fact, however, what emerged was a fanciful vision of Soviet life that trivialized the real suffering of the millions of people conquered and forced to live under brutal Nazi occupation.

Initially Milestone and Hellman collaborated peacefully, but they eventually came to blows. The main source of disagreement seems to have been over the visual style, which Hellman had envisioned as "dirt-farmer realism" of a documentary sort—perhaps something like Pare Larentz's *The Plow That Broke the Plains*. Milestone and Goldwyn, however, wanted a pretty peasant village to be constructed on a back lot at great expense. They also added more music and dancing to the script; the first half resembles a movie musical featuring happy peasants dressed in lavishly embroidered and spotless clothes. Milestone took literally what the old peasant Karp says in Hellman's script: "All Russians sing too much and too loud."

The bitter disagreement between Milestone and Hellman over the screenplay eventually led Goldwyn to fire Hellman, which brought to an end their long-standing collaboration.

As for Hellman, she defended herself to the *New York Times* by charging, "I had not yet reckoned with Mr. Milestone's inveterate tendency to take upon himself the writer's function with or without benefit of the writer himself." She blamed Milestone and Goldwyn for turning the long "festival" scene into an "extended opera bouffe peopled not by peasants, real and alive, but by musical comedy characters without a thought or care in the world." Finally, she complained about the subservient position of writers in Hollywood and predicted the rise of unions in the movie business that would occur just a few years later. "An author's final security probably can come only in finding craftsmen with whom he can work harmoniously and, if need be, join in an independent unit as so many craftsmen in Hollywood are beginning to do."[33]

Milestone's relationship with the film's composer, Aaron Copland, was considerably more congenial. Very different from the psychologically probing music he created for *Of Mice and Men*, his simpler score for *North Star* includes a great deal of diegetic, or "source" music, and relies heavily on imported tunes, both folk and popular songs. Here Copland came much closer to the role of arranger-composer, the sort of approach used with such great success by Max Steiner in *Casablanca* in 1942, whose score offers variations on the imported theme of "As Time Goes By." The first half of *The North Star*, before the German invasion, adopts a Broadway-musical song-and-dance style poorly. David Lichine, another Russian émigré who had danced with Anna Pavlova and the Ballets Russes de Monte Carlo, provided the choreography, giving the dance sequences an uptown concert-hall polish that seems wildly inappropriate for a provincial farming town.

For the English lyrics, Copland collaborated with Ira Gershwin, who supplied mostly plodding lines like "We're the younger generation and the future of the nation." Only four of the eight songs are original compositions by Copland and Gershwin. Copland also provided an orchestral arrangement of the Communist hymn "The Internationale," broadcast on Soviet radio after the news of the Nazi attack.

The North Star did not suffer from a lack of creative talent—or a small budget. The production cost more than $3 million and boasted sets by the legendary William Cameron Menzies. No expense was spared in creating the dramatic conflagration of the village at the film's end. Unlike *Edge of Darkness, The North Star* did not use models or any trick shots. "The $260,000 set was razed with dynamite and gasoline. Extras, instead of the customary $8.25 a day, received a daily 'stunt' check of $35. Over 100 persons—including Walter Brennan and Von Stroheim—were injured by flying debris during the filming of the scene."[34]

The cinematographer James Wong Howe's work includes several dynamic sequences: the climactic torching of the village and the German aerial attack on the town's young people walking on their way to Kiev. As in *All Quiet on the Western Front,* the accompanying sound direction is masterful, one of the few moments when the real horror of war emerges. Elsewhere, Howe favored repeating patterns of concentric circles, especially in the pre-attack picnic scene of singing and dancing.

Besides Walter Huston and Erich von Stroheim as the good and bad doctors, the cast includes such veterans as Walter Brennan (as the old peasant Karp) and Anne Baxter (as Marina). She was a big box-office draw on the strength of her recent appearance in Orson Welles's *The Magnificent Ambersons.* Joining them were two newcomers, Dana Andrews and Farley Granger.

Andrews (1909–92) was already in his mid-thirties, but he had yet to make it big in Hollywood. Still to come were *State Fair* (1945) and *The Best Years of Our Lives* (1946), fine films that would turn him into a star. *The North Star* was the first of four features that Andrews would make with Milestone; *The Purple Heart, A Walk in the Sun,* and *No Minor Vices* would follow in rapid succession in the 1940s. In *The North Star,* Andrews was cast in the minor role of Kolya Simonov, a patriotic bombardier. In his most important and final scene, Simonov takes over the controls from a pilot who has been shot and aims the plane toward a German convoy on the road below, shouting, "I'm coming down, and it's going to hurt you. And I'm coming down just where I want to. Because I'm a good bombardier and a good pilot too!" His is a creditable performance, as the sort of taciturn, enigmatic, tough, and unsentimental character that became his trademark. On the set, Andrews struck other actors as "grumpy" and unapproachable (especially in the early morning), a result of his excessive drinking, which worsened with the years.

When Farley Granger (1925–2011), a wide-eyed seventeen-year old taking his first movie role as Andrews's screen younger brother Damian, tried to make friends with Andrews, he was not successful. "On set he was always line-perfect and always there for me, but I never felt a connection to him as I would with a brother who loved me. Of course, I thought that it was my fault."[35]

In Milestone, however, Granger found a kind and supportive mentor. "I had no way of knowing how lucky I was to have the great Lewis Milestone direct me and shape my performance in my first two movies."[36] At his audition, Goldwyn (with his "ball-bearing eyes") and Hellman ("an ugly little lady wreathed in clouds of cigarette smoke") intimidated a nervous Granger, but Milestone, "a friendly-looking, stocky middle-aged man, smiled at me and winked."[37] During the filming, the director gave Granger quiet reassurance, as he recalled years later:

> Each actor had his own beautifully honed technique, and every one offered something from which I could learn. Before each scene, Mr. Milestone, or Millie as everyone called him, would explain to those involved what was happening and how he expected them to react. He would then shoot the scene as many times as he had to in order to get a finished product that satisfied him. For the first few days, I went up to him after every scene to find out how I was doing. After the third time he took me aside and explained that I didn't need to check with him after each scene. He would let me know when he wanted me to do anything different. Up until now he was very happy with my work. I was pleased as could be, but I also got the message not to bother him.[38]

As Damian, Granger projects a natural camera-ready innocence and humor in his scenes with Anne Baxter's Marina. Milestone was so pleased with Granger's performance that he convinced a reluctant Goldwyn to lend him to 20th Century Fox for his next film, *The Purple Heart*. Within a few years, Granger was discovered by Alfred Hitchcock, who cast him in leading roles in *Rope* and *Strangers on a Train*.

When *The North Star* was released, less than a year after the Soviet army had defeated the Nazi forces at Stalingrad, political considerations still predominated over aesthetic ones. But audiences still failed to show up despite a promising first week in New York. In the end, *The North Star* failed to make its money back. In the *Nation*, the writer James Agee identified the fundamental flaw: "In its basic design Lillian Hellman's script could have become a fine picture: but the characters are stock, their lines are tinny-literary, their appearance and that of their village is scrubbed behind the ear and 'beautified'; the camera work is nearly all glossy and overcomposed; the proudly complicated action sequences are stale from overtraining; even the best of Aaron Copland's score has no business ornamenting a film drowned in ornament: every resourcefulness appropriate to some kinds of screen romance, in short, is used to make palatable what is by no remote stretch of the mind romantic."[39]

Even so, the political climate was such that *The North Star* received six Academy Award nominations: Original Screenplay, Cinematography, Art Direction, Sound Recording, Music (Scoring of a Dramatic or Comedy Picture), and Special Effects.

Today *The North Star*, like all the pro-Soviet films made during World War II, seems primitive, heavy-handed, emotionally insincere, and historically false. Pauline Kael joked that the film "romanticizes the Russians so fondly that they're turned into Andy Hardy's neighbors." Even Lillian Hellman later virtually disowned the film. In her memoir *An Unfinished Woman*, she admits: "It could have been a good picture instead of the big-time, sentimental, badly directed, badly acted mess it turned out to be."[40]

Hollywood's pro-Soviet films provoked political controversy as soon as they were released. In particular, *Mission to Moscow*, released in May 1943, six months before *The North Star* opened, came in for severe criticism for its portrayal of the purge trials that occurred in the late 1930s in the USSR. The fact that *Mission to Moscow* (with its onscreen introduction by former Ambassador Davies) presented itself more as documentary than feature made it an easier target for those who found fault with its historical accuracy. On May 9, 1943, just ten days after Bosley Crowther's lukewarm review of *Mission to Moscow*, the *New York Times* published another lengthy essay by Crowther raising questions about the film's political and historical veracity, as well as its intentions: "It is just as ridiculous to pretend that Russia has been a paradise of purity as it is to say the same thing of ourselves."[41]

In the same issue, a long letter by John Dewey, professor of philosophy at Columbia University, and Suzanne La Follette, a cousin of Senator Robert M. La Follette of Wisconsin, attacked *Mission to Moscow* as "the first instance in our country of totalitarian propaganda for mass consumption."[42] Other letters to the newspaper on both sides of the issue appeared over the coming weeks. The director of the National Department of Americanism of the Veterans of Foreign Wars charged that "renegade Communists" were attempting to suppress the film.[43] On May 20, a statement signed by fifty-two leading American educators, historians, writers, and trade union leaders denounced the film as propaganda. The same day, at a rally held in Carnegie Hall, Ambassador Davies and Walter Huston were awarded a certificate of appreciation by the National Council of American-Soviet Friendship. On May 28 the New York City Board of Transportation ordered that placards placed in subway and elevated cars announcing *Mission to Moscow* as the "motion picture of the month" be removed after complaints were received about its distortion of "the facts upon which it is supposedly based."[44]

So heated did the controversy become that Howard Koch, the screenwriter of *Mission to Moscow* (and, not incidentally, of *Casablanca*), felt called on to defend himself in a long letter to the *New York Times:* "History provides us with the materials of drama, but it doesn't conveniently arrange them into scenes or bind them to any unifying theme. That is the province of the dramatist as distinct from the historian."[45] Meanwhile, in Moscow itself, *Mission to Moscow* was screened for Stalin and soon released for public consumption in the USSR.

Six months later, *The North Star* also stirred up fierce political controversy. Goldwyn realized that its glowing representation of Soviet life would probably offend the influential anti-Communist American press. He especially feared the reaction of William Randolph Hearst. Goldwyn persuaded Hearst not to prejudge the film, and he was pleasantly surprised when a positive review appeared in Hearst's *New York Journal-American.* But Hearst had not approved the notice and in a furious rage had the paper run in its next edition a negative review under the headline "Unadulterated Soviet Propaganda."[46]

In the Hearst-run *San Francisco Examiner,* Neil Rau continued the attack: "Written by Lillian Hellman, whose interest in Sovietism is well known, it should get more Communist converts among unthinking, sophomoric minds than the late Emma Goldman tried to snare before her deportation. It is not that 'North Star' comes out boldly labeled as Soviet propaganda. It is too insidious for that. The danger is that someone may take the picture's musical comedy version of life in the Soviet Union before the Nazi invasion as the real thing."[47]

Other anti-Soviet newspapers joined in, launching what *PM* magazine called "the most vicious and unprincipled smear campaign ever launched against a film in America, even more hateful than that against *Mission to Moscow*."[48] Some publications did defend the film's representation of Russia. An editorial signed by Manchester Boddy, editor and publisher of the *Los Angeles Daily News,* praised Goldwyn for attempting to "create a better understanding of Russia and her people. While the cast includes many of Hollywood's most eminent actors, it is Russia, rather than the cast, that dominates the drama."[49] *Life* magazine named *The North Star* the "movie of the year." *Time* called it a "cinemilestone."

Not surprisingly, Soviet officials in Moscow welcomed the appearance of *The North Star* with open arms. The members of the cinema section of VOKS, the Soviet agency controlling relations with foreign cultural organizations and creative artists, sent a telegram addressed to Goldwyn, Milestone, and Hellman signed by its chairman, the film director Vsevolod Pudovkin. "VOKS CINEMA SECTION GATHERED DISCUSS YOUR FILM QUOTE NORTH STAR UNQUOTE HIGHLY APPRECIATES YOUR TALENTED WORK WHICH SPEAKS OF AMERICAS DEEP AND LIVELY INTEREST IN OUR COUNTRY STOP YOUR TRUTHFUL FILM IS GREAT CONTRIBUTION TO VICTORY OVER OUR COMMON ENEMY AND PROMOTES BETTER MUTUAL UNDERSTANDING BETWEEN SOVIET AND AMERICAN PEOPLES STOP WITH CORDIAL GREETING AND BEST WISHES CONTINUED SUCCESS YOUR WORK SIGNED BEHALF CINEMA SECTION."[50]

Such lavish praise from an official Soviet source proved to be a Trojan horse for Milestone. The political controversy ignited over the favorable representation of Soviet Russia in *Mission to Moscow, Song of Russia,* and *The North Star* faded for a time but never went away. It would return with renewed force and more serious consequences after the Soviet-American wartime alliance broke down after World War II. Opportunistic journalists and politicians would revisit this debate with gusto in the early years of the Cold War, seeing these films—and those who produced and created them—as damning evidence of persistent and dangerous pro-Communist sentiment in Hollywood studios.

The New Klondike (1926). Milestone (sitting at center) with the cast and crew in Florida. Margaret Herrick Library.

Two Arabian Knights (1927). Milestone (center) clowning in the snow with costars Louis Wolheim (left) and William Boyd. Margaret Herrick Library.

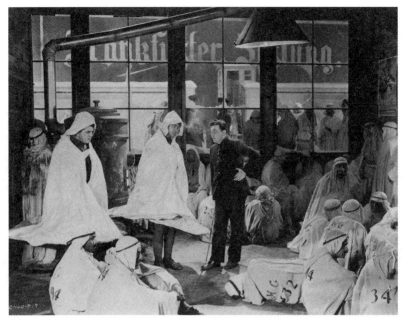

Two Arabian Knights (1927). Milestone directing a scene with Wolheim (left) and Boyd. Margaret Herrick Library.

Two Arabian Knights (1927). A United Artists/Caddo publicity shot. "One of the first and most thrilling bits of action in *Two Arabian Knights,* a comedy drama which follows the adventures of two doughboys from the trenches of France into a German prison camp and thence down into Arabia." Margaret Herrick Library.

Publicity photo of Milestone, around 1927. Margaret Herrick Library.

Milestone posing with an Oscar statuette, 1929, awarded for *Two Arabian Knights*. Copyright © Academy of Motion Picture Arts and Sciences.

Douglas Fairbanks presenting Milestone with the Oscar statuette, 1929.
Copyright © Academy of Motion Picture Arts and Sciences.

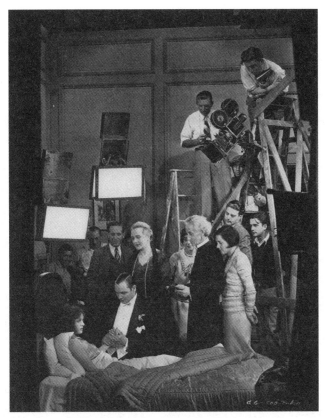

The Garden of Eden (1928). Milestone (at top right) filming a scene with the film's stars, Corinne Griffith and Lowell Sherman. Margaret Herrick Library.

Milestone (sitting with elbow on table at left) attending the eleventh anniversary dinner of the Photographic Division Association of the U.S Signal Corp at the Russian American Art Club in Hollywood, November 10, 1929. Margaret Herrick Library.

Milestone (standing by window at left, with cigarette) working in his
Hollywood apartment "around a wobbly card table" on the screenplay for *All
Quiet on the Western Front,* 1930, with Dell Andrews (seated at left), George
Cukor (standing at right), and Maxwell Anderson (seated at right). George
Cukor Collection, Margaret Herrick Library.

Milestone reading Erich Maria Remarque's *All Quiet on the Western Front,* in preparation for shooting his adaptation of the novel. Around 1930. Photo by Ray Jones, Universal Pictures Corp., Margaret Herrick Library.

A shot of the battlefield during filming of *All Quiet on the Western Front,* 1930. Gift of David Shepard, Margaret Herrick Library.

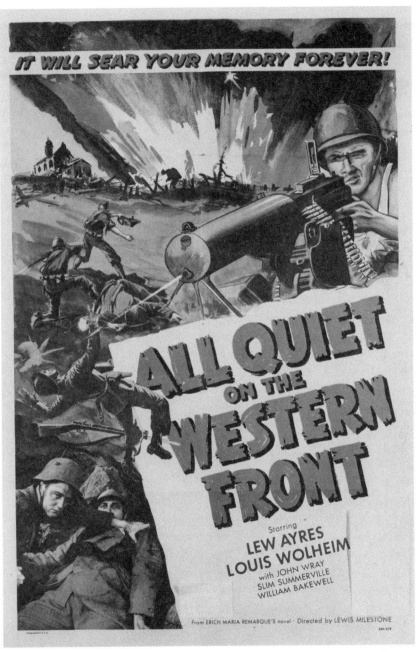

Poster for *All Quiet on the Western Front,* Universal Television. Gift of Andy Lee, Margaret Herrick Library.

Rain (1932). A group shot of the cast and crew. Milestone is at center (fourth from left, first row), with Walter Huston standing behind him. Louella Parsons Collection, Margaret Herrick Library.

Rain (1932). Milestone (kneeling at left), directing Joan Crawford (right). From the collection of Robert Cushman, Margaret Herrick Library.

Rain (1932). A shot of a scene in the hotel. Sitting at the table (left to right): Matt Moore, Beulah Bondi, Kendall Lee. Standing: Guy Kibbee, Joan Crawford. Beulah Bondi Collection, Margaret Herrick Library.

Rain (1932). Milestone during the shooting, on Catalina Island. Bison Archives Photographs, collected by Marc Wanamaker, Margaret Herrick Library.

The Captain Hates the Sea (1934). Left to right: Victor McLaglen, Milestone, Walter Connolly, Jack Gilbert. R. R. Stuart Collection, Margaret Herrick Library, gift of Michael Weekes.

Milestone and his wife, Kendall Lee, 1930s. Margaret Herrick Library.

The General Died at Dawn (1936). Milestone and Clifford Odets. The caption reads, "Clifford Odets, right, who rocketed to fame after years of precarious existence in a West Side lodging house, gets his introduction to movie writing." Paramount publicity photo, Margaret Herrick Library.

The General Died at Dawn (1936). The actor George Raft (left) visits Milestone (center) and Gary Cooper on the set. Paramount publicity photo, Margaret Herrick Library.

The General Died at Dawn (1936). The novelist John O'Hara (left) and Milestone. "NOVELIST TURNS ACTOR—author John O'Hara is playing a bit part to get material for a novel about Hollywood." Paramount publicity photo, Margaret Herrick Library.

Of Mice and Men (1939). Milestone reading the screenplay of Steinbeck's novel in preparation for shooting. Margaret Herrick Library.

Of Mice and Men (1939). Roman Bohnen (left) and Milestone discussing a scene on location at the Agoura Ranch. Margaret Herrick Library.

My Life with Caroline (1941). Milestone (left) discussing set designs with Art Director Nicolai Remisoff. Margaret Herrick Library.

My Life with Caroline (1941). Milestone on the set with the costars Kay Leslie (left) and Anna Lee. Margaret Herrick Library.

Edge of Darkness (1943). Milestone (left) with the film's star, Errol Flynn. Margaret Herrick Library.

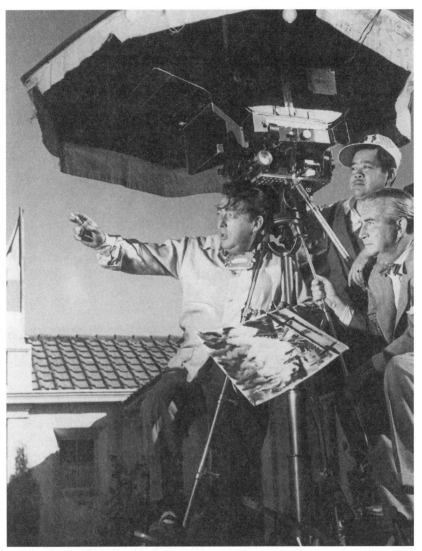

The North Star (1943). Milestone (left) planning a scene with the cinematographer James Wong Howe (center) and Milestone's friend William Cameron Menzies. Margaret Herrick Library.

The North Star (1943). Milestone (left) checking negatives with James Wong Howe during shooting. Margaret Herrick Library.

The North Star (1943). A scene of the village burning. Margaret Herrick Library.

The Purple Heart (1944). A shot of the cast and crew. Milestone is standing at right in the second row. Dana Andrews is standing at center wearing a leather jacket. Margaret Herrick Library.

A Walk in the Sun (1945). A shot of the cast. Norman Lloyd is second from left. Margaret Herrick Library.

A Walk in the Sun (1945). Milestone (left) and Robert Rossen, author of the screenplay. Margaret Herrick Library.

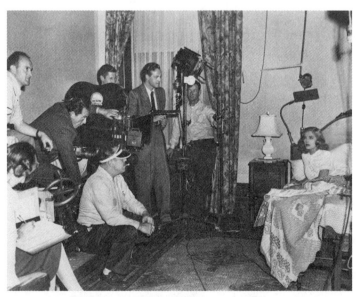

The Strange Love of Martha Ivers (1946). Milestone (bending over in front of the camera) directing a scene with Lizabeth Scott (in bed). Her costar, Van Heflin, is standing in front of the window. Margaret Herrick Library.

Arch of Triumph (1948). Milestone conferring with Edith Head, who designed Ingrid Bergman's clothes for the film. The studio's publicity caption reads that they are "keeping their eyes glued on the Swedish star who is en route to the set." Enterprise Studios publicity shot, Margaret Herrick Library.

Arch of Triumph (1948). Milestone (far right foreground) working with Russell Metty, director of photography (seated to Milestone's right), on a closeup of Ingrid Bergman and Charles Boyer. Margaret Herrick Library.

Arch of Triumph (1948). An Enterprise Studios publicity shot that was captioned, "Ingrid Bergman shares a chuckle with Lewis Milestone between scenes." Margaret Herrick Library.

The Red Pony (1949). The caption reads, "Bob Mitchum (left) confers on a question of acting technique with Lewis Milestone (right)." Margaret Herrick Library.

The Red Pony (1949). Milestone (left) and Peter Miles (on the pony) during a visit to the set by Roy Rogers. Margaret Herrick Library.

Halls of Montezuma (1951). Milestone (left) with Richard Widmark (center) receiving instruction in how to handle his rifle. Margaret Herrick Library.

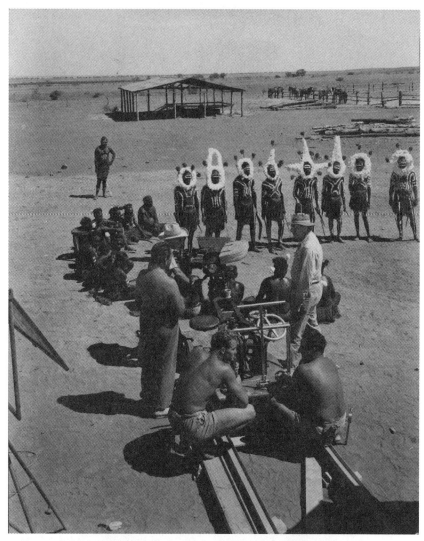

Kangaroo (1952). Milestone (standing at left, with his back to the camera, shirtless) preparing to shoot the rain dance scene with local tribesmen on location in Australia. From the Collection of Charles G. Clarke, Margaret Herrick Library.

Pork Chop Hill (1959). Gregory Peck (second from left) and Milestone (far right) during production. Gregory Peck Papers, Academy of Motion Picture Arts and Sciences, Margaret Herrick Library.

Ocean's 11 (1960). A group shot of the cast. Left to right: Richard Conte, Buddy Lester, Joey Bishop, Sammy Davis Jr., Frank Sinatra, Dean Martin, Peter Lawford, Akim Tamiroff, Henry Silva, Richard Benedict, Norman Fell, Clem Harvey. Margaret Herrick Library.

Ocean's 11 (1960). Milestone (standing, behind the camera) with Shirley MacLaine (seated, left) and William H. Daniels, director of photography (seated, behind the camera), during production. Margaret Herrick Library.

Mutiny on the Bounty (1962). Milestone with the star Tarita on location in Tahiti. Photo by Kendall Milestone, Margaret Herrick Library.

Mutiny on the Bounty (1962). Milestone (left) with Robert L. Surtees, director of photography, on location in Tahiti. Photo by Kendall Milestone, Margaret Herrick Library.

Mutiny on the Bounty (1962). Milestone (right) and Marlon Brando (left) and an unidentified man during production. Margaret Herrick Library.

Mutiny on the Bounty (1962). The arrival of the sailors and officers of the *Bounty* on Tahiti. Marlon Brando is in the center of the clearing, in an officer's uniform. MGM publicity photo. Gift of Mr. and Mrs. Lloyd Shearer, Margaret Herrick Library.

Milestone (second from left) with Hall Wallis (far left), Mrs. Jack Warner (center), Jack Warner (second from right) and Sidney Franklin, 1920s. Hall Wallis Collection, Margaret Herrick Library.

Milestone (far left) with (left to right) Ernst Lubitsch, Frank Capra, Marlene Dietrich, unidentified, Mervyn LeRoy, unidentified, Rouben Mamoulian. Undated, probably late 1930s. Margaret Herrick Library.

Milestone (far right) with his director colleagues (left to right) Rouben Mamoulian, William Wyler, Billy Wilder, Mervyn LeRoy. Around 1954. Margaret Herrick Library.

8

King of the Set

I also am tired of war pictures, but then I am tired of war, too. But the war goes on, doesn't it? And we can't ignore it. So war pictures also must go on.

—*Lewis Milestone*

Never one to waste a possible lucrative business opportunity, Milestone's former producer Howard Hughes suggested that he remake the World War I comedy *Two Arabian Knights,* but against the background of World War II. Milestone refused. "*Two Arabian Knights* belongs to the First World War. WWII is a different kind of war. We couldn't do it the way we did it before because World War II was not a lighthearted war. World War I had certain humorous overtones, but not World War II."[1]

The Purple Heart, Milestone's next film about World War II, provides precious few moments of comic relief. This time, the scene shifts to the Pacific War. Relentlessly serious and dark, it tells a disturbing story of the capture, torture, and trial of eight American airmen by the Japanese government. Perhaps Milestone's most obviously propagandistic film, it was made at a time when Americans called the Japanese "Japs" without a moment's hesitation and the American government was imprisoning tens of thousands of loyal Americans of Japanese heritage in internment camps. Today *The Purple Heart* seems uncomfortably nationalistic, racist, and one-dimensional in its portrayal of both the Japanese and Chinese people, but at the time of its release critics hailed it as a powerful "indictment of Jap atrocity" and even as Milestone's best film since *All Quiet on the Western Front.*[2] It was a movie that suited the mood of the times, when America found itself engaged in a life-and-death military struggle on multiple fronts and thousands of American sons, brothers, and fathers were fighting and dying on distant battlefields.

Milestone's old friend and collaborator from the silent days, Darryl Zanuck, now vice president for production at 20th Century Fox studios, gave him the idea for *The Purple Heart* at a party. "Darryl Zanuck whispered that he had a film for him, one that Milestone must direct. No, he couldn't tell him the name, nor would he even hint at the subject matter. Milestone must pick up the script himself; no one else must see it. The director, curiosity piqued, picked up the script the next day. It was a picture he felt he must make."[3]

The reason for Zanuck's secrecy was that the subject matter—Japanese atrocities toward American prisoners of war—was extremely sensitive. Fearful of inciting the Japanese to reprisals against POWs, the War Department wanted to minimize publicity. Zanuck went ahead anyway and wrote the screenplay for *The Purple Heart* himself, using a pen name. For the story, he used the few facts available about the Doolittle raid of April 1942.

Led by Colonel James Doolittle, a force of sixteen bombers took off from a U.S. aircraft carrier and carried out a bombing raid in Japan. But the B-25 bombers were too large to land on the carrier, so instead they flew on to land in China, in the expectation that they would be rescued by Chinese forces allied with the United States. Of the eleven airmen who survived the raid, three were killed, the remaining eight captured by the Japanese after crash-landing. Taken to Tokyo, they were put on trial for alleged war crimes. Three were executed, although the details of their trial and subsequent fate remained unknown until after the war. Zanuck, Milestone, and their production team therefore had to invent most of the courtroom and interrogation scenes. After the film's release, some journalists falsely accused the U.S. government of withholding information from them that it had supposedly provided to Milestone.

In the absence of hard facts, Zanuck and Milestone created a story that veers into wild speculation, stereotypes, and melodrama. Milestone admitted, "We knew nothing about wartime Tokyo . . . and had to more or less invent it in the studio."[4] They used as "technical adviser" a minister's daughter who had lived in Japan, but she did little to give the film a sense of realism. The characters of the Chinese who pick up the airmen after their crash landing, and all the Japanese soldiers, lawyers, and judges involved in their detention, interrogation, and torture, are universally loathsome, sadistic, evil comic-book villains. Equally despicable is the group of Nazi-sympathizing journalists covering the trial—especially the

Berlin correspondent Johanna Hartwig (played with malevolent gusto by the Romanian character actress Tala Birell, who had appeared in *The Captain Hates the Sea*), described in the screenplay as a "a blonde phlegmatic but almost pretty woman of thirty. Despite her prettiness her face is hard, her mouth grim though sensuous, her eyes brilliant, darting sadistic. She wears a Nazi swastika pin."[5] The only "good" journalist is a "huge gorilla-like amiable Russian" who is denied entrance to the trial—because the USSR is perceived as an enemy (although at the time the USSR was not officially at war with Japan).[6]

After they are taken to Tokyo, the eight airmen are imprisoned and informed that they are being put on trial as war criminals for allegedly bombing civilian sites such as hospitals and schools. Wild-eyed Samurai-style attorneys and judges wearing elaborate traditional robes dominate the courtroom scenes, speaking in strangely stylized English, stroking their grotesquely long beards, and grinning with sinister pleasure. Milestone hired Asian American actors for these roles and for those of the Chinese collaborating with the Japanese, including Benson Fong, better known for his recent appearance as Tommy Chan, Charlie Chan's "Number Three Son." This did not prevent them from indulging in stereotypical representations of Asians, however. One of the film's strangest moments comes when the courtroom guards and some spectators (including the supposedly objective journalists) launch into a frenzied ritual sword fight, screaming "Bonzai" as they celebrate the joyous news that the U.S. forces under General MacArthur have surrendered Corregidor in the Philippines.

Between their courtroom appearances, the eight Americans share a dreary cell and are taken off for individual interrogation and torture. As in most Hollywood war movies of the period, the group represents a cross-section of American life, from wise-guy ethnic city slickers to solid midwestern types to country bumpkins and innocent youngsters. Their "skipper," Captain Harvey Ross, is a "stalwart, decent American hero" from Texas played with impressive subtlety and control by Dana Andrews, who had impressed Milestone so favorably in *The North Star*.[7] Andrews's younger brother from *The North Star*, eighteen-year old Farley Granger, is Sergeant Howard Clinton, the group's "baby" or mascot, whose tongue is cut out (thankfully, offscreen) when he refuses to tell the Japanese interrogators where their planes took off from. Richard Conte plays tough and pugnacious Lieutenant Canelli, while Sam Levene's Lieutenant Greenbaum, the intellectual Jew, displays both his legal knowledge and street smarts.

In its portrayal of male bonding and the psychology of soldiers under stress in wartime, *The Purple Heart* bears a strong resemblance to *All Quiet on the Western Front*. Its most compelling scenes are those in the prison cell, where each man is left alone with his fears, fantasies, and memories. Here the style verges on Expressionism: symbolic stylized shots, ominous shadows, and exaggerated close-ups. Milestone provides glimpses into the men's prewar lives—we see Ross at home in an idealized vision of his ranch with a loving wife and young son, tending to a newborn colt. We hear of future plans, sweethearts, and even quotations from Shakespeare. Wisely, Milestone refrains from showing any of the actual torture, instead focusing on how each man responds to the situation. Predictably, one of them (Charles O'Shea, as Sergeant Skvoznik) snaps from the pressure, returning catatonic to the cell, his head bobbing uncontrollably from side to side.

The climax comes when the airmen are offered the opportunity to be released as prisoners of war if they will reveal the names of their commanding officers. Taking charge in a natural, paternal way, Ross suggests democratically that they all make individual decisions. Each man places into a vase the winged Air Force pin they all wear. As the judge has instructed, a broken wing means agreement with the Japanese demands, an unbroken wing refusal. If even one of the wings is broken, the men have agreed to provide the information the Japanese want. The judge examines the wings one by one, but finds none broken. They have all individually decided not to collaborate.

In the final scene, the eight men march off proudly down the long hallway to their deaths—to the stirring musical accompaniment of the Air Force song ("Wild Blue Yonder"). Dana Andrews suggested this finale to Milestone, who agreed and even had the music rerecorded to fit the exact rhythm of the soldiers' footsteps.[8] Since the film uses very little music elsewhere (with the exception of an impromptu group chorus of "The Battle Hymn of the Republic"), this scene makes a strong impression.

To create a sense of bonding among the eight actors, Milestone arranged for them to share a single dressing room (a technique he would repeat in his next war film, *A Walk in the Sun*) during shooting. Although "a few wary looks were exchanged," the actors acquiesced. According to the eager newcomer Granger, "As usual Millie was right. We quickly became a band of brothers."[9]

For Dana Andrews, *The Purple Heart* was a breakthrough film, the one that made him a star. It established his onscreen persona as an "ordinary guy" with excellent posture, a quiet confidence, and compassion for others. As Andrews observed in an interview in 1958, "The women all over the country, whose men were away at war, identified their husbands as being that sort of man. For some reason, this made a terrific impression on them. There was no romance in it at all. . . . But this was the picture that put me over."[10] In Milestone, Andrews was lucky to find a director who appreciated and understood his understated talent and knew how to nurture it. The two men became not only collaborators on four films, but also lifelong friends.

The Purple Heart earned mostly positive reviews after its opening in March 1944. James Agee called it "well organized, unusually edged, and solidly acted," and Milestone's "best in years." But some found the fabrication of the facts of the incident troubling, as well as the virulent dehumanization of the Japanese characters and nation. The novelist and critic Mary McCarthy denounced the film as "unquestionably the worst war movie I have seen, the apotheosis of a type in which the world conflict becomes a struggle between five or six Oriental character actors . . . and seven or eight recurrent American actors representing the forces of Democracy."[11] Milestone, like most other directors in Hollywood at the time, was working in the atmosphere of a war on a scale the world had never before experienced, and in response to very real fears that the forces of evil could triumph in the end.

When *The Purple Heart* opened in New York, Milestone was in town with his wife, Kendall. Their presence attracted attention in the society pages. The operatic soprano Grace Moore, "The Tennessee Nightingale," who had also appeared in numerous Hollywood movies, even threw a party in the Milestones' honor. Noted one columnist:

> Grace Moore sang a fine Tosca at the Met Monday. She proceeded to blow her not immodest stipend by throwing a wonderful party at her apartment at the Savoy Plaza. The reason this party was "hep" was that it was composed entirely of professionals—artists, musicians and writers. There were no outsiders to gape at the insiders . . . It was in honor of "Milly" and Kendall Milestone. Milestone is a Hollywood director and, more than that, he is one of Hollywood's GREAT directors. It was Milestone who directed "The Purple Heart," which you will see on Mar. 8 at the Roxy. Milestone is a Russian, and is a first cousin of my great friend the violinist, Nathan Milstein.[12]

While in New York, Milestone gave an interview to the *New York Sun*, which reported that "following his old custom, he is still freelancing." Already, however, he was selecting the cast members for his new project, to be made not for 20th Century Fox, but for United Artists—and not a war picture. *A Guest in the House*, his first psychological thriller, would star Anne Baxter (Marina in *The North Star*) as a mentally disturbed young woman whose arrival disrupts the life of her host family. Of Baxter, Milestone told a reporter with what turned out to be (considering her later performance as the ambitious young actress Eve Harrington in *All About Eve*) prophetic accuracy: "Once she gets a strong enough role she will be recognized as one of the screen's finest young actresses. He thinks this may be the role. It calls for an actress who can be pretty and appealing, and yet come near to wrecking several lives."[13]

This "Hitchcockian" story showed considerable promise, but unfortunately Milestone suffered a burst appendix in the middle of the shooting. As *Variety* reported on May 24, he "was stricken with attack Monday while on the set of 'Guest in the House,' but he went home, attempting to return to the studio yesterday morning. He collapsed just as he was leaving and was rushed to the hospital for the emergency operation."[14] John Brahm replaced Milestone as director, with some assistance from André De Toth and the actor and director John Cromwell (1886–1979), Milestone's long-time friend. Besides Baxter, the cast included Ralph Bellamy and Margaret Hamilton (the witch from *The Wizard of Oz*). In his autobiography Bellamy remembered Milestone as "a magnificent director and a fine gentleman."[15] After Milestone's departure, significant changes were made to the screenplay, especially the ending. Later Milestone said, "he wished to scare the characters," but Brahm "wished to scare the audience."[16]

The contract Milestone had signed with the producer Kurt Stromberg for *A Guest in the House* showed that he still commanded large fees. He was to receive $5,000 per week for a total of $75,000, plus 10 percent of the profits for the next seven years. This was in the same range as other fees he had received: $125,000 for *All Quiet on the Western Front*, $105,000 for *The North Star*, and $80,833 for *The Purple Heart*. In late May the payments to Milestone were suspended "by reason of your physical incapacity," and in late September the contract was canceled, "allowing the producers to remove his name from publicity and the film." The contract also had a "war clause" specifying what would happen if the director "should be called upon during the term to serve the United States

Government, either in the armed services thereof, or in some other auxiliary or representative capacity."[17]

Milestone's friend Nicolai Remisoff designed the sets for *A Guest in the House;* he also advised the director to seek a doctor's advice when he showed signs of appendicitis. Stromberg kept Remisoff on the project after Milestone left, and then used him for several more "because he found that this man was not only a brilliant art director but that he also understood how to achieve the most for the least amount of money."[18]

Even in the hospital, where he had an extended stay after his appendectomy, Milestone apparently did not lose his mischievous sense of humor. He "felt compelled to make some kind of wisecrack" to show his wife that he was on the mend. "The lighting was rather dim, and I thought she was dressed in black. My wisecrack was: 'What's the hurry—you're already dressed in black!' Kendall rushed out of the room crying and ran to the nun who was waiting in a room across the hall."[19]

After he recovered, Milestone began work on what was his most artistically successful film of the war years: *A Walk in the Sun.* For this project, he reunited with the screenwriter Robert Rossen to adapt a 1944 novel by Harry Brown. The two worked closely and productively together. Unlike *Edge of Darkness* or *The North Star, A Walk in the Sun* does not vilify the military foe (whether German or Japanese or Chinese)—we do not see a single enemy soldier's face. Instead, the film focuses entirely on one part of one day in the life of a small group of American soldiers launching an attack on a German-held farmhouse in Italy. The film attempts to provide not a panoramic view of war, but a microcosm, an intimate psychological examination of one small incident in an enormous global conflagration.

A Walk in the Sun took a circuitous route to the screen. In late summer 1944 the producer Samuel Bronston and Milestone agreed on a deal to film Brown's novel, recommended to them by the actor Burgess Meredith (who also provides the narration in the finished film). Shooting began in Agoura, north of Los Angeles, to Rossen's script. (*Of Mice and Men* had also been shot there.) But after two weeks, Bronston ran out of money. Milestone put in $30,000 of his own to keep the production going. There were other problems as well: torrential rains hit Agoura and buried the equipment in mud. Elephants from a circus troupe residing nearby came to the rescue, dragging the equipment to safety.[20]

Milestone eventually secured financial backing from a bookie, a one-time boxer and former convict named Johnny Fisher, owner of a bar on Melrose Avenue. Like many con men, Fisher saw the movies as a convenient way to launder money. According to the actor Norman Lloyd, who played the scout Archimbeau in the film and later became a close associate and friend of Milestone, the director got along well with Fisher and his shady Las Vegas friends: "Milly knew how to handle a man like Fisher."[21] Fisher's "friends" were hired to serve as extras—and to keep an eye on the proceedings, protecting their boss's interests. "Thanks to them, the picture became known as the greatest traveling crap game in Hollywood. Every morning, it was the first thing they wanted to do, and it went on all day long." Milestone sometimes joined in. "I remember an assistant coming to tell him that a shot was ready, when Milly was twenty dollars down in the game. He refused to shoot the scene until he was even again and had recouped his twenty dollars."[22]

With Fisher's support, Milestone managed to complete shooting, but he had lost the original distributor, United Artists, when Bronston dropped out. So Milestone turned again to his old friend Darryl Zanuck at 20th Century Fox. On the night President Roosevelt died (April 12, 1945), Milestone screened the film for Zanuck, who agreed to release it, but under a different title: *Salerno Beachhead*.[23] Later, it was rereleased with the original—more poetic and appropriate—title, *A Walk in the Sun*.

With its episodic and almost "plotless" structure, Brown's novel presented a challenge to Rossen and Milestone. The narrative follows a platoon as it walks six miles from the beach at Salerno to its target, a farmhouse and strategic bridge held in enemy hands. Along the way, various members of the platoon respond in different ways to their mission and the unrelenting reality of combat: some are wounded, some die, some gain strength and courage, others crack under the pressure. Filmed in a moody black-and-white pseudodocumentary style, *A Walk in the Sun* "praises not the special heroics, but the patient, even weary, heroism of the G.I.s."[24] The conversations among the soldiers are often mundane and fragmentary, conveying the tedium of endless waiting even as death stalks them at every turn.

The metaphor of the title's "walk" provides an image not of transformation or tragedy, but of people simply going about their business. It also lends the screenplay a natural movement toward a goal, which becomes the film's climax: the successful assault on the farmhouse, after terrible losses and suffering—most of which occur offscreen. Milestone and his cameraman Russell Harlan do not show us the gruesome wounds and deaths that occur along the way, instead focusing on the interaction of the soldiers and officers. Not a single female appears.

In its evaluation of the completed screenplay, the puritanical Production Code Administration took issue with some of the language used in the film. In a letter to Will Hays, Joseph Breen asked that the picture be approved "even though it has two uses of the word 'lousy.'" Hays agreed, although he warned that "such approval is not to be taken as a precedent."[25] In fact, some veterans later criticized the literary, mild language of the script as far too tame and unrealistic for a group of battle-hardened soldiers.

In what was his most innovative gesture, Milestone added a series of ballads that provided a sense of narrative unity and embodied the "folksy" atmosphere of the common man as hero. Milestone later claimed that he came up with this idea from a childhood experience in Kishinev.

> I . . . remembered street scenes in Russia. When veterans of various wars were demobilized, they had nothing like the veterans' hospitals and similar institutions to go to. When they were crippled they were through; they stood on the corner selling satchels or something like that. A lot of them played a Russian instrument, accompanying themselves as they recalled their glorious adventures. "If we can somehow use that device," I said, "then we can dramatize all of Harry's material without the usual dialogue. Let's have ballads. This can be an offstage thing; the singer is not going to be in the picture."
>
> We went through the book and marked off all the material we wanted to dramatize into ballads; the first time I think we came out with ten or eleven of them. We both felt that this was going to be a wonderful innovation in screen narrative; nobody had ever done it before.[26]

The texts of the ballads are poetic and lyrical, such as those heard at the film's opening, over the credits:

> It was just a little walk
> In the warm Italian sun,
> But it wasn't an easy thing . . .
> They took a little walk in the sun.

For the music to the ballads, Milestone engaged Earl Robinson (1910–91), a well-known composer and folksinger closely associated with the American labor movement and a longtime member of the Communist Party. (Robinson's music replaced most of the original score credited to Frederic Efrem Rich.) Robinson would be blacklisted in the late 1940s. Kenneth Spencer sang the ballads in a soulful, casual style to lyrics written by Millard Lampell. "The effect of the ballads was to take 'A Walk in the Sun' out of the category of an ordinary war film; it gave you a 'feeling,'" Milestone said. "For instance, one of the things I told Zanuck was that in a war the ordinary soldier never sees anything; you go here, you go there, you go some place else, and while you hear things you never see anything. You just wait."[27]

Originally, Milestone planned to include ten different songs in the film, but after preview audiences registered their disapproval, only four were used. To some listeners at the time of the film's release, the ballads seemed incongruous in a war movie, because they "associated the GI experience with the gritty world of American labour."[28] With time, however, this attitude changed, and the technique of using a ballad as a thematic unifying device was subsequently widely copied in other films, especially Westerns, including *High Noon.*

Just as he had done with *The Purple Heart,* Milestone housed the cast members together during the shooting to facilitate the male bonding shown in the film. They lived for the eight weeks of shooting at a vacant resort club nearby. By the end of the period, friendships had formed among some of the actors: "Friends in the movie were friends in fact, and similarly enemies in the script didn't like each other."[29]

The biggest star in the group was Dana Andrews, in the central role of Sergeant Tyne. When the commanding officer of the group, Sergeant Porter (Herbert Rudley), has a psychological breakdown, Tyne quietly takes over to lead the platoon, reassuring and prodding the men onward. This is one of Andrews's most masterful performances, minimalist and understated, reaching a climax as the camera follows him crawling on his stomach across the field in front of the heavily fortified farmhouse, his vision coming in and out of focus with exhaustion and dizziness.

As in *The Purple Heart,* Andrews's sergeant gains the respect of the men by treating them fairly and democratically, recognizing their individual strengths and weaknesses. But he never minimizes the danger and fear that envelop them on all sides as he addresses them before the final assault: "This is a bad situation. It stinks." Since this was their third picture together, Andrews and Milestone worked together with an uncommon, almost instinctual, sense of purpose. Andrews saw Milestone as a "poet with a camera" who knew "exactly when to cut to close-ups of the actors' faces" and how to use lighting and blocking to create images of war that were at the same time lyrical and brutal.[30]

Having worked behind the camera for twenty-five years, Milestone often took control of the cinematography. "I listen to my cameraman, but I expect him to listen to me too. I'm telling the story, and sometimes I don't feel obliged to discuss reasons for my setups—reasons for placing the camera—with the cameraman."[31]

In an interview around the time of the premiere, Andrews called Milestone "the kind of director who actually asks for an actor's advice instead of giving him orders. . . . He's not only the finest director in Hollywood. He's one of the grandest people. I've worked with him so much now, and we see so much of each other, that I'm beginning to get a Russian accent."[32] Milestone and Andrews became close friends offscreen, the director becoming a kind of father figure to the actor, fourteen years his junior. Andrews loved to listen to Milestone's tales of early Hollywood over the drinks they both enjoyed so much—in Andrews's case, too much. An excessive fondness for alcohol almost ruined Andrews's career in later years, although during the filming of *A Walk in the Sun* he could still turn up fresh and ready on the set even after a night spent with Jack Daniel's.

Some days, Milestone would drive in the early morning from his home in Beverly Hills to Agoura with Norman Lloyd, who was working with the director for the first time. They would stop by to pick up Andrews and continue on to the shooting location, where Milestone, Lloyd recalls, "loved to stand around in the winter cold of the mountains and tell stories."[33] Lloyd shared Andrews's admiration for Milestone, whom he has called "A King of the Set," one of the grand directors of Hollywood's Golden Age.[34] As Archimbeau, Lloyd, a serious actor who came out of the Group Theatre and had appeared in Hitchcock's film *Saboteur*, took the role of "the guy out front," a wiry, wisecracking intellectual who is forever repeating with a feigned weariness his trademark phrase: "You kill me." (Another phrase repeated as a sort of refrain by various characters is the ironically hopeful motto "No one dies!") Joining Lloyd and Andrews in the cast was a young Lloyd Bridges as the innocent apple farmer Sergeant Ward, in the years when the future star of the television series *Sea Hunt* had yet to make his mark in Hollywood; Richard Conte as the I've-seen-it-all Rivera; and John Ireland as Windy, who writes letters back home that are narrated throughout the film.

In its refusal to romanticize the business of war, *A Walk in the Sun* is the distinguished heir to *All Quiet on the Western Front,* as noted by numerous critics. Like its predecessor, it is an ensemble piece rather than a star turn. The film deeply moved many war veterans, although they pointed out some small inaccuracies, such as the platoon's failure to search two fugitive Italian soldiers they meet along the way.

As it happened, the film was completed after the war was over, which may help explain the incongruous, abrupt, and strangely triumphant ending. Having successfully taken the farmhouse from the Germans, the remaining members of the platoon are shown exiting the door as we hear the jingoistic tune of "The Caissons Go Rolling Along," which disrupts the more philosophical atmosphere created by the ballads. James Agee viewed this as seriously compromising the film. "At the end, with their farmhouse captured, various featured players are shown completing the gags which tag their characters—chomping an apple, notching a rifle, and so on—while, so far as the camera lets you know, their wounded comrades are still writhing unattended in the dooryard."[35] Other reviewers, however, praised *A Walk in the Sun* for not having a "message," and for capturing the "sight and smell of war" better than most other war films of the period.[36]

Recognized as a critical success, Milestone's last World War II film did not make him much money—especially since he had contributed some of his own funds to get it finished. But it did earn him respect and led to further offers and possibilities. *A Walk in the Sun* also deepened his important artistic collaboration with Robert Rossen. They immediately began work on another film, *The Strange Love of Martha Ivers,* completing it quickly, even before the delayed release of *A Walk in the Sun* on December 25, 1945.

A few months earlier, Milestone and Kendall celebrated their tenth wedding anniversary. In the society pages of the *Los Angeles Examiner,* Harry Crocker noted that the event was "the signal for the many friends of Kendall and Lewis Milestone to fill their home with flowers and gifts. It was a happy evening. Chatted with Lieutenant Oleg Cassini . . ."[37] A regular fixture on the Hollywood social scene, the always stylish Kendall was also seen "wearing that enormous aquamarine which we consider so vulgar ONLY because we don't own it!—325 carats—and gorgeous enough to make you turn vegetarian."[38] But Kendall, like so many other Hollywood wives, also contributed to the war effort by organizing shows for military hospitals in the Los Angeles area "in which the audience is encouraged to participate."[39]

One of Kendall's closest friends during this period was Claire McAloon, future wife of the actor Richard Boone. In the early 1940s she was a young dancer and actress newly arrived from New York. One of her New York acting teachers gave her a letter of introduction to Milestone. Kendall welcomed her warmly and took McAloon under her wing, introducing her to their many friends in the music and film business. She recalled:

In those days they gave big parties in Hollywood. Kendall was known for fabulous parties and all the prominent people in Hollywood would be invited. And it wasn't only Hollywood, because she knew everybody. People like Cole Porter would come from New York. I met everybody in the world at her parties— singers, writers, actors, composers, everybody who was anybody in the Hollywood scene. We'd stay up all night long, talking and singing and piano playing. Hoagy Carmichael used to play all night long. Artie Shaw, Humphrey Bogart, Lauren Bacall, Lloyd and Dorothy Bridges were regulars. Richard Conte, a popular actor of the time, and his wife were very good friends of the Milestones. Milly—everybody called Lewis "Milly"—was a wonderful raconteur; he'd tell wonderful stories, and you were just mesmerized. Those years in the 1940s that I spent with the Milestones were a golden era for me, and I learned so much from them.[40]

In 1943 Claire McAloon married Kendall's nephew Richard Lee Kent, the son of Rockwell Kent and Kendall's sister. That marriage lasted until 1950. Shortly thereafter, McAloon met Richard Boone during the shooting of Milestone's film *Kangaroo* on location in Australia, where she had been invited by Kendall.

One of those who took a new interest in Milestone after *A Walk in the Sun* was the powerful producer Hal Wallis. Wallis had recently left Warner

Bros. for Paramount Studios, where he hoped to have more independence. For one of his first major features, Wallis offered Milestone six story suggestions. One was a story by the writer Jack Patrick, originally titled "Love Lies Bleeding." Its prologue interested Rossen, with whom Milestone wanted to collaborate once again. Wallis agreed (thinking they were using the entire story) to hire Rossen as screenwriter, and they developed from the prologue what became *The Strange Love of Martha Ivers,* a powerful and cynical film noir tale of crime, corruption, greed, revenge, evil, social conflict, and murder. With a compelling A-list cast (including Van Heflin, Barbara Stanwyck, and the newcomer Kirk Douglas), crew, and narrative, Milestone had all the tools he needed to produce what was one of his most disturbing, carefully crafted, and admired films.

When Milestone started filming in autumn 1945, the term *film noir* was not yet in wide circulation, but the features of this distinctive style had already clearly emerged in such movies as Orson Welles's *Citizen Kane* and Michael Curtiz's recently released *Mildred Pierce.* Made in black-and-white, these and the many other films with similar themes to come in the late 1940s and 1950s reflected the pervasive anxiety and pessimism that followed the terrible personal and national experience of World War II and the dawning age of nuclear destruction, launched in earnest with the dropping of atomic bombs on Hiroshima and Nagasaki in early August 1945. As thousands of veterans returned from combat with physical and psychological trauma to homes not always happy, darker and more emotionally complex content replaced the escapism Hollywood had long supplied. As one historian of film noir has written, these films frequently offered "somber nocturnal settings, glistening rain-drenched streets, swirls of fog, evocative sets and deep visual fields segmented by patterns of light and dark."[41] A sexually dangerous and predatory female—the femme fatale—usually occupied the center of attention. She lures the hero (or, more likely, antihero) into crime and adultery in gritty urban and industrial settings. More recent critical readings of the femme fatale, however, have seen her as both a liberated and stereotypical figure.

Originally, film noir was relegated to low-budget B movies, but the genre gradually moved toward the Hollywood mainstream. Major stars such as Joan Crawford, Bette Davis, Rita Hayworth, Barbara Stanwyck, Humphrey Bogart, and Fred MacMurray all gravitated toward films in this style, which traced its origins to European and, especially, French cinema. David Thomson writes that film noir "did dirt on the American dream." Here "something like mistrust enters in the organism of American film . . . narrative unreliability, and an atmospheric uncertainty. It means being prepared to abandon happy endings and monotonously likable characters."[42]

Rossen's screenplay for *The Strange Love of Martha Ivers* has many of the features of a classic film noir narrative. It opens in 1928 in the grimy factory town of Iverstown (apparently in western Pennsylvania's coal country), where the Martha of the title is a teenager living unhappily with her cruel aunt, Mrs. Ivers. The Ivers family owns the factory and runs the town. Martha's parents have died some time before, and Mrs. Ivers has never forgiven her daughter (Martha's mother) for marrying a common worker below her social class who drank himself to death. (Alcoholism appears frequently in film noir.) The rebellious Martha has tried to run away several times, with the help of her lower-class boyfriend, Sam. A local schoolteacher, Walter, with lofty ambitions for his obedient son (Walter Jr.) tutors Martha, hoping to gain Mrs. Ivers's good graces (and financial support).

One night as one of many thunderstorms raged outside, Martha and Sam and Walter Jr. witness the crime that motivates the drama. Martha's beloved kitten wanders outside her bedroom, down the long curving staircase at the center of the gothic Ivers mansion. Since Martha knows her aunt detests cats, she follows, only to see Mrs. Ivers lifting her cane repeatedly to strike and kill the squealing kitten. Enraged, Martha grabs a poker and strikes her aunt on the head, causing her to fall down the stairs to her death. Sam disappears, but Walter Jr. stays with Martha. They confront his father. Martha lies that an intruder entered and killed her aunt, and Walter Jr., unwilling to contradict her, confirms the false story. Martha also believes—wrongly—that Sam witnessed the crime. The secret that Martha and Walter share about the truth of what happened binds them together irrevocably and tragically. Later, they collude to get an innocent man convicted and hung for allegedly committing the crime.

The action moves ahead eighteen years to the present: 1946. Sam, a hard-bitten loner recently discharged from the military after distinguished combat service, is driving west and unexpectedly finds himself entering Iverstown. This unlikely coincidence so distracts him that he drives his car off the road, necessitating a stop for repairs. (He also has a passenger, a sailor played by an uncredited young actor named Blake

Edwards in one of his first Hollywood jobs.) Now an impressive tough-guy physical specimen highly attractive to the opposite sex, Sam immediately meets a young woman down on her luck, Toni Marachek, and strikes up a friendship.

A "bad boy" himself, he finds the news that she is recently released from prison on a trumped-up charge of stealing a fur coat more appealing than dangerous. They take hotel rooms with a shared bathroom and develop a romantic relationship. In his review of the script, Joseph Breen of the PCA expressed concern to Wallis about the "sexual innuendos" in the script (including the adjoining hotel rooms) and warned, "It will be necessary for you affirmatively to establish it that Toni is, quite definitely, *not* a prostitute, and that her relationship with Sam is a clean one."[43] Wallis, Milestone and Rossen complied, of course, confining any sexual activity between Toni and Sam to sharing toothbrushes, cigarettes, drinks, and the front seat of a car.

Walter, his father having died, is now an attorney and Martha's husband. She has inherited her aunt's fortune and rules the town with an iron fist. When Walter learns that Martha's childhood pal Sam has turned up in town, he panics. Sam is both a potential romantic rival and a possible blackmailer concerning the covered-up details of Mrs. Ivers's death years before. A paranoid and barely functioning alcoholic, Walter also fears the repercussions for his campaign for the office of Iverstown D.A. So he enlists the vice squad to turn up some moral turpitude. They arrest Toni for a minor parole violation. The police give her a choice between prison and helping set up her new friend Sam for a good beating that will encourage him to leave town.

Lured to a restaurant by Toni, Sam gets roughed up and dumped in a ditch. But he returns to town anyway. He knows he has a strong protector in Martha, who wants to keep him safe and views him as an escape from her desperately unhappy marriage to Walter. In a final return to the scene of the original crime, the three meet at the Ivers mansion. Walter falls in a drunken stupor down the stairs. Unlike the elderly Mrs. Ivers, however, he does not die. Sam refuses to kill Walter and walks out the open door (as he did in the opening sequence) unharmed. Left alone with their misery and self-hatred, Martha takes the gun in Walter's hand and points it at herself and pulls the trigger. Walter follows suit, shooting himself.

In a short epilogue, we see Sam and Toni heading westward in his repaired car, escaping toward what seems to be marriage and better future, away from the ghosts and criminals of rotten Iverstown ("America's Fastest Growing Industrial City").

Rossen's screenplay seethes with hatred for the injustices of capitalism. At the time, he was still very visible and active in the Communist Party, although he would resign in spring 1946 as the party went through major organizational changes as the result of labor unrest in Hollywood that also affected the filming of *Martha Ivers*. His Marxist convictions color the script. Like her evil aunt before her, whom she hates but comes to resemble, Martha abuses her unlimited economic and political power as the employer of most of Iverstown's citizens. She bends the police, the courts, and the media—and her weakling husband—to her perverted will. As Manny Farber has written, the film shows "modern life as a jungle."[44] The Paramount press book promoted the film as "a picture which deals with people you won't like, but will like to see."[45]

In *The Strange Love of Martha Ivers,* justice comes only to the wealthy, whereas powerless individuals like Toni or the man wrongly accused of murdering Mrs. Ivers or the oppressed workers in Martha Ivers's booming factory count for nothing. Martha conforms in most ways to the model of the dangerous and scheming femme fatale, although she uses not only sexual but also economic power to dominate others. Any love she feels goes to Sam, but the twisted past of their relationship and her obsessive need for control prevent them from finding happiness. Instead, Sam seeks comfort with the vulnerable Toni, a victim (as he is) of social forces, whom he can protect and nurture.

Even the schoolteacher, Walter's father, is a pawn in Iverstown's economic machine. He panders to his wealthy patroness, and then to her niece Martha, in the hope that they will help him send his son to Harvard. His ambition even leads him to accept Martha's obviously false account of her aunt's death. He knows this will give him and Walter the power of blackmail over her. Martha confides to Walter's father in a cynical aside that Walter would probably be "happier driving a truck than going to Harvard."

Hall Wallis's clout in Hollywood gave him the ability to assemble an impressive cast. MGM lent out Van Heflin, winner of the Oscar for Best Supporting Actor for his performance in *Johnny Eager* (1941), for the role of Sam. As it happens, the rugged, deep-voiced Heflin had recently returned from military service, like the character he portrays. "When I read Sam, I knew he was for me," Heflin told an interviewer. "Sam is a guy you meet every day. He knows the score. He's painted in a number of colors. Not just as black or white. It's the Sams that promise a long life as an actor."[46] Milestone gave Sam a clever bit of physical "business" that defined his character as a gambler: habitually rolling a half-dollar coin across the back of his hand.

Originally, Wallis had considered Van Heflin for the role of Walter Jr., but he cast Kirk Douglas (1916–) instead. This was Douglas's first role, the start of a long and distinguished Hollywood career. Lauren Bacall recommended to Wallis that they try Douglas out, since she had seen him as a "promising Broadway actor."[47] Wounded in action while in the U.S. Navy in the South Pacific, he had just arrived in Los Angeles. Douglas's previous experience had been limited to the stage, and he was understandably nervous when asked to make a screen test (along with others considered for the role, including John Lund and Montgomery Clift).

"A camera can be a really frightening thing. I had a six-page scene to do. We kept rehearsing until finally the director, Lewis Milestone, said, 'Now, do you feel ready to shoot it?' I took a deep breath and said, 'Yes.' He said, 'Go home. I already shot it.' What a wonderful, painless way to do a screen test! I was grateful to him."[48] This experience taught him "the importance of relaxing in front of the camera, not feeling intimidated by it, not being self-conscious. . . . What Milestone did for me was the most marvelous thing for somebody just starting out in movies—the lesson being to forget that the camera is there."[49]

Not used to playing weak characters, Douglas found Walter a challenge. "I always worked on the theory that when you play a weak character, find a moment when he's strong, and if you're playing a strong character, find a moment when he's weak."[50] Like all the other characters in the film, Walter has to smoke incessantly, something Douglas had never done in real life, and at first it made him sick. Eventually, Douglas and Milestone became close friends. They shared similar backgrounds: Douglas's Jewish parents had immigrated from Russia in 1908 to escape anti-Semitism. Later, they also shared the experience of the blacklist.

But the biggest star in the cast was, of course, the imposing diva Barbara Stanwyck (1907–90) as Martha. By this point Stanwyck had been making movies for nearly twenty years and had already established herself as one of the reigning queens of what became known as film noir, especially as the villainous coconspirator (with Fred MacMurray) in her husband's death in Billy Wilder's *Double Indemnity* (1944). In promotional materials, Paramount exploited her reputation for on-screen meanness, suggesting such tag lines as "Lucretia Borgia was a baby compared to Martha Ivers," "Delilah was harmless compared to Martha Ivers," or "Mata Hari was guileless compared to Martha Ivers."[51] In person, Stanwyck intimidated nearly everyone in the cast and crew—including Milestone, who was known primarily as a "man's director" and whose experience of working with Hollywood's leading female stars was limited to a rather unhappy one with Joan Crawford on *Rain* thirteen years earlier. These two consummate professionals got along well, however, as he recalled in an interview some years later.

> Working with Barbara Stanwyck was among the most pleasant experiences I've ever had. In this respect she and Ingrid Bergman are rivals. Both were great, but Stanwyck is co-operative and tough. She can take all kinds of physical hardship. I can understand why everybody adores her. She's also very knowledgeable. She'll walk on the set and look up to see where the lights are in relation to the camera. She'll say to the cameraman, "I can help you. I need a key light, and that light over there is wrong. Readjust the key light and we're in business." She was that knowledgeable, and everybody is mad about her to this day.[52]

At first, Stanwyck hesitated to take the role because she feared being upstaged by Lizabeth Scott, the young actress playing Toni. (She needn't have worried.) Milestone promised to "protect" her, and she agreed. Playing opposite such a Hollywood icon was even more intimidating for Kirk Douglas. "Everyone had told me how nice Barbara Stanwyck was, so I was looking forward to working with her in this hostile environment. The crew adored her. They called her 'Missy,' and when she came on the set she went around hugging them, asking about their wives and children by name. She was a professional, she was there, always prepared, an excellent actress. But she was indifferent to me."[53] Stanwyck always made sure she was at the center of attention. She warned Van Heflin not to overdo his use of the "coin trick" during their scenes together.

"Van, that's a wonderful piece of business," Stanwyck told Van Heflin, "but if you do that during my important lines, I have a piece of business that will draw attention away from yours. Any time you start rolling that coin while I'm talking, I'm going to show them a trick a hell of a lot more interesting than yours. I'll be fixing my garter. So be sure you don't do that when I have important lines to speak." Heflin complied and used the trick only briefly during his scenes with her.[54]

Stanwyck's simmering, lustful performance as Martha completely overshadows Lizabeth Scott's strangely underdeveloped portrayal of Toni, her rival for Sam's affections. Scott (her real name was the more ethnic Emma Matzo) started out on the off-Broadway stage; oddly enough, her first dramatic lead role was as Sadie Thompson in *Rain*. (And, in fact, Joan Crawford would have made a much more effective Toni.) Sometime after meeting her at the Stork Club in New York, Hal Wallis brought Scott to Paramount, hoping to turn her into a star in the mold of Lauren Bacall. Like Bacall, Scott had a smoky, low voice, "a baritonal purr with a creamy huskiness."[55]

But even Wallis's careful coaxing of her career failed to make Scott the kind of sultry screen goddess he had hoped she would become, and she remained fated to be known as a Bacall wannabe. Her role in *The Strange Love of Martha Ivers* was designed to show her ability to hold her own with A-list actors, but her character seems oddly disconnected from the main drama of the script. (The Paramount press book describes Toni as "the girl from nowhere.") Although her performance earned fervent admirers in England, where she was mobbed at premiere screenings, most critics found Scott painfully stiff and self-conscious, given to striking poses not always appropriate to the required emotional situation. The scene in the seedy hotel room when Toni is interrupted while modeling a tacky new sundress for Sam by the grand entrance of Martha in a dazzling matching snood-and-dress ensemble approaches the level of camp.

In all fairness, Rossen's screenplay did not give Scott much to work with. She gets some of the film's weakest and most stilted dialogue. She is far too stylish to be an ex-con, and she and Sam never seem to click. The final shot showing them departing dreary Iverstown in a snazzy convertible for a happy matrimonial future looks forced and unmotivated.

So intent was Wallis on promoting Lizabeth Scott's career, however, that he even added close-ups of her in the final print after Milestone had left the project, adding a jarring note of cheesy Hollywood glamor to the director's typically masterful editing work.[56] (Milestone later said that Wallis had been a "nuisance" during and after the shooting.)[57] Even with Wallis's interference, *Martha Ivers* contains some of Milestone's most inspired visual imagery, most of it nocturnal: the prefiguring crane shot of the Iverstown bus station so important to the narrative; the cut between lighted candles that precedes the motivating scene of Mrs. Ivers's fall down the staircase; Toni's guilty view of Sam being beaten up through the rear window of a passing car. Obsessive attention is paid to physical details that create the atmosphere of overwhelming oppression and anxiety—the lighting and extinguishing of cigarettes, often with sexual undertones.

As the evil Mrs. Ivers, Judith Anderson took to a higher level the patrician brutishness she showed to such haunting effect as the demented housekeeper Mrs. Danvers in Hitchcock's *Rebecca*. Her brief appearance in one of Milestone's most effective opening sequences provides ample evidence for the origins of Martha's malicious, scheming personality. The Paramount press book for *Martha Ivers* includes Anderson's assessment: "It's the meanest part I've ever done. I'm really sinking low, for the script calls for me to be horrible to children and animals. It's bound to be a pleasure to audiences when I die my violent death. Oh, they'll love that moment."[58]

The churning, dense orchestral score by the Hungarian-born Miklós Rósza, one of Hollywood cinema's most distinguished and experienced composers, amplifies the emotional power of this and other crucial scenes throughout. It builds feelings of suspense (Rósza had recently written the score for Hitchcock's *Spellbound*) and gathering gloom. His dark, expressionistic music, reminiscent of Shostakovich, takes us "inside Martha's head and the way she sees and experiences things."[59]

Meanwhile, in the streets outside the studio in Burbank, a fierce labor struggle was being waged—with weird echoes of the economic inequality that pulsates through *Martha Ivers*. Around the time shooting began, in October 1945, the bitter conflict between two unions fighting to represent workers in some of the industry trades (the ruling International Alliance of Theatrical and Stage Employees, or IATSE, and the new Conference of Studio Unions, or CSU) that had been brewing since March escalated into violence. The main target of the striking CSU was Warner Bros. Studios in Burbank. A mob of eight hundred CSU members overturned several cars and engaged the police in pitched battles with knives, clubs, battery cables, and chains. The police and Warner Bros. guards responded with fire hoses, injuring eighty people. Hollywood's leftists and Communists promoted the cause of the striking CSU members, under the leadership of the radical union activist Herb Sorrell. Producers and conservatives, including the members of the newly formed and soon to be powerful Motion Picture Alliance for the Preservation of American Ideals (MPA), supported IATSE.

Strikers also picketed other studios, including Paramount. According to the testimony he gave in 1951 to a HUAC investigator, Milestone respected the picket line at Paramount for two days, until the strike was settled. During this period, Byron Haskin took over the direction of *Martha Ivers*.

Other sources have contradicted this account, however, and Milestone himself expressed doubt about whether he did in fact visit the site of the violence in front of Warner Bros.' Burbank studio. This is the version Kirk Douglas tells.

> We continued to shoot, but it meant we were locked in at the studio—if we went out, we couldn't get back in. . . . Thousands of people fought in the middle of Barham Boulevard with knives, clubs, battery cables, brass knuckles, chains, and saps. Two hundred police were called in, and subdued the crowds with fire hoses and teargas. . . . Milestone favored the strikers, and went across the street to Oblath's restaurant where a lot of strike supporters discussed it over coffee. For a while, the picture was directed by Byron Haskin. I felt guilty. What was I supposed to do? Stanwyck was working. . . . I was afraid that for me Hollywood would end before I began.[60]

The actors were ordered to arrive at the set at 4 A.M., before the pickets appeared.

The situation was resolved later in October by the Motion Picture Association of America's president, who fashioned a temporary compromise with the studios. The strikers were allowed to return to work along with some of those who had replaced them. Milestone resumed work on *Martha Ivers*, which was completed by December 7, 1945, but not released until July 1946.

The labor union violence in Hollywood would return just a few months later, however, with more serious consequences for the industry and for Milestone. From spring 1946 until late October 1947, Sorrell and the CSU staged more strikes, but with dwindling support. With the backing of powerful figures like Sam Wood, Walt Disney, and Gary Cooper, the Motion Picture Alliance was helping turn the sentiment in the film industry strongly against Sorrell and his "red-tainted CSU." Eventually the CSU lost the support of its own unions and collapsed.[61]

Not coincidentally, in Washington, D.C., the Un-American Activities Committee of the U.S. House of Representatives was opening hearings (on October 20, 1947) on the alleged pernicious influence of Communists in the Hollywood film industry. On September 21 Congress had issued forty-four subpoenas to executives, labor leaders, and filmmakers, requiring them to testify before HUAC about "Communist Infiltration of the Motion Picture Industry." Considering their shared history of involvement with leftist causes and sympathy for Communism and the USSR, it was not unexpected that Milestone and Rossen, creators of *The Strange Love of Martha Ivers,* a pointed denunciation of the evils of capitalism, were among those summoned to Washington. Milestone's career and personal life entered a new, dramatic, and dangerous phase.

9

Fallen Arch

If I came home from work and had to sit in the kitchen while my wife
cooked dinner, I'd get into another business.
—*Lewis Milestone*

For a time, the artistic success of *The Strange Love of Martha Ivers* boosted
Milestone's reputation with Hollywood producers. "There was always a
pattern in my career," Milestone said later. "I imagine there were moments
when producers would look at me and say, 'Forget about him. He's finished.' Then I'd do a picture that would reawaken all their interest, and
they'd come up with all kinds of offers."[1]

In early 1946 a new studio called Enterprise Productions chose him
to direct what was planned to be a blockbuster on the scale of *Gone with
the Wind,* a film adaptation of a best-selling novel by Erich Maria
Remarque, *Arch of Triumph.* Since he had so successfully brought to the
screen Remarque's *All Quiet on the Western Front,* Milestone was a natural choice for this high-profile project that Enterprise's idealistic and
well-connected founders—David Loew, Charles Einfeld and David
Lewis—hoped would put their new studio on the map. At Enterprise,
Loew and Einfeld proclaimed, they would create an atmosphere "where
people would feel happy, free and, regardless of their status, responsible."[2]
Unfortunately, their utopian hopes would quickly founder as the movie
business underwent a radical transformation in the postwar years. One of
the major reasons for the ultimate collapse of Enterprise Studios just two
years after its creation was the mismanaged, chaotic, and ruinously
expensive production of *Arch of Triumph,* which proved to be—despite
enormous initial promise, prestige, and star power—among the most
damaging (but fascinating) episodes in Milestone's Hollywood career.

Enterprise paid $235,000 for the film rights to Remarque's novel, a
record for the time. Initially serialized in *Collier's* magazine, the book

appeared at the end of 1945 and became an instant best seller; American sales alone exceeded two million copies.[3] An intense, gloomy, and atmospheric story of refugees in Paris on the eve of the Nazi invasion in 1939, written in a style reminiscent of Hemingway, *Arch of Triumph* was closely based on Remarque's own nomadic life after he was stripped of his German citizenship in 1938 by the Nazi leadership because of his "Jewish-Marxist" associations.

The hero, Ravic, is an anti-Nazi gynecologist seeking refuge in Paris after escaping from torture and imprisonment in Germany. Living undocumented in France, he performs "ghost" medical procedures, primarily abortions, illegally (since he cannot obtain a physician's license as a stateless person) as he assists French doctors who take most of the fees and credit. Occasionally caught by the police and deported from the country, he always manages to return to Paris. Living on the fringes of society in a seedy hotel inhabited by other refugees like himself (including a group of Spaniards displaced by the Spanish Civil War), he one night encounters a young woman on the verge of physical collapse wandering the streets. Taking pity on her, he takes her to his hotel and revives her. Also "stateless," Joan Madou is the daughter of an Italian mother and Romanian father and survives by singing in cabarets and occasionally selling sexual favors. When we meet her, the man she has been (unhappily) living with has just died, leaving her homeless and destitute. Ravic helps her find employment as a singer at the cabaret Scheherazade, a nightclub run by his Russian émigré friend Boris Morosov that caters to émigrés and outcasts of all sorts.

After initial hesitation on both sides, Ravic and Joan eventually drift into a love affair whose on-again-off-again progress is the novel's main story line and thematic focus. Joan, a seductive but willful woman, finds fidelity to one man in the uncertain circumstances of the time impossible; she was clearly modeled, as Remarque himself admitted, on his own tempestuous affair with Marlene Dietrich. Their liaison began shortly after their first meeting in Venice in 1937 and lasted for three years. Like Joan and Ravic in the novel, Dietrich and Remarque spent the most romantic interlude of their affair in Antibes, on the Riviera. But when Joan and Ravic return to gray, rainy Paris, the authorities deport him once again.

Unable to bear the loneliness and privation, Joan takes up with a man who offers her luxury and security—as well as the threat of violence. This does not prevent her, however, from continuing to pursue intimacy with

Ravic when he returns. In the end, the other man carries out his threats and shoots her, inflicting mortal wounds. Ravic rushes to her deathbed, and they renew their vows of eternal love. By this time, on September 1, 1939, the Nazis have invaded Paris and suspicious refugees like Ravic are being rounded up, probably to be sent to concentration camps. Tired of running and stripped of his emotional support in Joan, Ravic does not resist, joining the procession from his hotel into the waiting police van.

The novel's important subplot involves Ravic's successful attempt to exact revenge on the evil Nazi secret police official Haake, who earlier in Germany brutally interrogated and tortured Ravic and his wife, causing her death and leading Ravic to flee. Sitting in one of the cafés where he spends most of his time, Ravic suddenly sees Haake pass by. He becomes obsessed with finding and killing him. Eventually Ravic succeeds by trailing and befriending Haake (who does not recognize or remember him). Promising to take him to a whorehouse, Ravic instead drives Haake to a remote part of Paris and murders him.

Milestone had a special artistic bond with Remarque after *All Quiet on the Western Front.* He also found the themes of emigration and statelessness close to his own personal experience and that of many of his Russian and European friends. It didn't hurt either that Ravic's closest friend, a White Russian colonel, fled the Bolshevik Revolution and runs a cabaret very similar to the ones Milestone had frequented on his own trips to Paris. For the music, Milestone hired Louis Gruenberg (1884–1964), a Russian-born composer who supplied soulful Russian gypsy songs for the cabaret scenes that, "counterpointed with pelting rain, help to sustain the tragic aura of the film."[4] The large cast also included (playing a patron of Scheherazade) the renowned Hollywood owner of Romanoff's Restaurant in Beverly Hills, the so-called Michael Romanoff, a celebrated impostor of Russian royalty whose real name was Harry Gerguson (originally Herschel Geguzin). This seemed to be an inside joke for the many movie people who frequented his popular establishment.

Enterprise Studios engaged the novelist and screenwriter Irwin Shaw to adapt Remarque's lengthy novel to the screen. But Milestone (who always styled himself as something of a writer) refused to accept what Shaw had produced. Instead, he hired two people who had worked with him on *A Walk in the Sun* to help him prepare the screenplay: the actor Norman Lloyd and the writer Harry Brown. Milestone carefully extracted the dialogue from the novel's scenes he wanted to include and then gave it to Brown to "put into playable form." Milestone "was slavish in his devotion to the material," Lloyd writes in his memoirs. "He had worked this way on *All Quiet on the Western Front,* which had turned out to be a masterpiece; he believed that having bought a property, he felt he must stay with it."[5] For Milestone, the story's basic conflict was Joan's "futile attempt" to reconcile her needs for both love and security. Although she loves Ravic, he cannot supply the security she craves. The real villain, Milestone believed, was "the conditions of the times."[6]

Not surprisingly, the Production Code office raised objections to many aspects of the script. Ravic's unpunished murder of Haake (especially by strangulation) proved especially problematic, so Remarque's extensive and gruesome description was drastically shortened, robbing the film of the cathartic power the episode unleashes in the novel. The screenplay also excised the sordid details of Ravic's work as a gynecologist, performing abortions on prostitutes, as well as his dealings with various unsavory characters haunting the dark allies, dingy bars, and dirty hotels of the "other" Paris. Needless to say, Ravic's frequent visits to a brothel where he performs tests for venereal disease on the sex workers also had to go. As a result, the character of Ravic emerges as less politically committed and serious than in Remarque's novel, a condemnation of the exploitation by unscrupulous leaders of the abused working class.

Obvious similarities emerged between the screenplay of *Arch of Triumph* and the hugely successful *Casablanca,* released in 1942. Both feature refugees fleeing Nazi persecution around the time of the occupation of Paris in 1939. Ravic, like Victor Laszlo, has actively resisted the Nazis and is a hunted man. Joan, like Ilsa Lund, is a beautiful and enigmatic woman caught in the turmoil of the moment, forced to leave her homeland and seek protection with different men. In both films, a cabaret is a central setting for much of the action—although the Scheherazade is less prominent in *Arch* than Rick's Café in *Casablanca.* Both films have an evil Nazi officer eventually murdered by the forces of good. Unlike the happy ending ("This is the beginning of a beautiful friendship") of *Casablanca,* however, *Arch of Triumph* ends tragically, with the death of Joan and Ravic's capture. This proved to be an important difference at the box office—along with the changing tastes of postwar audiences, no longer so eager to relive the trauma of those years.

That the executives at Enterprise Studios were hoping to repeat *Casablanca*'s remarkable critical and popular success seems clear from the casting choices they made for the leading roles of Ravic and Joan. The French actor Charles Boyer was the only actor seriously considered as Ravic, because of his suave and mysterious Continental manner, and because of his friendships both with the founders of Enterprise and with Remarque. (Remarque was married to the actress Paulette Goddard, with whom Boyer had previously costarred in *Hold Back the Dawn.*) Like Humphrey Bogart (Rick in *Casablanca*), Boyer conveyed a cynical, devil-may-care, world-weary fatalism and dark sex appeal. What troubled him, however, was that he would be playing a German, against his well-established screen identity as a Frenchman (with a strong French accent). "I am a Frenchman," he told David Lewis. "For me to play a German, that would be ridiculous. And for me to play a *good* German, that would be impossible—I would not know how to begin to act such a part."[7] Remarque and the screenwriters responded by offering to remove specific references to Ravic's nationality, making him a "European of indeterminate origin." This change serves to weaken his motivation for pursuing and murdering Haake, however, and confuses his personal and political relationship with Joan.

During filming, Boyer, a loyal French patriot, acted almost as a propagandist for France and persuaded Milestone (after consulting with the French government) to remove material that showed the French in a bad light, especially their poor treatment of some refugees.[8]

Ingrid Bergman, who had appeared with Boyer in George Cukor's 1944 gothic psychological thriller *Gaslight,* was offered the role of Joan. Enterprise executives saw the Bergman-Boyer combination as a powerful and necessary box-office draw. Indeed, so badly did they want this pairing that they engaged in some shrewd old-fashioned deception to get it, telling Bergman they already had Boyer signed up and Boyer they already had Bergman signed up. Later, after its cool reception, Bergman claimed that "'Arch of Triumph' was one of the few films in my life that I felt 'wrong' about. I really didn't want to do it and I told them so, but they persevered and there was Charles Boyer in it and Charles Laughton, so I decided it was ridiculous not to do it. But I was always unsure of myself, concerned that I would not be 'believable.' Then it came out very long and they cut it to pieces, and it didn't make sense."[9]

Some in the industry wondered if Bergman was not too "wholesome" for the part of Joan, but Milestone defended the choice. "Nobody could have played the role better than she. Ingrid Bergman happens to be a good enough actress to look exceedingly forlorn in the beginning sequences, though she is so naturally beautiful it is impossible to disfigure her with the camera."[10]

When Bergman arrived to start filming in May 1946, at studios Enterprise had rented in Culver City, she was twenty pounds overweight. At the time, her twenty-year marriage to Petter Lindstrom was coming apart, and she was having an affair with the photographer Robert Capa. Capa followed her to Hollywood and got himself hired to take production stills for *Arch of Triumph,* partaking heartily in the nightly post-filming consumption of cocktails with Boyer, Milestone, and the crew. According to her biographer Donald Spoto, Bergman took refuge from the turmoil of her personal life in her work, "giving to a dark and claustrophobic picture an intensity that, in the finished film, is sometimes frightening."[11]

During the filming, Bergman and Remarque also developed a close friendship. In a letter after seeing a rough cut, he expressed his enthusiasm for her portrayal of Joan. "Strange, I know that having seen Joan on the screen, I will not be able to recall her face back from my imagination. It will be from now on always your face. . . . I believe she looked like you. . . . She died a beautiful death in your arms."[12]

Initially, the supporting role of the sadistic and decadent Nazi SS officer Haake went to Michael Chekhov, a Russian émigré actor (and teacher of acting) whose most important role in Hollywood to that date as the psychoanalyst Dr. Brulov in Hitchcock's *Spellbound* gained him an Oscar nomination for Best Supporting Actor. Close friends, Milestone and Chekhov often socialized with some of Hollywood's other Russian émigré artists. But just before shooting was to begin on *Arch of Triumph,* the frail Chekhov had a second heart attack and had to withdraw.

The famously "difficult" British veteran Charles Laughton, known for nasty roles such as Captain Bligh in *Mutiny on the Bounty* and the tortured Quasimodo in *The Hunchback of Notre Dame,* replaced Chekhov. Laughton soon declared the character of Haake not "German enough" and demanded a rewrite. For this task he recommended his friend the German playwright Bertolt Brecht, working with him at the time on an English adaption of Brecht's play *Galileo.* (In the end, none of Brecht's many suggestions made it into the final cut.) Laughton also demanded that the German film composer Hanns Eisler serve as his dialect coach. To further immerse himself in the mentality of a committed Nazi, the eccentric Laughton undertook to study Hitler's book *Mein Kampf* with Norman Lloyd—over a daily bottle of Scotch.

Milestone struggled to deal with the egos and conflicting demands of these three big-name and highly paid stars. In most of his previous films he had avoided casting stars, since he believed they distracted from the artistic mission. "One thing wrong was that it was supposed to be a realistic piece and it had two major stars in the leads," Milestone later remarked. "If you have two stars like that, then half your reality goes out the window; all you have is another film with Ingrid Bergman and Charles Boyer."[13]

Shooting was scheduled to last for ten weeks but dragged on for twenty. Since Bergman had another commitment in New York (a new Maxwell Anderson play about Joan of Arc) in late September, the crew had to rush to complete her scenes. The atmosphere on the set was tense and the script changed daily. In his memoir, Norman Lloyd provided a vivid account of this troubled film's difficult birth.

> Milestone was caught; he couldn't say no to Ingrid, she was dazzling to him. He wanted to keep her as a star, which is why he had Brecht write original scenes for her, to satisfy her objections. Boyer also had to be placated. At Enterprise, the situation was different from that at most major studios, where a director could go to the front office and ask the head of the studio to bring the stars into line. Einfeld was a publicity man, and Loew was a quiet, gentle personality, a talented painter and a collector of works of art. Milly became confused; he was trying to please Ingrid, trying to please Boyer, and when Laughton arrived, trying to please him.[14]

Milestone's temper frequently got the better of him during the shooting, as expenses mounted. "Even at his best," Norman Lloyd writes, "Milly had a lifelong problem with his temper; it was always too quick to come to the surface. . . . He was always irascible when working, and I suspected he really didn't like to work—it made him unhappy. But he wanted the money, and he loved pictures; he was deeply insecure."[15]

The production designer William Cameron Menzies, one of the best in the business, was commanding a virtual army that constructed 112 different sets, including a lavish reproduction of Fouquet's Restaurant, an important meeting place in the story. (Just a few years later, a film like *Arch of Triumph* would have been filmed on location in Paris.) Albert E. Van Schmus, the newly hired second assistant director at Enterprise

Studios, later recalled, "They opened two ends of the stage and built ramps up. The café was about in the center of the stage, but they had the actual street there, so they could drive cars in one door and out the other and pass on the street. Oh, it must have cost a *fortune* to do that! But it was a delightful set, absolutely entrancing. Visitors would come in just to *see* the bloody thing, it was so realistic."[16]

For publicity purposes, the studio ordered a large replica of the Arch of Triumph, made of plaster, that was displayed at theaters. So profligate did the spending become during the shooting that there was a running joke around the studio that if you had "anything you wanted to charge, you'd just mark it 'Charge it to ARCH.' Oh, they just spent way too much money."[17] Originally budgeted at $750,000, the film eventually cost $5 million—an enormous sum for the time.

Arch of Triumph also suffered from bad timing. Between 1946 (when Enterprise Studio came into being) and 1949—exactly during the period of the shooting and release of *Arch of Triumph*—the film industry changed profoundly. Numerous antitrust court decisions came down that forced the major studios to divest themselves of their theater chains. The economy took a serious downturn after the boom years of World War II, which affected the box office. Studios began drastically cutting costs in response to the unfavorable market conditions that developed in 1947. The many independent studios (like Enterprise) formed in the optimistic immediate postwar period were particularly hard hit by the tightening of credit, a reduction in box-office revenue, and new tax laws. Many—like Enterprise—could not survive and folded.

When *Arch of Triumph* went into production in spring 1946, the film industry was still booming, but by the time it was completed later that year, the situation had deteriorated rapidly. Initially, Enterprise had envisioned a four-hour epic film in the style of the recently reissued *Gone with the Wind*. Milestone claimed that he had wanted to shorten the script before shooting began, but that the Enterprise executives, who wanted to get as much as they could out of their highly paid stars, overruled him. But by the time the film was finished, audiences were no longer interested in lengthy screen epics—no matter who was starring.

Until 1947, "movies were the best thing you could get for your dollar in the way of entertainment," Van Schmus observed. "There was nothing to rival it. Well, when they started making ARCH, that suddenly stopped. People had to buy gas to drive their cars, they had many other things to do, so they *stopped* going to movies in great numbers. Nobody knew that while we were making ARCH. By the time it came out, the audience was not there anymore, not the one they *needed,* at least."[18]

In October 1946, as shooting was wrapping up, the *Los Angeles Times Magazine* ran a long profile of Milestone at home that focused on the eagerly anticipated *Arch of Triumph*. Its author, Mary Morris, was clearly dazzled by the high style in which the director was living at the time, a reflection of what he had attained after more than twenty years as a "king of the set." He was one of the founding fathers of Hollywood and a member of its power elite.

> Today Milestone lives in Benedict Canyon, Beverly Hills, in a large, white-brick Georgian house surrounded by romantic olive and pepper trees. Like most movie homes, it has changed hands many times. Milestone bought it from Louis B. Mayer; Mayer got it from Robert Montgomery.
>
> Milestone was wearing an expensive dark-brown business suit, a collarless knitted sport shirt and a silk scarf tucked around the neck that Sunday morning. His manner was reserved and his face masked his feelings. He spoke with only the faintest trace of accent. He met me in the living room, pulled back a sliding door, and we stepped out onto a bricked terrace overlooking formal gardens with a kidney-shaped swimming pool below. We sat here on reclining garden chairs in the warm sunshine. . . .
>
> The dining room was lovely and sophisticated, done in various tones of gray-green. The breakfast-lunch consisted of melon, curried eggs, and elegant paper-thin pancakes with jelly, all served by an expert butler in a correct starched white jacket but with a surprising red-and-blue-striped tie.[19]

Just one year later, Milestone's life of luxury and esteem would be shaken to its foundations.

Not long after he gave this interview, the original 224-minute version of *Arch of Triumph* (three minutes longer than *Gone with the Wind*) had its first preview screening, in Santa Barbara. It was "a disaster."[20] Milestone and his crew went back to work to try to fix it. They tried adding documentary footage of German soldiers marching across Europe to link the sections, then discarded it after wasting $25,000. Franz Waxman (who had compiled the extremely successful score for *Casablanca*) was briefly brought in to write different music that was also eventually thrown out. All but one short scene with the character of Ravic's American friend Kate (Ruth Warrick), an important presence in Remarque's novel, dropped to the cutting room floor. After these and other changes were made, a new, much shorter version was screened in Florida, but it fared no better, and Einfeld withdrew it from distribution.[21]

Uncertain how to proceed, the Enterprise executives hesitated, withholding the film until April 1948, when it had its official opening in New York at a much shorter (and considerably less coherent) 115 minutes. By then, word had gotten out that *Arch* had serious cracks, and the critical and popular reception was mostly negative. By then, too, in Milestone's words, "the bottom had fallen out of the market."[22] In the end, the film grossed $1,428,490 in the United States against expenses of around $5 million—the most expensive picture made until that time, rivaling the cost of King Vidor's 1946 "adult western," *Duel in the Sun*.[23]

For Milestone, the failure of *Arch of Triumph* came as a crushing blow. Van Schmus was there the day that the reviews were brought to the director, already at work on his next picture for Enterprise, *No Minor Vices*. "Somebody brought in a group of them to him, and he took them into his dressing room and read them and they were disastrous. Absolutely disastrous. The poor man was just shattered, because this was, hopefully, one of the *big* steps in his career, to make that a successful movie. And it just flattened him terribly. He suffered for *days* about that. . . . Here was a real chance for a crowning achievement, that, shall we say, just fell apart."[24]

One of the most damning assessments of *Arch of Triumph* came from Charles Boyer, who, when asked by Edwin Schallert of the *Los Angeles Times* how he felt about the drastic cutting of the original version, replied: "It has improved it considerably. It was terrible for four hours, but now it is terrible for two hours."[25] In one of his famous memos, David O. Selznick, producer of several of Bergman's most successful films, wrote, "Her downfall started with her very first picture after leaving us, *Arch of Triumph*."[26]

Other reviewers were not much more charitable. In the *New York Times*, Bosley Crowther wrote: "From within Lewis Milestone's roving camera, we watch love as it is made by two of the movies' most able craftsmen, repetitiously and at exceeding length. And to the inevitable question, 'Is that bad?' we can only say that too much of a good thing—even of Bergman and Boyer—is too much."[27] Even worse, when *Arch of Triumph* fell, not only did it severely damage Milestone's subsequent career as a director—its failure would bring down Enterprise Studios as well. In the end, what doomed the project was Milestone's noble insistence on remaining faithful to Remarque's pessimistic vision, at a time when audiences no longer wanted to revisit the terrible days of 1939. Such an "old-fashioned" film would have been much more successful five years earlier, before the dawning of the Cold War confused the political and cultural milieu.

For all that, *Arch of Triumph* boasts some inspired and powerful moments. The film's masterful and meticulous re-creation of the noir pre-war Paris underworld, crisscrossed by shadowy ghosts and permeated with anxiety, seduces us from the outset. The opening sequence of Ravic's encounter with Joan on a rainy bridge trembles with pathos and compassion, Milestone teasing us as her beautiful face slowly emerges from the dark shadow underneath the brim of her hat. Convincing in her early scenes, Bergman seems to lose focus in the film's melodramatic later ones; her extended, heavy-breathing deathbed throes fail to convince, launching the final moments into the realm of operatic cliché.

As always, Boyer casts a spell with his cigarette-soaked voice and unfailing composure. But he is rather too suave and debonair to capture the raw anger and outrage in Remarque's Ravic, a victim of political forces and venality he cannot accept or control. Laughton's Haake, while the interesting work of a brilliant actor still in his prime, seems rather too artificial, studied, and insufficiently sinister, a performance, in the words of his biographer Simon Callow (himself a distinguished actor), with "the potential for something interesting which he had neither time nor perhaps encouragement enough to achieve."[28] Milestone did use music very skillfully to create atmosphere; the lively and engaging scenes in the Scheherazade received the most praise, even though casting the American actor Louis Calhern as its proprietor, Morosov, seemed a missed opportunity. An actual Russian character actor like Vladimir Sokolov, Akim Tamiroff, or Fyodor Chaliapin Jr. would have been a much better and more realistic choice.

In the end, Milestone could not control this unwieldy production and the outsize creative personalities he was given to direct. If Enterprise Studios had possessed a strong creative head (like David O. Selznick or Sam Goldwyn or Jack Warner) with the kind of forceful vision and command necessary to guide this unwieldy project through to completion, *Arch of Triumph* might have fulfilled the high hopes it initially inspired.

Nor did the world outside the studio offer much respite to Milestone during these difficult times. On September 21, 1947, he received a subpoena from the Committee on Un-American Activities of the U.S. House of Representatives, "inviting" him (along with forty-three other men from the Hollywood film industry) to appear in Washington on October 20. When nineteen of those subpoenaed announced their hostility to HUAC and its goals, the *Hollywood Reporter* labeled them as "unfriendly." They quickly became known as the Unfriendly Nineteen.

Besides Milestone, the group included only three other directors: Edward Dmytryk, Irving Pichel, and Robert Rossen. With the exception of one producer, Adrian Scott, the rest were writers, including such distinguished figures as Bertolt Brecht, Howard Koch (*Sergeant York, Casablanca*), Ring Lardner Jr., and Dalton Trumbo. Only four members of the Nineteen had *never* belonged to the Communist Party—including Milestone. That Milestone was included in this first group summoned by HUAC is not so surprising, however. He was born in Russia (actually Ukraine, but part of the Russian empire at the time); his native language was Russian; many of his close friends and associates shared strongly left-wing and Communist sympathies; he was known for his friendships with Soviet film people; and he had directed a film—*The North Star*—regarded as pro-Soviet.

"While there is no evidence or indication of his membership in the CPUSA," Alan Casty writes of Milestone, "he was a regular and faithful presence in left-wing Hollywood circles."[29] Another important factor was that his film *All Quiet on the Western Front* had become "the celluloid Bible of pacifists," and pacifism was associated with left-wing sentiments. That its leading actor, Lew Ayres, had become a conscientious objector in 1942, "the most famous CO during the war," only further linked Milestone to antiwar movements, which were in the popular view closely tied to Communist convictions.[30]

Nearly four years later, on June 25, 1951, Milestone had the following exchange with William Wheeler, an investigator for HUAC, in closed private testimony in Los Angeles.

Q Have you ever been a member of the Communist Party?
A No, sir.
Q Has anybody ever asked you to become a member of the Communist Party?

A Never. I never gave it any thought until this thing started and I was wondering why nobody ever asked me.[31]

In the same interview, Milestone was asked why "many people have said or believed, or made statements to the effect that you are a Communist."

I suppose it has something to do with the origin of my birth, A; B, in some circles, I have expressed myself freely, which was probably misconstrued by the other people as being too far to the left. . . . Because I was more concerned about the prop man than I was about the big star I think was a contributing factor. And because wherever I could, in debates at home, at parties and places like that, if I thought that something was right I would say that. I was never afraid, you see, to express my viewpoints. . . . I never considered my statements as being pro-Communist, but if they were construed so, you see, there is nothing I could do about it.[32]

In the 1930s Milestone had belonged to the Anti-Nazi League, later regarded as a Communist front organization. A lifelong Democrat and admirer of FDR, in 1944 he had also served on the executive board of the Hollywood Independent Citizens Committee of the Arts, Sciences and Professions (HICCASP), an organization that grew out of the Hollywood Democratic Committee and aspired to "retain the humanistic approach to politics that had grown nationwide during the New Deal Days."[33] Not all the members of HICCASP shared left-wing convictions, however: Ronald Reagan belonged.

Milestone also believed that he was denounced by a writer he had once met on a train. "I was supposed to pick up a writer in Kansas City and bring him out here; he was going to be under contract to Paramount. And I found out that he was the guy who said that aboard the train we had long conversations and I told him that nobody over forty should be allowed to live because it was too late to change their minds. . . . So that was one enemy, and who knows who else?"[34] The HUAC hearings and resulting blacklist proved to be a fertile opportunity for those who wanted to take revenge on others they envied, resented—or simply disliked—in the business.

As soon as they had received their subpoenas (which were not entirely unexpected given preceding events), the Hollywood Nineteen began to meet to plan strategy for their upcoming appearance in Washington. Milestone hosted the group's first meeting at his lavish home on San Ysidro Drive. As he told Wheeler, "Since I landed with the unfriendly witnesses I decided that collective action would probably be stronger than individual action."[35] Along with eighteen of the unfriendly witnesses, the attorneys they had hired to defend them attended: Bartley Crum, Charles Katz, and Robert W. Kenny. Ben Margolis, a Communist Party member, also joined the legal team.

"The first meeting, which was to place the stamp of inevitability on the future events of all our lives, took place at Lewis Milestone's home in Beverly Hills," Dmytryk wrote in his autobiography. "Milestone was not a Communist—he was an easygoing liberal and a soft touch for any leftist with an honorable cause. As a director of great reputation, he had been singled out for a subpoena. Actually, in the group of nineteen, there were a few sheep to go along with the majority of goats, and I believe the committee knew that. But it couldn't hurt to scare hell out of them and teach them a lesson, now could it?"[36] No evidence has ever turned up to suggest that the Unfriendly Nineteen received any support or instructions from domestic or global Communist organizations, as was widely rumored at the time, and as Dmytryk later falsely claimed.

The actor Larry Parks described the group as "19 men you'd never have been able to get together for a dinner party" who had "nothing in common but the conviction that this Committee was itself un-American and had to be fought."[37] Milestone was meeting most of the them for the first time. With only three of the eighteen did he have a personal relationship.

I knew who John Howard Lawson [a prominent screenwriter] was and I think I had a speaking acquaintance with him, but I never sat down and talked to him, never shared coffee with him. Dalton Trumbo lived next door to me and we exchanged a series of telegrams about my dog, but the first time I ever talked to him was at one of those meetings. I knew Rossen, I had worked with him. . . . I never knew Mr. Trumbo until one morning about 3:00 o'clock when I received a telegram from him complaining that my dog was barking and kept his new-born baby awake. And he thought that he was more entitled to the baby than I was to my dog. I agreed with him and I sent my dog to the Valley to be educated not to bark."[38]

At this and subsequent meetings (several more of which took place at Milestone's house), the Nineteen discussed how they should respond to the questions they would be asked by HUAC. They agreed, after heated debate, to observe the "unanimity rule"—meaning that all members of the group had to abide by the decisions made by the majority, a tactic associated with Communist ideological discipline. Only Bertolt Brecht, a German citizen, refused to go along with this strategy, no doubt fearing for his status as an alien. At the time the subpoenas were served, Brecht was in New York, and he did not meet with the other members of the group. He would leave the United States for Berlin on October 31, the day after his testimony in Washington.

The lawyers recommended that when called to testify, they should use both the First and the Fifth Amendments, refusing to reveal their political or union affiliations. But the group decided that taking the Fifth Amendment ("no person . . . shall be compelled in any criminal case to be a witness against himself") implied that membership in the Communist Party was a criminal act. So instead they agreed to invoke their First Amendment rights, in the hopes of discrediting the committee—although by doing so they risked being convicted of contempt of Congress.[39] "What they wanted to make clear was that the essential question involved here— and ten of them went to jail on this very point—was freedom of speech."[40]

One of those who protested this tactic most vehemently, according to Milestone, was Howard Koch. "He didn't feel it was right. He figured it out for himself . . . he felt that the Congress had a right to know if they asked you the questions."[41] Milestone (who was in the end not called to testify publicly) also felt ambivalent about hiding behind the First Amendment, and he admitted he was unsure how he would have acted if called. "This is a very difficult question to answer," he said in his 1951 HUAC testimony. "What I was going to do I had no idea. I don't know whether I would have gone through with it. It is just difficult to tell."[42]

Some of the members of the Nineteen, including Milestone, also attended a party at the home of the actor Edward G. Robinson to meet and consult with Senator Claude Pepper, Democrat of Florida, a fierce critic of HUAC's activities. Later, Pepper came to a meeting with the group at Milestone's house.[43]

Not long after the subpoena, however, another notification arrived that HUAC had canceled Milestone's invitation to testify, along with Robert Rossen's and several others'. The reason for the cancellation was not made clear. In the end, only eleven members (ten American citizens and Bertolt Brecht) of the Unfriendly Nineteen were called before the committee. But in comradely fashion, Milestone continued to support the group's other members and helped raise money for their defense and other expenses. He attended a fund-raising rally attended by seven thousand people at the Shrine Auditorium on October 15, sponsored by the Progressive Citizens of America, and signed a two-page ad that appeared in industry publications: "An Open Letter to the Motion Picture Industry on the Issue of Freedom of the Screen from Political Intimidation and Censorship." If HUAC was allowed to continue its activities, the letter warned, the result would be "a lifeless and reactionary screen that will be artistically, culturally, and financially bankrupt."[44] Some prominent Hollywood actors (including Humphrey Bogart, Lauren Bacall, Danny Kaye, Gene Kelly, Jane Wyatt, John Huston) rallied behind the Nineteen to form the Committee for the First Amendment, which sought to publicize the predicament of the Nineteen.

Milestone also decided to accompany the group on its trip to Washington in late October for the hearings, as he explained in an interview years later. "I just wanted to know what was going on. . . . I watched the performance, and I saw all of it. I was in the caucus room every day, and I saw the whole development—how from nineteen they became ten, leaving the rest of us (free) to do anything we wanted."[45]

In his 1951 testimony, Milestone added that "there was quite a bit of emotionalism involved in the doings of that time and I feel that my subpoena was unjustly served and I went there anyway. In case they wanted me I was there."[46]

So Milestone heard the question (posed by J. Parnell Thomas, HUAC's chairman) that became the refrain of the HUAC crusade against Communism in the film industry: "Are you a member of the Communist Party or have you ever been a member of the Communist Party?" By the time Thomas asked this question of the first of the Unfriendly Nineteen called to testify, John Howard Lawson, on October 27, a parade of "friendly" witnesses (including Gary Cooper and Adolphe Menjou, both of whom had previously worked with Milestone) had already taken the stand to describe widespread Communist influence in Hollywood. Some of them named names, including Dalton Trumbo's. The atmosphere in the packed room, according to Ring Lardner Jr., was "one-sided" and "frightening."[47]

A young congressman from California, another HUAC member, Richard Nixon, made a strong impression on Milestone (and many others). "From watching him sitting with the committee on the stand, I knew he was headed for a career. There were several big picture companies that were backing him."[48]

When called to the stand, Lawson was not allowed to read his carefully prepared opening statement, which called HUAC's mission into question and was designed to elicit public sympathy. Asked whether he belonged to the Communist Party, Lawson refused to answer, instead attacking the committee for invading his rights as an American citizen. Repeatedly interrupted by Thomas's gavel, Lawson lost his cool and started shouting: "It is unfortunate and tragic that I have to teach this committee the basic principles of American . . ."[49] Thomas abruptly ended his testimony and Lawson almost had to be dragged away from the stand in a spectacle that won little support for the cause of the Nineteen. Shrewdly, Thomas followed up with a recitation of Lawson's many known Communist affiliations by one of the committee's investigators. Similar scenes were repeated in the following days as other members of the Nineteen took the stand.

Asked later whether he approved of the antagonistic tactics employed by those called to testify (with the exception of Brecht, who answered the question in the negative), Milestone replied: "No. I thought it was a little too violent. I remember Lawson's first appearance, and it scared everybody to death, including me, because he screamed and shouted and yelled. It was quite a scene. A little too violent, see, for the opening for almost anything."[50] Some of the influential members of the Committee for the First Amendment were also dismayed by the reluctance of the Ten to cooperate with questions from HUAC. Trumbo's biographer Bruce Cook observed, "Those who had come across the country together, so full of high purpose, began leaving in ones and twos, feeling vaguely betrayed by the very men whose cause they had come to Washington to fight for."[51]

At first it appeared that the eleven who testified had succeeded in turning public opinion against HUAC. The media coverage of the way the hearings had been conducted was overwhelmingly critical, and Thomas halted the hearings after Brecht's appearance on October 30. But on November 24 the House of Representatives voted in favor of issuing contempt citations against the ten who had refused to answer the committee's questions, opening the way for their prosecution under federal law. At the same time, film industry executives were wilting under the pressure and bad publicity, and they began to distance themselves from the group. After a meeting of studio heads and production companies at the Waldorf Astoria Hotel in New York, Eric Johnston, president of the producers' association, announced that "we will not re-employ any of the ten until such time as he is acquitted or has purged himself of contempt and declares under oath that he is not a Communist."[52] The Unfriendly Nineteen had become the Hollywood Ten.

The consequences for the Ten became immediately clear. All were indicted, tried, convicted of contempt of Congress, and sentenced to prison terms. They were unable to work (at least under their own names). The consequences for the members of the Unfriendly Nineteen who had not been called to testify—including Milestone—were less clear. "I don't want to go through that goddam thing again," Milestone said years later, revealing how painful the experience had been, "but the fact remains that people like Rossen and myself, who weren't touched at all, didn't land on a blacklist but drew something worse, a gray list—which was bad enough. It took a long, long time to get rid of it. You had adversaries, you see, but you never knew who they were, so you couldn't face them."[53]

For the next ten years, until HUAC was completely discredited, Milestone remained under suspicion. He was regularly visited and called by HUAC and FBI investigators who asked him questions about people he had known or worked with. Despite his repeated denials (he even went so far as to sign a notarized affidavit filed with the Directors' Guild stating that he had never been a member of the Communist Party), conservative newspapers and magazines continued to call him a Communist and to question his motives. Eventually, like many others in the same position, he decided to leave the United States and work abroad until the situation improved.

"It was pretty silly," Milestone said of the HUAC hearings years later in a joint interview with the director John Cromwell. "But it drove me out of the business."[54]

But not immediately. For the moment, Milestone continued to work at Enterprise Studios. After the epic scale of *Arch of Triumph,* Einfeld proposed something entirely different, a light romantic comedy, *No Minor Vices,* to be shot in the spring and early summer of 1947. According to Norman Lloyd, Milestone and Harry Brown "started with the title and wrote a script."[55] In fact, however, they were adapting a story by Arnold

Manoff, whom Milestone described as "an excellent writer with left-wing sentiments."[56] A strained intellectual farce about art and psychiatry set in Manhattan, it stars Dana Andrews as a doctor whose wife (Lilli Palmer) becomes infatuated with (but eventually rejects) an upscale Italian artist (Louis Jourdan). The plot recalls that of Milestone's earlier film *My Life with Caroline.*

Although it was a small-scale project with a running time of only ninety-six minutes, the cast and crew boasted some impressive talent: the actors Dana Andrews, Jane Wyatt, Louis Jourdan, Lilli Palmer, and Norman Lloyd; the composer Franz Waxman; and the production designer Nicolai Remisoff. *No Minor Vices* attempts to explore the world of the subconscious mind and the subjectivity of "reality" and emotions: "Everyone sees what he has to see." A large eye adorns the door of the artist's studio, as if peering into the depths of anyone who enters. Long portions of the script take the form of stream-of-consciousness internal dialogues of characters with themselves (especially the artist). But the film feels like a workshop experiment rather than a finished product, as if Milestone were taking a break from the Hollywood studio system to indulge himself, without caring much about the audience. The performances are generally too earnest and forced to give *No Minor Vices* the light touch it needs. Dana Andrews and Palmer do not generate much energy as sparring spouses, and much of the arch humor falls flat.

Screen Director's Playhouse broadcast a more successful—and condensed—television version of *No Minor Vices* in 1951, performed before a live audience.

By the time *No Minor Vices* went into production, Enterprise Studios was on the ropes. For a time Bertolt Brecht was regarded as the studio's last best hope. Lloyd recalled, "Milestone had the hope that Brecht would provide us with a treatment that Ingrid [Bergman] would be keen about, and that she would agree to do, which would put us all back in business."[57] But Milestone rejected several scripts that Brecht produced, and he flew into a rage at what he considered to be Brecht's lazy working habits. After one of their many shouting matches, Brecht told Lloyd that Milestone "is not an artist. That man is a heavyweight prizefighter."[58] Not long afterward, Brecht left the United States, never to return.

The last hurrah for Enterprise Studios production was Stanley Kramer's first feature, *So This Is New York,* based on Ring Lardner's novel *The Big Town.* Although Kramer would go on to a very successful directing career, this film failed so badly that it never even opened in Manhattan. Enterprise Studios folded.

Once again, Milestone was on his own. What saved him this time was a project he had put on hold for nearly ten years: a film version of Steinbeck's *The Red Pony*. Milestone and Steinbeck had discussed filming this collection of short stories around the time they were making *Of Mice and Men,* in 1939, but the outbreak of World War II and other more pressing projects repeatedly postponed those plans. In September 1946 Milestone made a formal agreement with Steinbeck for the rights to the story, the screenplay to be written jointly by Milestone and Steinbeck—the only time the author adapted one of his own works.

In March 1947, with the assistance of the prominent agent Charles Feldman, Milestone (actually, Lewis Milestone Productions, of which Milestone served as president) signed a contract with Republic Studios, a successful producer of B movies—especially Westerns. Under its terms, Milestone was to receive $100,000, and Republic would provide 60 percent of the production costs, up to a maximum of $1 million.[59] (His salary was considerably lower than what the stars, Myrna Loy and Robert Mitchum, received: $200,000 and $130,000, respectively.)[60] Milestone acted as both director and producer, on what was also his first color film—and his first Western, with horses in starring roles.

Republic Studios "saw an opportunity here," according to Albert Van Schmus, who followed Milestone from Enterprise Studios to work on the project. "I think they saw a chance for stature, for class. A touch of class. . . . The Republic lot, they were kind of penny-pinchers and we always kind of ridiculed them for that, but we were used to the Enterprise posh style of production. . . . That was really, I guess, the biggest effort, up to that point, that they had ever made, in trying to make a quality film."[61]

Six years earlier, Milestone and Steinbeck had spent considerable time near Steinbeck's home in Monterey working on a screenplay. Now, meeting in a hotel in New York, they undertook revisions. In a letter to the author John Hersey, Milestone described their unusually congenial collaboration.

> John understood all the problems involved in telling it on the screen. He was most cooperative in helping to bring the story into screen form. Thus, we were able to remain closer to the basic conception of the story. This is the chief advantage of the

author-director relationship such as Steinbeck and I established. There is a consistency of style in dialogue and character only John could have executed.

All changes from the basic conception are invention. But if invention is demanded, it is better that the author and director do it together rather than at cross purposes which usually makes for a negative result. This latter condition has been the usual story between first-rate writers and Hollywood. If we are to improve the quality of pictures, one way is for our outstanding authors to remain close to their work when it is transferred to the screen; to help; to guide. John has done this with "The Red Pony."[62]

Unlike the novella *Of Mice and Men*, *The Red Pony* is a collection of four stories written at different times and originally brought together with other stories in 1938 in *The Long Valley*. In 1945 they appeared together as the slim volume *The Red Pony*, unified by the place of the action (the Salinas Valley) and some common characters. The stories could be classified as children's literature, since the hero is a ten-year-old boy, Jody Tiflin, growing up around 1910 on a ranch where he learns to love and care for a variety of animals, particularly horses. In "The Gift," he receives a pony named Gabilan from his father, but he learns some hard lessons about life and death when Gabilan dies after catching a chill when inadvertently left out in a drenching rainstorm. A tale of the inescapable cycles of nature, "The Great Mountains" focuses on an old Mexican farmhand, Gitano, whose life of labor comes to its natural end along with that of the horse Easter: "Too old to work. Just eats and pretty soon dies." In "The Promise," Jody's father and the young ranch hand, Billy Buck, promise him the colt of one of their mares, but they have to kill her to save the colt when problems arise at the birth. The final story, "The Leader of the People," introduces Jody's grandfather, an aging pioneer whose endless tales about "westering" now bore his listeners, and shows how the world has changed since his adventurous youth crossing the plains to the Pacific.

In adapting the stories to the screen, Steinbeck and Milestone decided to add a new element of conflict. Jody's father becomes a transplanted city slicker (from San Jose) who struggles to find his place in a rural farm community, which causes friction with his wife. She in turn finds solace in a close relationship with their hired hand, Billy Buck, whose character (a brawny man's man) becomes much more important in the film as a contrast to the bookish and stiff father. The screenplay drops the story of Gitano, focusing on the relationship between Jody (who becomes Tom), his parents, Billy Buck, the visiting grandfather, and the two horses. Steinbeck and Milestone also expanded the role of the local schoolteacher, a plum character role assigned to the witch from *The Wizard of Oz*, Margaret Hamilton, in a deliciously nasty cameo. In an unfortunate concession to Hollywood's need for "happy endings," the film ends with the successful birth of the new colt, without the traumatic death of the mare, as the farm family gathers around, laughing heartily at their good fortune.

Concerned that the material was insufficiently commercial, Feldman, the producer, insisted from the outset that Myrna Loy be cast as Tom's mother. Milestone had known Loy for many years—she had made her first major film appearance in his silent film *The Cave Man*. But Loy, then in her early forties, seemed an odd choice both visually and dramatically, recognized as she was for her work in sophisticated comedies, particularly as Nora Charles (playing opposite William Powell) in *The Thin Man* and its numerous debonair sequels. She looked too prim, dignified, and patrician for the part of a ranch mother—even though Loy had in fact been born of frontier stock in rugged Montana, one of the reasons she wanted to take the role in *The Red Pony*. Milestone was concerned that putting Loy ("a big star with sex appeal") together with handsome screen idol Robert Mitchum as Billy Buck would create too much romantic tension and change the atmosphere of Steinbeck's stories.[63]

RKO Studios lent Mitchum, one of Hollywood's legendary leading men, to Republic for *The Red Pony*, the actor's first color film. As it happens, Steinbeck was one of Mitchum's favorite writers, and he was happy to participate in what he viewed as a "prestige" project. Alfred Van Schmus, the second assistant director, remembered Mitchum as "an interesting man. A bit of a hell-raiser, but that kind of goes with the job in some respects. He never took himself very seriously as an actor."[64] Mitchum got along well with Loy, although he loved teasing her on the set, as she remembered in her autobiography. "He just about tortured me with his pranks during shooting—particularly when he had an audience. . . . Oh, yes, Bob clowned around, but when it came to actually working he was all business. He is one of those artists that make it look easy, a fine actor and intriguing man with so many sides to him. He has that smooth, masculine face, seemingly without a care in the world, yet you saw an underlying sensitivity and intelligence."[65]

Mitchum's reputation as one of the "bad boys of Hollywood" received considerable reinforcement when he was arrested for marijuana possession on August 31, 1948, not long after completing shooting on *The Red Pony* (and before its theatrical release). He spent sixty days in jail, although the experience seems only to have enhanced his allure.

During the shooting, however, Milestone did not confront the sort of problems handling actors that he had on *Arch of Triumph*. Weather conditions at the Agoura Ranch (where Milestone had shot *Of Mice and Men* and *A Walk in the Sun*), a long drive from Los Angeles, were far from ideal during the early winter of 1948, but the well-paid cast members did not complain. The shooting of Loy's scenes was frequently disrupted, according to Van Schmus. "You know, it would have taken her two hours to go through the hair and the makeup every morning, and she'd come out and for such a *long* period of time, it seemed like it went on for weeks, the weather was just not good for shooting. And she'd sit around, and I would come to her about one o'clock and say, 'Myrna, we're not going to be able to shoot you today. I'm *so* sorry about this.' She would say, 'Van, don't *worry* about it. I'm an actress, I have to expect this."[66]

Adopting the appearance of Buffalo Bill, with long gray hair and a collection of arrowheads, Louis Calhern shed the Russian identity he had developed for *The Arch of Triumph* to portray the endearing but useless figure of the grandfather.

Animals play a central role in *The Red Pony;* directing them was a new experience for Milestone (and one that would help him in his upcoming Australian film, *Kangaroo*). He relied on the trainers to deal with the horses and with the buzzards that attack Tom's sick pony (and then Tom himself, played by Peter Miles) in one of the film's most dramatic and powerful scenes. According to Van Schmus, Milestone got along well with Miles and the other child actors on the set—including seven-year-old Beau Bridges, a son of Lloyd Bridges (Lloyd had appeared in *A Walk in the Sun*), who would go on to his own distinguished career in the movies.

In another first, Milestone used several episodes of animation to represent Tom's daydreams. In one, he sees himself with Billy Buck (a visibly uncomfortable Mitchum), both dressed as knights in armor traveling on horseback. In another, he is the ringmaster in a circus, surrounded by prancing steeds. A group of animators who had originally worked for Walt Disney designed both sequences. But neither seems well integrated, and

Milestone shortened both in the course of production. Their inclusion creates a certain confusion about the film's intentions: is it escapist fantasy fare for children, or something more serious, as Steinbeck intended?

Aaron Copland's colorful, highly accessible, and idiomatic musical score proved to be the production's most successful and enduring element. The composer's third collaboration with Milestone, after *Of Mice and Men* and *The North Star*, it is their best. For ten weeks of work, Copland received $1,500 a week (a pittance compared to what the stars were receiving) for fifty-two minutes of music that he composed, orchestrated, and conducted. Copland went to Agoura for the shooting, immersing himself in the film's atmosphere. What he liked about the project was the possibility of composing longer sequences instead of the small forms (two or three minutes) required in most films he had worked on before. For Tom's fight with the buzzards, for example, he wrote six minutes of "dissonant music with complicated rhythms."[67]

As Copland wrote later, "Much of the story called for simple harmonies and clear melodies and, of course, some of the inevitable steady rhythmic accompaniment to simulate cowboys on horseback." When Tom watches as his beloved pony undergoes surgery, three bass clarinets convey the emotional gravity. "The only problem I had with *The Red Pony* was that it was shot on the same ranch that was used for *Of Mice and Men*. Now I ask you: If you had to look at the same landscape every day, could you think up different music?"[68]

But the score for *The Red Pony* seems fresh and novel, sounding indelibly "American" in the same unique way as his recent ballet scores for *Rodeo* and *Appalachian Spring*. Like them, it conveys a feeling of "folksiness," although all the tunes are original. Steinbeck told Copland he admired what he had produced because "you let the somber come into your music to balance the gaiety and to give it proportion and significance."[69] When Copland later created a concert suite from the music he had composed for *The Red Pony* for the Houston Symphony Orchestra, it enjoyed enormous success, and today it ranks among the composer's most widely known and frequently recorded (and broadcast) scores.

Curiously, Copland had been nominated for (but lost) the Academy Award for Best Score for both of his preceding collaborations with Milestone—including *The North Star*, whose music was vastly inferior to that of *The Red Pony*. In 1949, however, he finally won the Oscar—but for his score for William Wyler's *The Heiress*, released the same year as *The*

Red Pony (whose score wasn't even nominated). Only a few years later, Copland, like Milestone before him, would fall under the suspicion of HUAC for his long history of embracing leftist causes and his collaborative friendships with Russians.

Perhaps because it was difficult to categorize as a picture for either children or adults, or because of the lack of romantic appeal, *The Red Pony* did not fare well at the box office or with critics. Released in March 1949, it generated lukewarm reviews, such as Bosley Crowther's in the *New York Times*, which praised its "considerable sincerity" but bemoaned its "indifferent dramatic success.... In directing the picture, Mr. Milestone has adopted a frankly casual style which further invests the proceedings with a languid quality."[70]

Whatever the critics said, in *The Red Pony* Milestone returns to his roots in simple, straightforward storytelling. Many of its scenes simmer with a burnished, nostalgic lyricism that suits Steinbeck's vision and has weathered well. Much more personal and genuine than either *The Strange Love of Martha Ivers* or the overblown *Arch of Triumph*, this film comes from the director's heart and conveys a longing for a more innocent time in America history, before the catastrophic wars of the twentieth century. Like the grandfather, Milestone as a young man had gone west to California in search of fame, fortune, and a better life.

To the cast and crew of *The Red Pony*, Milestone—despite his recent struggles—still stood as a larger-than-life figure, nothing less than a Hollywood legend. He never forgot his own humble beginnings, and he treated everyone on the set with compassion and respect. They responded in kind. "I think they respected Milestone," said his assistant director Van Schmus. "They sensed that he knew what he was doing, and he *did*. He was a damn good director. I don't care if he has the best track record in the world in the industry or not. He was a *damn* good director."[71]

Since *The Strange Love of Martha Ivers*, however, Milestone's films had fared poorly with audiences and critics. He needed a fresh start, and an old friend would give it to him.

10

On the Graylist

Everybody's not a hero; everybody's not made of hero material.
—*Lewis Milestone*

After the release of *The Red Pony,* and with no other projects on the horizon, Milestone and his wife, Kendall, made a dramatic change in their lives. Like many others in Hollywood who had fallen under suspicion for their alleged Communist associations, they left the United States to live abroad until the political situation improved, to escape the paranoia and uncertainty.[1] Their financial situation had deteriorated significantly, and the future looked menacing. The Hollywood Ten had been sentenced to prison terms they would begin to serve in June 1950. The Cold War seemed only to be intensifying. It would turn hot on June 25, 1950, when the Korean War began.

By early 1950 the Milestones were living in an apartment they had rented in Paris. Soon after, they sold their beloved house on Benedict Canyon in Beverly Hills, the site of so many memorable parties. "Don't feel sorry for the old house," wrote Milestone in a letter to Kendall. "We are well out of it and perhaps soon we'll have another. Wouldn't it be nice if it wasn't in Hollywood?"[2] During their early time in Paris, they encountered Brenda Helser, who reported on their meeting to her friend the gossip columnist Hedda Hopper. "I see a great deal of Lewis Milestone and his wife, Kendall. They've just moved into a flat and go about almost entirely with our group (mostly under thirty) and they have the time of their lives. They're studying French daily and Millie says that he upsets the teacher so much she's a nervous wreck by the time she gets to Kendall and Kendall is mad because she wastes half the lesson trying to calm her down."[3]

Just a few weeks later, Helser wrote another letter that expresses a very different opinion of the Milestones. It seems she had received new information from Hopper, very active in ferreting out suspected Hollywood Communists.

> I was horrified to read about Milestone's communist leanings and said so to a mutual friend who said "of course he is, I thought I'd told you!" . . . Not that the rest of the group is, but they like Milly and I did too, however, I'm still too immature to be blazed about it. I'm glad you told me and that they have left Paris (to go back to make some nice capitalistic dollars). I'm a little ashamed of myself for turning tail, but I'm about as uncommunistic as a girl can be and I don't care to find myself stuck one day because an investigating committee discovers I dined with the Milestones. I guess I have a lot to learn.[4]

The Milestones lived in various rented apartments in Paris over the next five years, until late 1955, using them as a base for their new nomadic life, with occasional trips to Los Angeles and elsewhere during the first few years. They continued to pay rent on a Paris apartment until August 1957, not sure what the future would hold.[5]

The "nice capitalistic dollars" that Milestone returned to Hollywood (temporarily) to earn not long after they settled in Paris were to come from a new project proposed by his old friend Darryl Zanuck. Since their first meeting and collaboration twenty-five years earlier, in 1925, on the silent comedy *Seven Sinners,* Zanuck had risen rapidly to become one of the most powerful men in the industry. Appointed vice president in charge of production at 20th Century Fox in 1935, he presided over the studio's most prestigious and glorious era.

Zanuck admired Milestone's work as a director of war pictures and had produced both *The Purple Heart* and *A Walk in the Sun* at Fox a few years earlier. Now he offered him another chance when he really needed it: a film project (in Technicolor) about World War II, *Halls of Montezuma.* This time the setting was the War in the Pacific, the realistic tale of an assault by American marines on a Japanese-held island. Michael Blankfort's screenplay, based on his own story, focuses on the psychological struggles of seven members of a patrol sent ashore to dislodge Japanese rocket launchers concealed under a hillside. Their lieutenant, Carl Anderson, a former high school chemistry teacher, suffers from psychosomatic migraine headaches. Other members of the group come from various ethnic, geographic, and professional origins—as is usually the case in Hollywood war movies of the time. One suffers shame because his sister had married a Japanese man in Hawaii. Another is a hard-bitten war correspondent who sees the war as material for writing. Another spends most of his time trying to brew alcohol in a portable still. Another is an effete translator with valuable knowledge of Japanese and a fondness for smoking cigarettes with a cigarette holder. Another is nicknamed "Doc" because of his basic medical skills.

In the course of their dangerous and bloody operation, the Americans take a group of Japanese soldiers prisoner. Several of them, it turns out, speak English quite well; one was a baseball star in Japan. The subtle interaction of the Americans and Japanese emerges as one of the film's most unusual features. ("A good Jap is also a prisoner who tells us things.") Blankfort resisted the temptation to treat the Japanese as villainous caricatures (although the labels *Jap* and *Nip* fly about freely in the dialogue), instead showing their humanity and their own fevered patriotism. Like the Americans, they are pawns in a much larger struggle they cannot control. This treatment recalls Milestone's humane portrayal of the French soldier trapped in a hole with Paul, the German soldier in *All Quiet on the Western Front*.

In other ways, too, *Halls of Montezuma* displays a strong kinship with *All Quiet*, as a study of how different ordinary men react under the pressure of combat, avoiding simplistic heroics and bravado in favor of a gritty emotional realism. "Always treat a human being like a human being—you'll be surprised what happens," the translator Johnson advises.

Zanuck and Milestone secured the assistance of the U.S. Marine Corps in the filming, much of which took place at nearby Fort Pendleton. The opening credits include the message that "This story is dedicated in gratitude for its help in making it possible—but most of all for its stalwart defense of all we hold dear to our lives, our people, and our future." Documentary footage of real combat in the Pacific theater appears throughout. Sol Kaplan's minimal musical score mostly offers arrangements of patriotic anthems, including the U.S. Marine hymn and "My Country 'Tis of Thee."

Halls of Montezuma is propaganda, of course, but it still manages to offer a mostly engrossing examination of a wider issue, the psychology of war, and the trauma suffered by those who engaged in combat. Short flashback scenes flesh out the personalities of the main characters and help explain why they react the way they do to the extreme situation. In a few early scenes, we hear the internal monologue of certain characters, mostly Anderson, musing on his anxiety. At the end, however, the film veers into one-dimensional patriotic-religious preaching, including a recitation of the Lord's Prayer and Doc's dying message: "We must keep our country strong—we are on God's side."

With Zanuck's clout, Milestone was able to assemble an impressive all-male cast. (A tough-talking female nurse makes a brief appearance in an early hospital scene, but the actress doesn't even receive screen credit.) Richard Widmark is Lieutenant Anderson, a well-meaning officer whose distaste for the hell of war comes out in his headaches, barely controlled by handfuls of painkillers that he conceals from his soldiers. His own emotional vulnerability makes him more understanding of the fear experienced by those he commands. When the Production Code Administration reviewed the screenplay, Joseph Breen raised objections about Anderson's use of morphine. "The unacceptable element in this story is the use of, and addiction to, narcotics by Lieutenant Anderson—this, in spite of the fact that the morphine originally is administered by a doctor for the alleviation of pain. The use of drugs in this story, in our judgment, is in direct violation of the Production Code."[6] So pills replaced morphine in the final version.

Besides Widmark, already an Oscar nominee for Best Supporting Actor for his role in Henry Hathaway's 1947 *Kiss of Death,* the distinguished (mostly young) cast included Jack Palance, Richard Boone, Karl Malden (as Doc), the foppish Reginald Gardiner as the translator Johnson, and the handsome newcomer Robert Wagner as the innocent Coffman.

By June 1950 the production of *Halls of Montezuma* was in full swing. Zanuck wrote to Milestone at Camp Pendleton in a long memo, "I want to tell you that I am highly pleased with the manner in which you are directing. . . . The battle scenes have scope, authenticity and a good broad sweep of action. The intimate personal scenes are sound and effective." What follows, however, is Zanuck's blunt appraisal of where Milestone now stood in the film industry, one of the most honest and incisive commentaries on his inconsistent career as a director.

Now purely as your friend and on a personal and confidential basis I will tell you what I think about you and your work. You are a highly talented individual. Your main talent is your ability to *direct.*

195

I believe you can contribute business and ideas to a finished script and that you can give much in the way of characterization. I think it is *fatal* for you when you try to do anything in addition.

You have a perfect knack for picking the wrong story, and I think that more than anything else this has contributed to the "bad luck" you have had in the past four or five years. Not one of the pictures you were associated with, with the exception of *Arch of Triumph*, should ever have been attempted, and on *Arch of Triumph*, where you had practically complete authority as both producer and director, you made one of the worst pictures I have ever seen in my life—and there was no need for it, although I would never have picked the story for myself. . . .

You were blessed with the talent of directing and the ability to enthuse a company You know your job in this category and you know it well. You do not have to take a back seat to anyone.

Right now you will need more than the one good credit for *Montezuma* to rehabilitate yourself in the eyes of this suspicious and calloused industry. In all probability you will not listen to me and you will embark on another adventure which will end up unproduced like the last one. . . . If you listen to me you will settle down, at least for the next year or two, to the job of doing what you can do best—directing.

I am saying the above not because I am trying to encourage you on the idea of going on this next expedition but because I admire anybody with real talent and I hate to see it wasted or diffused.

Best always,
Darryl[7]

Zanuck's frank assessment of Milestone's recent career doldrums must have stung, but it contained some hard truths. When Milestone focused on directing—rather than writing or producing—he produced his best results. When he tried to assume other responsibilities on a picture, he became distracted and often made bad choices. And despite his belief in his literary acumen, he had a poor record in choosing subjects for adaptation to the screen. His proudly stated inability to get along with the front office led him to trust too much in his own judgment without listening to well-meaning advice from knowledgeable colleagues.

In this same memo, Zanuck offered Milestone another big project that would start after the filming of *Montezuma* finished in summer. It was a Technicolor adventure film "with four remarkable characters" to be shot during a six-month period in a remote area of Australia—Milestone's first on-location shoot. "It would be a tough location, more or less in the back country," Zanuck warned, "but we are planning to send our own chef and put up good living quarters with a 16mm. movie service. Other than this you will be cut off from civilization."[8] Considering Milestone's own precarious political and financial situation, it was a very attractive proposition from a major studio, and he accepted. By the terms of the contract he signed on July 13, 1950, he was to depart for Australia on August 7, and he would receive a fee of $65,000 for a projected shooting period of twenty-four weeks.[9] The production would keep Milestone in Australia until January 1951. One of the only consolations for the long separation from Kendall (she did come to visit for a while) was being so far away from the Cold War chill. "You are so right about Australia being a long vacation from wars and politics," he wrote to Kendall. "You'd never know there's a Korea or a Russia or any of the bugaboos."[10]

Originally entitled *Sundowner*, the film's title changed several more times during production, to *Australian Story, Bush Ranger*, and finally *Kangaroo*. (Currently it is released on DVD under the title *Australian Story*.) *Kangaroo* was the first American film shot in Australia, and one of the first large Hollywood features to be shot at a distant exotic location, something that would become much more common in following years. One of Fox's motivations for filming in Australia was to use some funds the studio had accumulated there.

Having wrapped production on *Halls of Montezuma*, released in January, Milestone set off on the long and arduous journey from California to Sydney, Australia—via San Francisco, Honolulu, Canton Island, Fiji, and New Caledonia. In a cranky letter to his wife, he joked that Honolulu "now resembles San Pedro, California, more than it ever did before." As for Sydney, it "is the largest and the most cosmopolitan city in Australia—about as cosmopolitan as Pomona, California. Well, maybe during the state fair! . . . It's dull—its people look drab—its restaurants are mostly bad, even places like Romano's—are third-rate Romanoff's. . . . The city goes to sleep early and we go with it. I have never had so much sleep in my life."[11]

Milestone and the crew traveled about a thousand miles across the southern portion of the continent to the shooting location in Port

Augusta, to what he called "the end of the world. . . . Zanuck better come up with a hell of a lot to make up for this Siberia."[12] Some time later, as he struggled with the project, he confided to Kendall, "Well, I suppose I have no one to blame but myself—Since my only reason for making the picture is money."[13]

Zanuck was a strong presence throughout the shooting, if only through correspondence. At one point he criticized Milestone for trying to take too much control, which led the director to respond: "It is true that my last three pictures were flops (I am paying for them). But I have done ten times that many pictures that were successful, both at the box-office and artistically. And I had as much to do with them as the others."[14] Zanuck also complained about the budget, which eventually rose to $1,900,000—$400,000 more than originally anticipated.[15]

Milestone disliked the screenplay he was given to direct, a generic and stereotypical Western written by Harry Kleiner from an original story by Martin Berkeley. The director attempted to persuade Fox to use several novels by a famous Australian journalist, Brian Penton, instead, but the studio insisted that he shoot the script "as written." Zanuck insisted that he wanted an action film, not a character study.

The story revolves around four characters: Michael McGuire, a cattle ranch owner with a bit of a drinking problem; his lovely (and very eligible) daughter, Dell; and two drifters who meet up in a Sydney gambling den—an ex-con named John W. Gamble and the petty swindler Richard Connor. Gamble and Connor meet a very hungover McGuire in Sydney and come up with a scheme to take advantage of his feeble memory and guilty conscience. When they learn McGuire had given up his son for adoption years before, Connor persuades him that he is that son. They travel with him to his ranch, hoping for a windfall. But McGuire's daughter, Dell, charms Connor and he finally goes straight—after murdering the much more sinister and ruthless Gamble. The action at the ranch takes place during a catastrophic drought that is decimating the huge herds of cattle.

To his credit, Milestone inserted as much local color and authenticity as he could, creatively filmed in an almost travelogue style by the cinematographer Charles G. Clarke. Using an Australian crew along with those who had been brought from Los Angeles, he shot in houses, saloons, and natural interiors, "utilizing as many historic locations as possible" both in Sydney and in Port Augusta—including scenes on board a coastal ship.[16]

Since the outback location looked much like the American southwest, Milestone concentrated on historic landmarks in Sydney to maximize the exotic effect of being "down under." He also used a large group of Aborigines in some of the ranch sequences, most effectively in an almost documentary-style filming of a traditional rain dance, something new in Hollywood cinema.

The climactic sequence, one of Milestone's most successfully executed ideas, is a desperate cattle drive, starring hundreds of thirsty animals and ending in an action-packed stampede that can bear comparison with similar scenes in Westerns directed by John Ford or Howard Hawks. The pervasive dust seems to filter off the screen. Initially, Milestone intended to set the cattle drive to the music of Dmitri Shostakovich's dramatic Sixth Symphony, but problems with securing the rights unfortunately made this impossible. Instead, he had to make do with Sol Kaplan's rather pallid score.

Other set pieces feature vivid vignettes of surviving in such a rough natural environment: bullwhip fights, blinding dust storms, a broken windmill water pump spinning wildly out of control, poisonous snake bites. And, of course, kangaroos jumping around with wild abandon.

During the filming, the cast and crew lived in some World War II Quonset huts near Port Augusta. "They called it Zanuckville after Darryl Zanuck," recalled Claire Boone. She was there as a guest of Kendall Milestone, and met her future husband, Richard Boone, cast as the ex-con Gamble, during the shooting. "The whole company was out there. The food was catered; I don't know where in the devil they got the food."[17]

The film comes to its predictable end with a torrential rainstorm that finally brings the drought to an end and Dell into Richard Connor's arms. Milestone anticipated (after enduring weeks of heat that reached 126 degrees during the day) that the downpour would have to be shot on a set back in Hollywood. But amazingly, after the Aborigine rain dance, a storm really did arrive, allowing the scene to be filmed on location after all.

As Milestone had correctly judged, the weak screenplay of *Kangaroo* (it seems highly improbable that McGuire and his daughter and his large entourage would have so easily accepted Connors as his long-lost son) proved an insurmountable problem, despite his heroic efforts to take advantage of the Australian scenery. Nor did the odd casting choices help matters. Zanuck had hoped to get Orson Welles or James Mason for the part of the debauched Michael McGuire, but he had to settle for the rumpled British actor Finlay Currie. For box-office reasons, Maureen O'Hara was eventually chosen to play his daughter, Dell, although at age thirty-one she seemed too old, and certainly rather too elegant and delicate, to be believable as a rough-and-tumble ranch girl. During the cattle drive her absurdly red lipstick never smudges. Her feeble horse-riding skills led Zanuck to warn Milestone to be sure to use a double in those scenes whenever possible. Peter Lawford played very much against type as a wannabe low-class swindler. During the exhausting shooting Lawford lost twelve pounds and started losing his hair. *Kangaroo* wrapped in February 1952 and was released in June.

While Milestone was shooting in Australia, *Halls of Montezuma* opened to some unwelcome political controversy back home. Most reviewers praised the film. In the *New York Times,* Bosley Crowther compared it to *A Walk in the Sun* but noted that "the span is a little broader, the violence is more vivid and intense, and the comprehensions of human tension are somewhat more abstruse and involved."[18] Fox Studio's head, Spyros Skouras, raved, telling Zanuck that "this picture can be the most definitive film produced on World War II."[19]

At the New York premiere at the Roxy on January 4, 1951, in a typical 20th Century Fox spectacular, thousands lined the streets to see marines march down Broadway, joining such celebrities as "Eleanor Roosevelt, the Duke and Duchess of Windsor, Gene Tierney, Basil Rathbone, Gertrude Lawrence, Mr. and Mrs. Vincent Astor, Reginald Gardiner and many others."[20] At both the Roxy and Grauman's Chinese Theater in Los Angeles, the opening box office was very strong, although Zanuck complained that business fell off sharply soon after, mainly because women did not find the film appealing.

Much less welcome news for Milestone was the appearance of a prominent publication accusing him of Communist sympathies, a harbinger of the revival of the HUAC hearings on Communism in the film industry that would resume in Washington, D.C., two months later. At the time, the United States was "in the grip of something like a national panic over what was seen, at all levels of society, as a plausible domestic and international threat of communism."[21]

Numerous factors stoked this paranoia: the recent establishment of a Communist regime in China; the ongoing Korean War and the escalation of Cold War international tensions with the USSR; the conviction of a former State Department official, Alger Hiss, for passing secrets to a

Communist spy ring; and the highly publicized trial of the Rosenbergs, accused of giving the Soviets information on the development of the atom bomb. Senator Joseph McCarthy shrewdly and maliciously capitalized on these fears in a ferocious anti-Communist crusade that began in earnest with a speech in Wheeling, West Virginia, in February 1950, in which he claimed to have a list of several hundred Communists employed by the U.S. State Department. In Hollywood the new president of the Motion Picture Alliance, John Wayne, was calling for a "complete delousing" of the film industry.

As a member of the Hollywood Nineteen, Milestone remained a prime target of the witch hunt. In January 1951 the newsletter *Alert: A Weekly Confidential Report on Communism and How to Combat It* devoted an entire issue to *Halls of Montezuma,* describing Milestone and the screenwriter Michael Blankfort as "two notorious participants in Communist fronts and causes." The article goes on to charge that both "lurked for years in the murky circles of the criminal Communist front, *Arts, Sciences and Professions Council,*" apparently referring to the Hollywood Independent Citizens Committee of the Arts, Sciences and Professions (HICCASP), an innocuous organization that included Ronald Reagan among its members, as noted earlier. A list of the supposedly pro-Communist organizations to which Milestone and Blankfort belonged followed.[22]

Understanding the danger to the reception of *Halls of Montezuma* and other Fox films, Zanuck responded quickly. In a letter sent to Milestone in Port Augusta, in an envelope marked CONFIDENTIAL (underlined in red), Zanuck reported that an "outside influence" had tried to persuade the marines to cancel their participation in the premiere festivities for *Halls of Montezuma* after the article appeared, but that he had successfully intervened. "At one point it looked as if Spyros [Spyros Skouras, head of 20th Century Fox] would have to fly to Washington to appeal directly to General Marshall and President Truman. . . . I did not want to write you sooner because I did not want to alarm you but now that the picture has been launched I think you should know of what occurred. The important thing now is for you to think only of KANGAROO. Nothing is more important than having another good picture under your belt."[23]

A few weeks later, Milestone composed a letter to Zanuck that places the incident in instructive historical perspective and provides an eloquent rebuttal to the charges made against him by HUAC and others.

Soon after we released ALL QUIET, a hue and cry went up in Germany: "We don't need Jews to tell us of how we fought the war." Twenty years later, after HALLS OF MONTEZUMA, another hue and cry, this time from a rag called ALERT but smacks of the "Sturmer."

I have not the time or money to sue over these libelous attacks. . . . I am sure that you know there is a notarized affidavit on file with the Directors Guild prepared by Martin Gang and signed by me: stating that I have never been and am not now a member of any Communist Party. . . .

My indignation at these people, whose very actions are against our American principals [*sic*] of freedom, would never allow me to write a groveling letter in answer to such unfounded charges. Therefore dear Darryl, I think you are more capable with your astuteness and good judgement, of handling this any way you see fit.

I thank you for all you have done in my behalf, and I shall always endeavor to prove worthy of your trust in me.

Gratefully[24]

In winter 1951, after seven months, Milestone departed "this God damned wilderness" of Australia.[25] Although he initially intended to sail directly to Europe, he went to Los Angeles instead, arriving there at the end of March. That same month, another batch of subpoenas was sent out to Hollywood movie people, ordering them to appear before HUAC in a new wave of hearings in Washington. Milestone was again spared, although his former friend and collaborator Robert Rossen, another member of the original Unfriendly Nineteen, was not. But Milestone was not completely ignored: he was ordered to give closed testimony to the FBI in Los Angeles in late March, at which time he was questioned about his entire career and political associations.[26]

On June 25 Rossen testified before the committee in public testimony and admitted that he had once belonged to the Communist Party, although he no longer did. This tactic was different from the refusal to answer any such questions that had earned the members of the Hollywood Ten prison sentences for contempt. Rossen did not name any names of other members, however. Rossen was not indicted, but his career was interrupted for a number of years and his health suffered. Soon after his appearance before Congress, he also left America for Europe, and he never returned to Hollywood. In May 1953 Rossen was again called before HUAC, and on this occasion he did discuss what he knew of other members of the Communist Party—although all had already been named in earlier testimony.

Many in Hollywood regarded Rossen's 1953 "friendly" testimony as cowardly, especially his insistent denunciation of the Communist ideals he had once embraced. He became a pariah among most of his former friends and associates. Rossen told the blacklisted actor Mickey Knox: "I did a terrible thing. I named my friends. But I have to work."[27] Milestone, however, refused to condemn Rossen. "It was part of the climate of those years," he later said. "We don't know why he did it—there must have been all kinds of reasons. . . . Everybody's not a hero; everybody's not made of hero material."[28]

Milestone made this comment before it was widely known that he, too, had provided testimony to HUAC, but in a closed private session in Los Angeles. On the very same day—June 25, 1951—that Rossen was testifying in Washington, Milestone was in the Taft Building in Los Angeles answering questions posed by William Wheeler, an investigator for HUAC. Such closed testimonies became quite common in those years, and they have recently been made available.[29] As transcribed in this seventy-two-page document, Milestone was asked to answer a wide variety of questions about his career, his films, his political associations, and his colleagues and associates. Wheeler showed particular interest in Milestone's membership in and contributions to the Hollywood Democratic Committee, the Hollywood Anti-Nazi League, the Joint Anti-Fascist Refugee Group, the Russian-American Club, HICCASP, and the legal fund for the Unfriendly Nineteen.

When asked if he knew if any of the Hollywood Ten were members of the Communist Party, Milestone replied in the negative. He also denied knowing that Rossen and Dmytryk were Communist Party members. Indeed, the only people he stated that he knew for certain were Communists were the Soviet writers Ilya Ehrenburg and Konstantin Simonov and the Soviet film director Mikhail Kalatozov, whom he met during World War II when Kalatozov was in Hollywood as an official representative of the Soviet film industry. Milestone also stated he had been a guest at a social event on a Soviet ship in Los Angeles in 1943, when the USSR and United States were allies.

In the testimony's last section, Milestone was asked about his role in the 1945 studio strikes and his political convictions, including his vote in the presidential elections of 1940, 1944 ("FDR"), and 1948 ("I started out being for Wallace and voted for Truman"). "I consider myself a Democrat."[30] Milestone also discussed his film *The North Star*, and he blamed the perception that it was excessively pro-Soviet on the production designer, William Cameron Menzies: "We presented Russia in glowing colors because of the sets and the beauty of the sets and the exterior settings. We had no idea for propaganda, or trying to introduce to the American people the idea that this is the most wonderful existence in the world."[31]

Nowhere in his testimony to HUAC did Milestone name any names or incriminate others. But in the conservative anti-Communist atmosphere of the 1950s, his name, reputation and earning power had been badly damaged. As he recalled later, "My own personal condition had changed; I couldn't choose like I used to choose."[32] Even after his official closed testimony in June 1951, HUAC agents continued to question him periodically when he came to Los Angeles. "The direct effect was a grey list, which meant that nobody was hiring you. You couldn't put your finger on it; you couldn't accuse anybody because they were all looking out the window—everybody was innocent. That's when I went to Europe: I left in 1950, and I didn't come back until the middle of 1955."[33]

Throughout it all, however, Darryl Zanuck and 20th Century Fox stood by Milestone—despite the commercial failure of *Kangaroo*. At first, Zanuck declined to show the film to preview audiences and sent it out for distribution. A few months later, after some screenings on the East Coast, he demanded that Milestone film a new ending, but without extra compensation. "I went in and volunteered my services because I wanted to rescue as much of the film's quality as I could. But we had to do whatever Mr. Zanuck wanted. He can be good but, boy oh boy, he can also be very, very bad."[34] *Variety* judged after a preview screening that "Lewis Milestone's direction is particularly good in the out-door action moments provided by a cattle drive, a stampede and a bush fire, but he's not able to endow the script with much dramatic merit."[35] The *Hollywood Reporter* noted the "unhurried" tempo and praised Milestone's ability to keep "the suspense at a high level."[36] But *Kangaroo* failed to appeal even to audiences in Fox's Australian theaters.

By the time these reviews appeared in spring 1952, Milestone had already completed filming his last picture for Zanuck and Fox: *Les*

Misérables. Victor Hugo's popular novel about the Parisian underclass had already inspired dozens of films in many different countries, and Milestone had little enthusiasm for the project: "Twentieth Century-Fox got into the habit of doing *Les Miserables* when they didn't know what else to do."[37] (Zanuck himself had produced Richard Boleslawski's successful 1935 version, starring Fredric March and Charles Laughton.) But Fox was determined to go ahead, believing it to be a guaranteed box-office success, and Milestone was not in a strong bargaining position, so he agreed. "Oh, for Chrissake it's just a job—I'll do it and get it over with."[38] "I didn't have anything better to do, and I didn't feel that I could pass up the money."[39]

Richard Murphy adapted the novel for the screen. Milestone urged Zanuck to include portions of the novel that had not been included in previous film versions, but the producer insisted on covering the same familiar ones. In many ways, *Les Misérables* represented a step backward creatively—a studio production in black-and-white without "marquee names." Michael Rennie, recently seen as the alien who visits Washington in *The Day the Earth Stood Still,* took the leading role of Jean Valjean, sent to prison for stealing a loaf of bread. Robert Newton was cast as his relentless police pursuer, Javert, and Sylvia Sidney as the whore-with-a-heart-of-gold, Fantine. Milestone had seen Newton on Broadway in a production of Noel Coward's *Private Lives,* and he'd been trying to cast Sidney in a film since the early 1930s, when he wanted her for *The Front Page.* When she first walked onto the set, Milestone is reported to have said, "Welcome, Sylvia, it took me 23 years to make a bad girl out of you."[40]

Never less than competent, Milestone's direction feels old-fashioned and academic, with the exception of a few scenes—especially the crashing of the prison ship on the rocks that frees Valjean from his labor as a galley slave. Here models were used to surprisingly dramatic effect, to the accompaniment of Alec North's soaring score. Sidney's pathos-laden deathbed scene elicits tears, and her performance garnered the most attention from critics, who generally damned the film with faint praise. Newton's Javert suffered greatly by comparison with Laughton's earlier, operatically obsessive, and infectiously malicious interpretation. For Milestone, what Laughton did with the role was too "hammy," which perhaps explains why he elicited such a restrained performance from Newton.

As was his usual custom, Milestone had the actors rehearse scenes before they were filmed, a technique that received particular attention in an advance piece on *Les Misérables,* where he was credited with pioneering the practice (which had recently become more common in the industry). "He can also be credited with the first concerted effort to make pre-production design a standard procedure for movie making."[41]

During the shooting, Milestone developed a warm working relationship with the screenwriter Richard Murphy, who expressed his respect for the director in a thank-you letter. "I wanted to say how much fun I'd had working with you. . . . It was fun, Mill—exciting, stimulating and instructive, and I'm happy I had the chance to do it. I think you did a wonderful job, so until we square off again—all my best, thanks again and God Bless. . . . If by some odd chance it does turn out to be a bomb, we can each blame the other and the hell with it.[42]

Les Misérables was not a bomb, but it failed to give Milestone's career the lift he badly needed at that moment. After selling their grand mansion on San Ysidro Drive, the Milestones had purchased a much more modest dwelling on North Doheny Drive just below Sunset Boulevard, where they had been living during the filming of *Les Misérables.* But staying in Hollywood held little appeal for them now, given the uncongenial political environment as the HUAC hearings continued. So they rented out their house and returned to Paris, which would serve as their base for the next few years, as Milestone shifted his creative operations to Europe.

11

Abroad

You can make a good script bad; but you can't ever make a bad script good. Never forget that.

—Lewis Milestone

From 1952 to 1955 Milestone and his wife lived the uncertain life of American expatriates. They used various apartments in Paris as their home base while he traveled around Europe for three different film projects. None ranks with the director's best efforts, but they kept him in the business and generated enough income for a comfortable lifestyle with Kendall—including frequent vacations in glamorous resorts like Biarritz. They also kept him out of the United States and beyond the reach of the HUAC. The three films have little in common. The first, *Melba*, was a biopic about the Australian opera star Dame Nellie Melba. *They Who Dare* brought Milestone back to the subject of World War II. *La Vedova X* (*The Widow*), a joint Italian-British production, treated a tragic romantic triangle.

In later years Milestone dismissed *Melba* as a "pot-boiler." "My 'biopic' of Dame Nellie Melba should have been called *Melba* like I should have been christened Napoleon. It had nothing to do with Melba. The script was worthless."[1] Dame Nellie Melba (1861–1931) was one of the most celebrated operatic sopranos of all times. Born in Australia, she later moved to Europe and sang at all the major opera houses of Europe and America, including the Metropolitan Opera in New York. Although the project didn't particularly interest Milestone, he needed the money, and the producer was his friend Sam Spiegel, working with United Artists. Spiegel was attempting to copy the success of other British biographical musicals, such as *The Story of Gilbert and Sullivan* and *The Great Caruso*.

The rising young American opera star Patrice Munsel (1925–2016) was cast as Melba. Her strong American accent and mannerisms seemed wrong for the part, but Munsel was more than equal to the vocal demands. In fact, the film is little more than an excuse to present long excerpts of Munsel singing some of Melba's signature roles: Cherubino in Mozart's *Marriage of Figaro,* Rosina in *The Barber of Seville,* Mimì in *La Bohème,* and Violetta in *La Traviata,* among others.

Harry Kurnitz's banal screenplay buries the real details of Melba's life under a heap of romantic and show-business clichés. Her Australian husband, Charles Armstrong, in real life an alleged wife beater to whom she was married for a single year, becomes a charming companion, willingly stepping aside to let her pursue her admirable dedication to art. The film's most vigorous and vivid dramatic moments come from Robert Morley as the insistent impresario Oscar Hammerstein and the versatile character actress Martita Hunt as Melba's influential and capricious teacher, Mathilde Marchesi. Another high point: the moment when a kitchen accident produces the singer's famous namesake dessert, Peach Melba. It doesn't help that the story unfolds as a clunky flashback, in which Melba describes to an elderly Queen Victoria (Sybil Thorndike) in an audience at Windsor Castle the saga of her unlikely rise to stardom.

Because it turned out that Munsel was pregnant, the shooting had to be rushed to be completed in just a few weeks. (Many years later, Munsel wrote Milestone a friendly letter remembering "the dreadful traumas I must have given you all those mornings . . . when there was a laundry tub just off the set for me to heave into after my love scenes.")[2] Unable to find suitable studio space, Milestone opted to shoot mostly outdoors in locations around London. Later he bragged about his ability to improvise. "The production looks as if we spent millions on it, but I can point out to you one place in Fire Lane, directly across the way from the Dorchester Hotel, from which we managed to extract five sets: a casino upstairs, a restaurant bar as you walk in, and so on."[3] The Russian art director André Andrejew did a reasonable job with the sets and costumes, considering the limited budget and condensed shooting schedule. But *Melba* lacks the psychological depth and incisive editing of Milestone's best work; it is work for hire, and not from the heart.

Melba did not fare well with critics, either. The *Hollywood Reporter* called Milestone's direction "static and unimaginative. The pacing is slow and the editing somewhat choppy. Film is overlong at 113 minutes."[4] Milestone had signed a contract for an initial $10,000 advance, plus an expense allowance, with a percentage of the profits to come later, but more than a year after its limited release (mostly in art cinemas), he had received nothing.[5]

Milestone returned to more familiar territory for his next effort, *They Who Dare*. Produced by the British company Mayflower Pictures, it was set on the island of Rhodes and based on a true occurrence, as adapted by the writer Robert Westerby. A group of eight British soldiers, members of the Special Boat Service, are assigned to blow up the planes on two airfields used by the Nazi air force to harass Allied forces in the Mediterranean. A young Dirk Bogarde plays the squadron leader, Lieutenant David Graham, coping with his own insecurities, the inhospitable terrain, and the uncertain loyalties of the local Greek population. The film was intended to be part of a two-picture deal with Mayflower Pictures, but the second was never made. Most of the filming took place on location on the island of Cyprus in spring 1953.

By then Bogarde had made fifteen films and had already become one of the most popular British actors on screen. The project's main appeal for Bogarde was working with the legendary Milestone. "He it was who would direct this film, and I was very happy and proud to be asked to participate. The fact that I had not much cared for the script didn't really worry me, for I felt sure that if Mr. Milestone had agreed to direct it then he must also have liked what he read. Another serious miscalculation."[6] Bogarde had flown with the RAF during the war, so he knew something of airplanes and combat. The opportunity to collaborate with Milestone excited Westerby, too, which demonstrates the high regard the director still commanded among movie people worldwide. "If he gives me an ulcer I'll keep it as a pet and keepsake," said Westerby of Milestone.[7]

Bogarde rightly perceived the weakness of the script, still unfinished when filming began. He was wrong, however, in believing that Milestone liked it. On the plane from London to Athens, Milestone read Westerby's latest version. When they arrived, Bogarde and the other members of the cast were "rather disconcerted to see him shredding the new material into confetti and chucking it over his shoulder into the cool Greek air. 'I don't mind,' he said, 'people carrying shit about with them in their pockets. What I do mind is that they don't know it's shit.' Milestone was a man of few words; all of them effective."[8]

In his memoirs, *Snakes and Ladders*, Bogarde (1921–1999) left an amusing and colorful account of his work on *They Who Dare*. On location in Cyprus, Milestone had the eight cast members "practice" by carrying commando packs that weighed ninety pounds each along rocky ravines and cliffs, dodging goats along the way. "The first time we all struggled into them we fell flat on our faces before him; Muslims in Mecca." When they complained, Milestone insisted. Bogarde recalled: "Mr. Milestone (we had by now actually overcome fear of him by fear of our exercises and called him Millie to his face) had a perfectly valid point. You cannot act weight." Eventually the actors got used to the burdens and "managed to give the impression, anyway, of a respectable band of brave desperados, tough, rough and bloodied."[9]

But *They Who Dare* still didn't have a script. The studio sent another writer from London to assist Milestone, who saw him as a spy and went about tormenting him so persistently that the fellow fell from his stool and cracked his skull. The film's cast admired Milestone for constantly challenging the studio executives and insisting on retaining artistic control. Bogarde noted: "We all worshipped him; he was funny, scathing, hated the Front Office, and was splendidly irreverent about everything. Except his work. Even though we had not much to go on as far as a script was concerned, we all worked together with him, as a great adventure, and did the best we could. And if nothing else, and there wasn't much else alas, we all enjoyed ourselves tremendously."[10]

Joining Bogarde was Milestone's old friend Akim Tamiroff, as a local Greek scout. The two hadn't worked together since *The General Died at Dawn*. Here Tamiroff turned his considerable talents to the portrayal of a tough Greek patriot determined to drive the hated Germans from his land: "The war sits heavy on your stomach." The rest of the cast were lesser-known, including the character actor Denholm Elliott as a high-strung and unreliable coward who cannot bear the stress of waiting for a submarine to pick them up after they have successfully executed their mission.

They Who Dare reprises many of the same conventions Milestone employed in his other war movies, especially *A Walk in the Sun* and *Halls of Montezuma*. Like them, it focuses on a small group of soldiers sent to carry out a specific mission. On the way, they develop strong and sometimes antagonistic relationships, and Graham as their lieutenant matures from a callow young officer into a mature, seasoned, and optimistic leader. Shot in Technicolor by Wilkie Cooper, the film takes full advantage of the rugged scenery of Cyprus, making us feel the searing heat and harshness of the rocky, mountainous terrain. Nighttime sequences filmed in a spooky half light intensify the suspense and the environment's rough contours. Dissolves and optical wipes move the action along efficiently. Robert Gill's better-than-average score incorporates the ploy of a shepherd playing on his pipe as an important plot device. Milestone again demonstrated his mastery of sound direction in the film's later scenes, where the rumble of planes and tanks merges with the offscreen orchestra and the shepherd's pipe to create a palpable sense of the soldiers' dread and tension.

Despite Milestone's strenuous efforts—including an impressive montage of planes blown to bits—the film ultimately falters because of the scenario's weaknesses. The opening in a Cairo nightclub nicely captures the exotic flavor of the Middle Eastern setting and the physical appeal of Dirk Bogarde's character. But later, relationships between the characters fail to develop fully. The final moments are nearly incoherent; suddenly we are back on the submarine, only two of the eight having survived. How they got there and what happened to the others remains unclear. Although Milestone assured Bogarde that he would find an ending for the epic, in the same way that he had suddenly found the brilliant last scene of *All Quiet on the Western Front*, Millie could not come up with anything this time around.

During the shooting, Milestone had no trouble keeping up with the actors as they negotiated the rough terrain. Bogarde recalled that although he was "a thick-set, heavy man, . . . he never seemed to sit down." And really, many younger men would have been hard-pressed to keep up with the schedule the director, now approaching his fifty-eighth birthday, was maintaining during the eleven weeks of on-location shooting.

7 a.m.   I'm knocked up with tea.

7:30   Breakfast.

8–8:45   a dull ride in a local taxi to the location

8:45–6   a dull ride back in a local taxi to our dull hotel

6–7   Bath—shave and change clothes—and for what!?

7–8   Bar and a nightly lecture to the local bar-man on how to make a martini.

8–9   Dinner. Tell 21, The Colony, the Pavilion, etc., that they have nothing to fear from Cyprus.

9–1   Work on script with Bob Westerby, and M.C.A. will probably claim commission.[11]

Westerby also marveled at Milestone's apparently inexhaustible energy and stamina:

> He has endless ideas and inventions which he thinks up on every scene—and I have to tag behind, writing dialogue. When we got back from Cyprus after exterior shooting he saw through six solid hours of rushes without a break and then turned to me, fresh as a daisy, and began dictating details and alterations from memory with appalling accuracy. . . . He's got a trick of being so darned right that I get almost suicidal. Whenever he's wrong he makes me glad that he's got the guts to be so confoundedly wrong with such assurance. . . . heh . . . I wouldn't have missed making this film with him for five years of my life. . . . Which it's probably cost me, anyway.[12]

Milestone wrapped up shooting and postproduction on *They Who Dare* by early summer 1953 in London. Because Cyprus had no sound equipment available, the film was post-synched, using notes from dialogue recorded during shooting.[13]

The film played in England but received only limited distribution a few years later in North America, and it was not widely seen or reviewed. In Toronto a critic wrote that "Milestone has worked plenty of action into *They Who Dare,* but aside from that there isn't much about the picture that justifies putting it in the company of the director's other films."[14] Even more disappointing, however, was the news that the second promised feature with Mayflower Pictures had fallen through. For the two pictures he had made in England, Milestone realized only $32,000.[15] Once again, he was on the hunt for a new project.

By summer 1954 he was in Turin, Italy, working on a feature for an Italian-British company, Venturini Express. Entitled *La Vedova X* in Italian and *The Widow* in English, it used Louis Stevens's adaptation of a novel by Susan York. Originally the property had been developed by Paul Kohner, a Hollywood agent, as a vehicle for Bette Davis and the director Max Ophuls, with a very different screenplay by Howard Koch, but that version never progressed past the planning stage. In Milestone's version, the British actress Patricia Roc, the cast's only bona fide star, plays Diana, widow of a European nobleman, now in love with a younger racecar driver (the newcomer Leonardo Botta). Sure of her appeal, she introduces him to a younger woman (Anna Maria Ferrero) to test her power, with predictably tragic consequences. Akim Tamiroff, also living in Europe at the time, appears in a small role as the uncle.

Few people ever saw *La Vedova X,* released in the United States later as a foreign art film. Milestone had spent six months on the project, in Montecatini, Rome, and Turin. But even he thought little of this minor effort. In "Milestones" he calls it a "potboiler. . . . I don't even remember what the film was all about."[16]

Since the blacklist environment still enveloped Hollywood, Milestone had no desire to return to California. He even considered applying for citizenship in a European country. They were living in a Paris apartment, had rented out their Beverly Hills home, and were trying to sell property they owned in Malibu. One of Milestone's closest consultants during this difficult period was his financial adviser, Rex Cole, president of Equitable Investment Corporation in Los Angeles. In a long letter to Milestone in early 1955, Cole advised him to return to Hollywood, where "business is booming," and warned him that he would soon be forgotten there if he remained abroad. "Any longer absence from Hollywood where you and I know they forget quickly is to me the very worst of tactics. That is unless you are going to be perfectly happy in Europe during the remainder of your professional life."[17]

Milestone still had misgivings about returning to the United States. He told Cole that in Europe "We live a little more interestingly than Hollywood would permit an unemployed director."[18] But Cole's advice, and the gradual fading of the HUAC terror, apparently persuaded Milestone to go home. By the end of 1955, they were in New York, and back in Los Angeles shortly afterward. Apparently still uncertain about the future, they kept their apartment in Paris until 1957, however. When they gave it up, a Paris-based society columnist for the *Hollywood Reporter* posted a farewell tribute to their hospitality.

Happy reminder of dining with Kendall Milestone at her beautiful flat, where she and "Millie" have entertained so graciously in the past four years. Now, unhappily, this was a farewell dinner because they are giving up this Paris pied-à-terre. "It devastates me to do it!" sighed Kendall. "It was wonderful when Millie was filming abroad and we spent so much time here, but now that he is working in Hollywood again it is just too impractical to run two establishments." "Are you taking your cook back with you," I asked as I feasted on mushrooms and onions, as only the French can prepare them. "If only I could, but it's too complicated for too many reasons," was Kendall's reply. "However, I've given her to a friend!"[19]

Back in California, Milestone for the first time started working in an industry he had previously avoided: television. Between 1958 and 1964, he did a handful of television jobs. Three were collaborations with Richard Boone, an old friend from *The Halls of Montezuma*. In 1958 Milestone directed two episodes of the long-running series *Have Gun Will Travel*, featuring Boone as the gunslinging fixer Paladin: "The Girl from Piccadilly" and "Hey Boy's Revenge." For his work on "The Girl from Piccadilly" he received the very modest fee of $1,250.[20] In 1963 he directed an episode of *The Richard Boone Show* ("The Hooligan"), a Western adaptation of Anton Chekhov's short story "The Bear." Milestone joked that this was his first real Western.

The Schlitz Playhouse engaged Milestone to direct two episodes that aired in 1958: "Guys Like O'Malley" and "No Boat for Four Months," starring James Mason. The same year, he directed an episode of Alfred Hitchcock's show *Suspicion* called "The Bull Skinner," with Rod Steiger. But Milestone never viewed television with much respect or interest. Used to extensive preparation and rehearsal, he found the small scale and relentless production-line speed of what he called "the box in the corner" depressing and limiting.

Fortunately, another major film project came to the rescue. By early 1958 Milestone was already involved in preparation for *Pork Chop Hill*, his first work in Hollywood since *Les Misérables* six years earlier, and his seventh film about war. "I do not go out of my way seeking war themes. They just somehow seem to find me." Rather disingenuously, he stated, "I never accept an assignment unless I believe in it," a claim that rings hollow considering the many inferior projects he had taken on purely for financial reasons in the preceding years. This film, he said, would be a work of "uncompromising realism at its sternest."[21]

Pork Chop Hill was the first feature produced by Melville Productions, a new outfit created by Gregory Peck and Sy Bartlett. The financing came from United Artists, the film's distributor. By this time Peck had been making movies for fifteen years and was one of the biggest stars in

Hollywood, having worked with such major directors as Hitchcock (*Spellbound*), King Vidor (*Duel in the Sun*), Elia Kazan (*Gentleman's Agreement*), William Wyler (*Roman Holiday*), John Huston (*Moby Dick*), and Vicente Minnelli (*Designing Woman*). Peck exercised considerable control over the screenplay, the casting, and—as it turned out—the editing. James Webb wrote the screenplay, based on the book *Pork Chop Hill: The American Fighting Man in Action, Korea, Spring 1953,* by Brigadier General S. L. A. Marshall. Marshall had interviewed the battle's participants to achieve maximum authenticity.

The script adapted one of the book's chapters, concerning the story of K Company, under the command of Lieutenant Joseph P. Clemons Jr. Their assignment was to take a heavily fortified Pork Chop Hill from the Koreans and Chinese, a bloody and futile exercise since the Korean War was about to end with the conclusion of peace talks between the Chinese and Koreans and the Americans. But the American military brass believed it was important to show continued American commitment to the conflict in order to secure more favorable terms at the negotiating table. In the end, the Americans withdraw from the hill, having sustained horrific casualties, when the treaty is signed.

Peck took the leading role of Lieutenant Clemons, but most of the rest of the actors were relatively unknown. Several would become stars in years to come: George Peppard, Rip Torn, Martin Landau, and Robert Blake. (Once again, the cast did not include a single female.) Casting unknowns—and filming in black-and-white rather than in color—reduced the budget to $1.75 million, a relatively small sum for the time.[22] *Pork Chop Hill* did manage to turn a profit, grossing $1,845,962 in the United States and $1,737,571 abroad.[23]

The shooting took place near Los Angeles, in the Goldwyn Studios and at the Albertson Ranch in Thousand Oaks. There, trenches were dug up a hillside and tracks built alongside to allow the camera to move up and down along with the soldiers—a technique Milestone had used to dramatic effect in *All Quiet on the Western Front* nearly thirty years earlier. To ensure authenticity, Peck enlisted Joseph Clemons Jr. himself as an adviser on the set. Peck noted, "It's quite a thrill to play a part such as this, and at the end of the scene, turn to the man you are portraying, a few feet behind you, and ask how it looked."[24] Peck wanted Milestone to direct because of his long history of making war movies, especially *All Quiet on the Western Front,* where he had shot scenes of trench warfare similar to those needed for *Pork Chop Hill*. For Milestone, this would also complete a trilogy of films dealing with the three major world conflagrations in which the United States participated in the twentieth century.

As shooting progressed, it became clear that Peck and Milestone had very different artistic visions. Milestone wanted to show Clemons the way he was portrayed in Marshall's book, as a young, rather inexperienced officer not entirely sure of himself. But Peck, used to playing strong leading-man roles, insisted that he should be a more confident, even heroic, character. Peck wanted a realistic, but still relatively conventional war movie, whereas Milestone envisioned a more thoughtful reflection on the futility of war in the semidocumentary style of *A Walk in the Sun*.

Even more important, Milestone intended to include more episodes showing the enemy both on the battlefield and at the negotiating table. He believed (in this case, unlike his approach in *A Walk in the Sun*) that it was important to show whom the Americans were fighting. His original conception featured ironic crosscutting between the peace talks and the battlefield, but these scenes were lost in the editing room, primarily at the urging of Peck's interfering wife, Veronique. ("You know, darling," she reportedly said, "nothing happens until you come on the screen, so why don't you just lop it off?")[25] In the end, the enemy is seen (and heard) mainly in the character of the propaganda broadcaster (played with malicious pleasure by Viraj Amonsin) who intermittently taunts the American soldiers in English through a loudspeaker perched at the top of the hill. He also plays recorded screaming and music intended to sap their morale, such as Vernon Duke's nostalgic, jazzy American show tune "Autumn in New York."

When Peck, Bartlett, and Webb saw Milestone's final cut, they found it too slow and "a bit self-conscious and artsy." So they "sharpened it up and speeded it up."[26] Milestone protested, but Peck was calling the shots. The released version of *Pork Chop Hill*, Milestone said later, "became a picture I am not proud of, because it looked as if it were 'cut with a dull axe.' All that remained was Gregory Peck and a gun."[27] That even the actors perceived that Peck was deeply involved in the film's direction is clear from a letter Peck received from Viraj Amonsin. "I especially enjoyed our rehearsals and our discussions as to the character of the broadcaster. Frankly I was overwhelmed by your sensitivity as a director (for all practical purposes where I was concerned, you directed). Before that, I had thought of you as a fine actor! And I look forward in the near future to a work in which you will star as well as direct."[28]

For all that, *Pork Chop Hill* contains many compelling moments. Peck's performance is straightforward and stoic, but without the emotional nuances Richard Widmark brought to a similar character in *Halls of Montezuma*. As the reluctant African American soldier Franklen, Woody Strode makes a deeper impression. On the verge of deserting the hopeless mission of winning back the hill, he projects a seething anger at the impotence and injustice of his situation, calling attention to the racism that awaits him in America. "You should see where I live back home," he says with bitter fury.

We clearly see and feel the emotional trauma endured by the men as they witness their buddies slaughtered next to them, their exhaustion and doubt. But we also sense their deep commitment to their duty as American fighting men, even for a cause they do not entirely understand or embrace: "There's no use trying to figure it out, you just have to keep going." Leonard Rosenman's spare and anxious music, highly reminiscent of Leonard Bernstein's hard-hitting score for *On the Waterfront,* lends the action an appropriately modern edge, devoid of romance and clichés.

If Milestone had been allowed to pursue his more nuanced vision, highlighting the irony and futility of the situation, *Pork Chop Hill* could have been a better film. In light of his recent experiences with HUAC, it could not have been easy for Milestone to hear one of the American negotiators remark simplistically, "These aren't just Orientals—they're Communists." In the final moments, as the camera pulls back to a long shot of the Americans retreating down the hill, Peck's voice-over assumes statesmanlike command as he proclaims with a stilted confidence, "Millions live in freedom today because of what they did." Milestone envisioned a different, more provocative ending: a shot of the newly demilitarized zone where the hill stood, with this voice-over message: "The men who fought here know what they did and the meaning of it." Milestone believed the enlisted men—not the officers or architects of war—deserved the most credit and sympathy.

Pork Chop Hill received for the most part positive notices, but no Academy Award nominations. *Time* magazine named it as one of the five best pictures of 1959. One of the most insightful reviews, in *Variety,* pointed out that Milestone did not bring us as close to the individual characters as he had in his earlier war films. "Some features of 'Pork Chop Hill' recall Lewis Milestone's two great war films, 'All Quiet on the Western Front' and 'A Walk in the Sun.' Like those earlier pictures, this one has the truth of a Matthew Brady photograph. But despite its candor and a steady flow of action, the Sy Bartlett production for United Artists lacks emotional grasp. There are not enough hooks on the audience to pull it into the conflict on the screen. Interest is achieved, but not involvement."[29]

Pork Chop Hill did, however, revive Milestone's flagging career, and it marked his successful return to the Hollywood scene. It proved that he could still make a profitable film and deal with big-name stars. Once again, Milestone was rising like a phoenix from his period of exile. He was back in the game. And gaming would be the subject of his next and most unlikely creation.

12

"Where the Devil Has He Been?"

Plenty of money is a hard habit to kick.
                    —*Peter Lawford as Jimmy Foster in Ocean's 11*

Milestone's next project, *Ocean's 11,* bears only a faint resemblance to his earlier films. But it turned out to be one of the most profitable and strangely enduring. This amoral, light comic caper about the heist of five Las Vegas casinos on New Year's Eve, starring Frank Sinatra and the rest of his notorious "Rat Pack," trades on Hollywood stardom—something Milestone had dismissed as empty and frivolous since his earliest days as a director. Just a few years earlier, Milestone had declared, "I never accept an assignment unless I believe in it."

That this "message director" could have found much to believe in in a vanity glamor project glorifying wealth, materialism, and deceit is hard to swallow. But however unpalatable it may have been, it was a job—a good, well-paying job with a major studio—that also returned him to the Hollywood spotlight after years in the wilderness. In more recent years, *Ocean's 11* has also inspired a franchise of similarly plotted (and titled) films directed by Stephen Soderbergh (*Ocean's Eleven, Ocean's Twelve, Ocean's Thirteen*) and Gary Ross (*Ocean's 8*).

The idea that eventually became *Ocean's 11* originated in a story told by a gas station attendant to a Hollywood assistant director, who told it to Peter Lawford, one of Sinatra's closest buddies. The attendant had served in the U.S. Army in Germany during World War II. His outfit managed to dismantle some valuable radio equipment and smuggle it piece by piece out of the country. Said Lawford: "We thought the idea could be applied to a fictional story for a movie [about a group of war veterans who] rob six gambling casinos simultaneously in Las Vegas on New Year's Eve when the lights go out."[1] Eventually, Lawford and his wife, Patricia

Kennedy, bought the story from the assistant director (Gilbert Kay) for $10,000.

When Lawford shared the story idea with Sinatra, Frank "flipped." Immediately, Sinatra saw the project as a golden opportunity to showcase, carouse, and make money with the rest of the Rat Pack: Lawford, his fellow crooner Dean Martin, Sammy Davis Jr., and Joey Bishop. Sinatra's company, Dorchester Productions, still owed a film to Warner Bros., so he and Lawford went to Jack Warner and described the project. Warner's alleged reaction was to joke: "Let's not make the movie—let's pull the job."[2] Warner gave the go-ahead, paid the Lawfords $50,000 for Kay's script, and hired a succession of writers to rework it. Sinatra took over artistic control, including script approval, casting, and the division of profits. But he still listened closely to Lawford, who suggested that Milestone, with whom Lawford had worked on *Kangaroo,* be hired as director. According to Milestone, Warner at first resisted, apparently because of Milestone's reputation for independence and temperamental behavior, but Sinatra insisted. Warner summoned Milestone and warned him he had to "look out for our interests."[3] Milestone had not worked for Warner Bros. since *Edge of Darkness,* in 1943.

Under the terms of the contract Milestone signed with Dorchester Productions and Warner Bros. in November 1958, he was to receive $37,500 upon signing and $6,250 per week for each of twelve weeks of shooting, for a handsome and very welcome total compensation of $112,500.[4] This amount paled, however, in comparison to the $230,000 Sinatra eventually received ($30,000 for the story and $200,000 to act). Dean Martin got $150,000 and Sammy Davis $125,000. Milestone was also named as the film's producer, and he was promised 2.5 percent of any future profits, which proved to be a nice, steady windfall. Lawford took one-sixth of the gross—almost $500,000 in total.[5]

Milestone worked with the crime screenwriter Richard Breen to improve the script. They viewed other caper films for inspiration and even asked Billy Wilder for advice, but the result still failed to please Sinatra. Harry Brown and Charles Lederer then replaced Breen, adapting a story supposedly created by Jack Golden Russell and George C. Johnson. In the end, as Milestone told the *Los Angeles Examiner,* "the only thing left of the original story when we started was the basic idea that 12 ex-paratroopers robbed five Las Vegas casinos."[6] There was so much confusion that Sinatra's costar Dean Martin allegedly asked him "You will give me a chance to read the script before we're through shooting it, won't you?"[7]

One constant in all the rewrites was that the men assembled to carry out the heist are army buddies from the 82nd Airborne Division, daring parachutists who had fought side by side in World War II. This explains their deep sense of camaraderie and shared history. They approached the complex heist "like a commando raid" and a "military operation." "Why waste all those tricks that the military taught us because it's a little peaceful now?" "Think of how proud all the brass in the Pentagon would be." "Think of this as a full-fledged battle."

One of the script's early versions had a tragic ending. After a police pursuit, some of the team's members died in an airplane crash. In the final version, however, the heist is successfully executed, but with an ironic twist. One of the coconspirators dies of a heart attack just after completing the theft. The gang's remaining members decide to stash the stolen cash in his casket, thinking it a perfectly safe hiding place. What they do not know is that his widow has decided on cremation. So the money goes up in smoke as they sit helplessly at his funeral listening to the flames consume their prize. Dazed, they file out into the harsh daylight, all their clever planning for naught. The End.

Sinatra enjoyed putting his closest buddies in the leading roles. Peter Lawford is typecast as Ocean's sidekick and confidant Jimmy Foster, a rich boy raised in privilege trying to escape the suffocating control of his patrician mother. Dean Martin is Sam Harmon, a suave Las Vegas nightclub singer and lady-killer. Sammy Davis Jr. is Josh Howard, the cast's sole African American, a former baseball player now working as a (singing and occasionally dancing) garbageman. Joey Bishop is the always accommodating Mushy O'Connors. Tough guy Richard Conte (from *Walk in the Sun* and *The Purple Heart*) plays Anthony Bergdorf, an ex-con with bad luck and failing health. Henry Silva, Buddy Lester, Richard Benedict, Norman Fell, and Clem Harvey round out the eleven. Cesar Romero, as a mobster trying unconvincingly to go straight, plays the I've-seen-it-all fiancé of Jimmy Foster's impeccably stylish mother (Ilka Chase). Milestone's old friend Akim Tamiroff bear-hugs the ancillary role of the always exasperated fixer (and ex-con mafioso) Spyros Acebos, who assembles and tries unsuccessfully to control the unruly team from his Beverly Hills mansion.

Women assume a backseat (or maybe even the trunk) in the male-dominated proceedings. The angelic Angie Dickinson stands by her cheating man as Ocean's former wife. Sinatra's pal Shirley MacLaine shows up in a funny cameo as a pretty drunk ("I'm so drunk I couldn't lie down without holding on.") Other females appear to massage and serve the men, who ogle them as sexual objects, or as jealous shrews, like Ocean's girlfriend, Adele (Patrice Wymore). Sam Harmon proclaims that he wants to use the money he will get from the heist so he can "take the vote away from women and turn them into slaves." The film's unabashed sexism startles us today. So does its racism. When the gang decides to hide the bags of money in the coffin, some of them don blackface to accompany Josh to transport it in his garbage truck—as though only African Americans could make credible garbagemen.

In her review of the 2018 all-female spin-off, *Ocean's 8* (directed by Gary Ross), the *New York Times* film critic Manohla Dargis described Milestone's original not incorrectly as "a lead soap bubble of a movie, a nostalgia item that's memorable only for its Rat Pack stars, who seemed to have made it between martinis and rounds of golf. It's best enjoyed as a relic of Playboy-era masculinity, with Angie Dickinson and assorted disposable women floating in and out like moths."[8]

Sinatra arranged for most of the shooting to take place at his Las Vegas hangout, the Sands Hotel, of which he was a 9 percent owner. They deliberately chose to shoot in February, when business slowed, and the town rolled out the welcome mat. The five hotel casinos featured (and robbed) in the film—the Sands, the Riviera, the Sahara, the Flamingo, and the Desert Inn—provided free rooms for the 225 actors, extras, and crew members. The publicity proved to be a godsend for Las Vegas, at the time on shaky financial ground.

Sinatra had carefully planned the shooting schedule to coincide with the Rat Pack's appearances together at the Sands as "The Summit," a mostly improvised nightclub act featuring Sinatra, Martin, and Davis singing, as well as Bishop and Lawford joking, jiving, smoking, and drinking around the edges. The act had the atmosphere of a college fraternity roast—and audiences loved it. For Sinatra and his show-biz brothers, this was the real show, and the movie that Milestone was directing was not much more than an afterthought. The men partied most nights until dawn. During the twenty-four days of shooting in Las Vegas, Sinatra showed up for only nine. The other "actors" were not much more punctual. Sammy Davis would show up after a few cocktails "at 9:00 or 10:00 in the morning, and Dean and Peter would show up at 9:00 or 10:00 in the morning, and Joey—who was lucky to be here at all, let's face it—would be there at 7:00 or whenever they said so, showered and alert. But Frank: 4:30 in the afternoon, maybe 5:00, and twice, *twice,* before lunch; and most days not at all."[9]

Milestone, a veteran gambler, drinker, and "man's man" used to dealing with macho egos, somehow brought order to the chaos. Amazingly, he even managed to bring the film in under budget, at around $2,000,000. His long experience of making movies about groups of men under deadline pressure to complete a tricky mission came in very handy. Joey Bishop paid tribute to Milestone's tact: "It would have taken a great director to have been able to take this gang of people and get a good picture out of them. He had to be as *little* a director as possible and still get his points across when the time came."[10]

Angie Dickinson agreed: "The director was very easy. He knew exactly who was signing his check."[11] Milestone claimed (or, perhaps, wanted to believe) that he and the Rat Pack had "a pact" that "the film came first, the show second," as he said in an extensive interview published in the *Los Angeles Examiner* just before the film's premiere in August 1960.

> Discipline was probably the answer. Although they made light of their chores, this talented group was always in the right place at the right time. We never could have worked this picture at the usual nine-to-five hours. The casinos are always too crowded. So we worked early—from 1 to 5 a.m. And also around dusk. We had only one major problem and that was how to set the lights in the casinos so they wouldn't reflect or be seen. Bill Daniels, our cameraman, mastered it. Another factor in our favor was that the production assistants were all great. We never had a delay. Plus Frankie and his clan. Wait until you see the performance Cesar Romero turns in. Richard Conte has the fulcrum role. We worked together in A WALK IN THE SUN and I found out you can always be certain Conte will turn in a good performance. . . . This picture was really a ball.[12]

Perhaps because of Jack Warner's warning that he should "look out for our interests," Milestone was careful to remain upbeat in talking publicly about *Ocean's 11.* Although he boasted about the "discipline" of his boy actors, in fact he had to put up with many indignities that must have felt demeaning to a director of his stature. He had to defer to Sinatra on matters of content and acting that he had always decided himself. Most of the cast didn't bother to learn their lines and relied on cue cards. Sinatra became known as "One-Take Charley" because he demanded that most sequences involving him be done in a single take, no matter the result. In later years, when he could afford to be more honest, Milestone told Sinatra's biographer Michael Freedland: "Ask me which was my least favourite film that I ever made and it has to be *Ocean's 11*."[13]

Sinatra, on the other hand, thoroughly enjoyed the project. Besides the control he exercised over the script, casting, and shooting schedule, he hired the composer (Nelson Riddle) and the designer of the opening and closing credits (Saul Bass). Both were accomplished craftsmen at the top of their game and made original and memorable contributions to *Ocean's 11*. Riddle and Sinatra were old friends who had been working together for years. For his jazzy opening music, Nelson used a variety of percussion instruments, including xylophone. Elsewhere he provided a "bluesy harmonica-and-strings accompaniment" for Sammy Davis Jr.'s opening song, "EO 11," sung while he is driving a gleaming garbage truck through the Nevada desert. Riddle's cocktail lounge–style music departs radically from the more traditional symphonic scores Milestone had used in his previous films.[14] Sammy Cahn and James Van Heusen wrote the forgettable songs performed by Martin, Sinatra, and Sammy Davis Jr.

Saul Bass created innovative and trendy designs. Bass had provided titles for *The Frank Sinatra Show* in 1957. For *Ocean's 11*, he devised a complex opening animation sequence combining moving multicolored dots in vertical and horizontal rows, circles and columns that spell out the actors' names, in rapid sync with musical leitmotifs. His design also plays with the gambling theme, showing dot-matrix images of rotating slot machines, roulette tables, and rolling dice. As Jan-Christopher Horak has written in his study of Bass's work, "The opening titles for *Ocean's 11* are jokey, fun, and not very deep."[15] In his production design, Milestone's longtime collaborator Nicolai Remisoff expertly maintained Bass's contemporary, abstract style—including the Picasso-esque paintings on the walls of Spyros Acebos's home. Shot in Panavision with new high-speed Eastman color film, *Ocean's 11* is a visual feast, saturated with color and detail that emphasize the bright palate of the desert environment.

Because of all the publicity generated by the antics of Sinatra and the Rat Pack, *Ocean's 11* opened with a splash. Sinatra and his cronies staged a gigantic party for the Las Vegas preview on August 3. All the cast members flew in, along with assorted bit players and "hangers-on and glad handers," including Danny Kaye, Sophie Tucker, Tony Curtis, Janet Leigh, and Nick the Greek—"a perfectly representative snapshot of the cream of Vegas royalty circa 1960." The film was screened at midnight after a cocktail party for the dozens of journalists, a dinner party, and a show. Thousands turned out on the street for a glimpse of the celebrities. Warner Bros. shrewdly decided to publicize the film more as a happening than a serious work of art.[16] Even before it opened, *Ocean's 11* had been sold "into more than 200 theaters, sight unseen."[17]

By association with the hoopla, Milestone found his own reputation resurrected. In a letter, one of the publicity agents working on the film informed him, "In the eyes of the industry, Millie, you are 'on fire,' and we intend to keep it that way. Just the other night I overheard a conversation in the next booth at Romanoff's, and one sentence was music to my ears: 'I read that Milestone has really got a big one in this Sinatra picture—I read that he's got some big things coming up—where the devil has he been all this time?'"[18]

When the film opened in New York and Los Angeles later in August, it received mixed reviews. *Variety* judged that "Milestone has failed to curb a tendency toward flamboyant but basically unrealistic behavior, as if unable to decide whether to approach the yarn straight or with tongue-in-cheek. In trying to blend both approaches, he has succeeded in contradicting one with the other."[19] The *Hollywood Reporter* wondered about the film's amoral message. "No one ever mentions that fact that stealing money is wrong; just that it's hazardous. The film itself, in fact, is a good-humored lark, in which most of the stars play their own public characters rather than anything created by Brown and Lederer. But the very humor with which they most often speak fits the man, and this is one of the reasons for the overall success of the film. But the film is intended really only to be an elaborate and brightly painted joke, an up-to-date O. Henry twisteroo."[20]

Audiences didn't seem to care about the message. They enjoyed the entertainment. *Ocean's 11* turned out to be the highest-grossing film of Sinatra's career, at $5.5 million. Just two years later, Sinatra's much more important and serious performance in John Frankenheimer's chilling *The Manchurian Candidate* could not match its box-office success.

"On fire." It didn't take long to see just how "hot" Milestone had become with the solid financial success of *Ocean's 11*. In Hollywood, as the saying goes, "You are only as good as your last picture." Milestone was back.

Working with Frank Sinatra prepared Milestone well for his next project. *Mutiny on the Bounty* revolved around an even bigger star— Marlon Brando. Like Sinatra, the temperamental Brando was used to calling the shots on the set, rewriting the script and overruling directors. In fact, Milestone was the second director to work on *Mutiny*. The original director, Carol Reed, handed in his resignation to MGM's studio head, Sol C. Siegel, in late February 1961, primarily because he found it impossible to work with Brando. By the time Milestone took over, *Mutiny* had been in production for a year and was incurring mounting costs that would eventually rise to the colossal sum of $27 million. (Film historians disagree over the exact cost; Brando's biographer Peter Manso puts it at "more than $25 million.")[21] For the tidy sum of $750,000, and after multiple delays that held up the start of shooting, MGM had even built a replica of the late eighteenth-century British vessel *Bounty*, on which the action takes place. Sailed with great fanfare and publicity from Nova Scotia down the Atlantic coast, it reached the Pacific and Tahiti via the Panama Canal.

Siegel chose Reed, a soft-spoken British director known best for the classic film noir *The Third Man* because he seemed "safe . . . and unlikely to take any financial risks."[22] But Reed was inexperienced in the ways of Hollywood—and especially the extent to which studios, including MGM, had become willing to cater to the whims of their biggest stars. With box office declining in the face of competition from television, studios believed they had to produce epics like *Cleopatra* and *Mutiny on the Bounty* featuring big names (Elizabeth Taylor, Brando). It proved a risky and ultimately ruinous strategy. The extravagant whims and financial demands of Brando at MGM and Taylor at 20th Century Fox ultimately severely damaged those studios, and they have received part of the blame for bringing the great studio era to an end.

The late arrival of the newly constructed *Bounty* meant that production in Tahiti started when the rainy season had already begun, which made shooting slow and tedious. Even worse was the absence of a working script. Brando kept changing his mind about his character, Fletcher Christian, the first officer who leads the mutiny against the ship's sadistic Captain Bligh (Trevor Howard). The screenwriter Eric Ambler had conducted extensive research in the Royal Navy archives to uncover new details about Bligh not included in the popular novel about the mutiny by Charles Nordhoff and James Norman Hall. Their novel was the source for the screenplay used in MGM's own 1935 Oscar-winning version, starring Clark Gable as Christian and Charles Laughton as Bligh. But Brando had ideas of his own that he insisted be included in Ambler's work. What most interested the star was the fate of the mutineers after they took over the *Bounty* from Bligh and sailed to Pitcairn Island, where they settled permanently. But Ambler refused to continue in this uncomfortable subordinate position and returned to Los Angeles.

Without a screenplay, production slowed almost to a halt. Meanwhile, Brando engaged in liaisons with the very available local women, particularly the nineteen-year-old Polynesian Tarita Terriipai, who played Brando's love interest (Maimiti) in the film. (In doing so he also risked contracting the venereal disease rampant in Tahiti.) When Brando refused to follow his directing instructions, Reed took the company back to Hollywood. To save the film, he suggested to Siegel that Trevor Howard should replace Brando as Christian, and that the role of Bligh be recast. But Siegel disagreed, believing that the film's financial success depended upon Brando's box-office draw. So Reed quit (or was fired, in any case receiving full pay), inciting a real mutiny among the members of the mostly British cast loyal to Reed.

This was the snake pit into which Milestone descended when he took over direction of *Mutiny on the Bounty*. How much he knew about what had already transpired on the set is unclear. But the money MGM offered him surely played a role in his decision to accept the job. Under the terms of his contract, he was to receive $50,000 in 1961, $50,000 in 1962, and $50,000 in 1963. If necessary, he would also get $2,000 per week in 1964, and $5,769.23 per week for possible retakes.[23] But this hefty sum was a mere fraction of Brando's total compensation for the film: $1.25 million, one of the largest salaries ever paid to an actor in Hollywood at that time.[24]

Milestone apparently assumed that Reed had shot a substantial amount of usable material, and that his services would be required for only two or three months. But he discovered that only a few minutes could be salvaged. (Brando's biographer disputes this version, however: "Reed had in fact shot most of the spectacular, epic sequences that would eventually garner most of the film's meager praise.")[25] In the end, Milestone spent four months in Tahiti, and an entire year on *Mutiny on the Bounty*.

It became Milestone's film; Carol Reed's name does not appear anywhere on the final credits. Charles Lederer, who had also worked on *Ocean's 11,* came on board as the screenwriter.

Milestone started working with the production in February in the MGM studios in Los Angeles. For the first few weeks after Milestone took over, Brando behaved himself. But soon he was disregarding Milestone's instructions and talking privately to the cameraman. As Bill Davidson described in an unusual tell-all exposé in the *Saturday Evening Post,* published with Milestone's participation a few months before the film's release, the actor and director came into conflict when Brando began to take control of the scenes in which he appeared.

> Milestone's idea of moviemaking is to set up the camera, tell the actors what to do and get on with the job. Brando's idea of moviemaking is for the actor to have endless discussions with the writer, director and producer to attain the proper mood, and then when said mood has descended on the actor, to set up the camera to catch the actor's genius in flight. Milestone would tell Brando, "Do so-and-so," Brando would say, "Why?" Milestone would not answer. And the tug-of-war would be on.
>
> Brando quickly indicated to associates his dissatisfaction with Milestone. Milestone was not aware of this criticism for about three weeks. "Then," he told me, "Charlie Lederer, the writer on the picture who had recommended me to be the director, came to me and said, 'You're working too fast. You better slow down a little.' I said to Charlie, 'Of course I'm working fast. Don't you think enough time has been wasted on this picture already?' Charlie said, 'Yes, but Brando says you're not really interested in the picture and you're speeding things up because you're just trying to get it over with as soon as possible.' I said to myself, 'Aha, it looks as if we're in for a rocky voyage.'"[26]

And a rocky voyage it was. On March 1 the production moved to Tahiti. Production costs reached a staggering $50,000 per day. Brando's insistence on discussing every change in the script that affected his character slowed shooting to a crawl. "It wasn't a movie production; it was a debating society," said Milestone.

Brando would discuss for four hours, then we'd shoot for an hour to get in a two-minute scene because he'd be mumbling or blowing his lines. By now I wasn't even directing Brando—just the other members of the cast. He was directing himself and ignoring everyone else. It was as if we were making two different pictures. But I was having trouble not only with his private mutiny; he had rallied to his side every punk extra who claimed he was a Method actor. . . . It got so bad that one eighteen-year-old punk walked off the set when I refused to reshoot an entire scene in which he "emotionally felt" his performance was not quite right. I said, "OK, walk. But don't come back." Like his master, he sulked for a while—but he came back.[27]

Besides Brando, there were other obstacles. During the shooting of the canoe race at the end of the first part, one canoe hit a reef, killing a Tahitian extra and seriously injuring others. Production halted for two weeks around Bastille Day (July 14), the French national holiday, which was celebrated on Tahiti. The incessant heat and bugs were a constant nuisance. When word leaked out that only one-third of the film had been completed by spring, MGM's stock began to fall.[28]

Concerns were also raised about the screenplay's alleged portrayal of Captain Bligh as a deeply closeted homosexual. In his review of the original script, Geoffrey Shurlock of the Production Code Administration warned MGM that he had received the "distinct impression" that "Captain Bligh is a homosexual." He reached this conclusion, he continued, because of Bligh's "sadistic enjoyment in having men flogged"; his "unnatural reaction to the men making love to the women"; and his reaction to a tattoo on the arms of one of the sailors—"Those are the arms that held the woman who smiled." Shurlock went on to admonish that the Production Code "specifically prohibits sex perversion or any inference of it."[29]

But other critics have pointed out that it is Brando's portrayal of Fletcher Christian that seems "gay." Although he enjoys sexual relations with the local women who throw themselves at him, Christian is a fop who fusses about his clothes, speaks in a prissy fashion that irritates Captain Bligh, and minces as he walks the deck.

When he agreed to take the role of Fletcher Christian, Brando had been promised by MGM that he would have considerable control over the film's concept and screenplay. The conflicts that constantly erupted between Brando and Reed, and then between Brando and Milestone, focused primarily on the star's insistence on altering the script as the shooting progressed. The uncertainty over the direction of the story line undermined the efficiency of the production, led to lengthy delays, and weakened the narrative continuity of the finished film. The gap between Bligh's departure from the *Bounty* after the mutiny in a small boat with his band of supporters and his appearance before a naval court-martial in England months later seems especially abrupt.

Changes to the screenplay continued to be made until the very end of the shooting period, through the summer of 1962. Brando insisted on reshooting the ending several times. The first version showed Christian sitting in a cave on Pitcairn Island, contemplating the debauched behavior of his fellow mutineers on Pitcairn Island and "man's inhumanity to man." But after seeing the rough cut, Brando demanded that another ending be shot—although he did not have one.

In desperation, the production team even considered—and accepted—a suggestion from an outsider, the director Billy Wilder, who provided what became the final version. Christian proposes to the men that they return to England to face justice. Some violently disagree and decide to burn the *Bounty* to make a return impossible. Desperate, Christian rushes to the ship, where he is horribly burned. He dies an agonizing death, as a heartbroken Maimiti looks on.[30] This scene was shot in Culver City in August 1962, and Brando agreed to work for free. By this time relations between Brando and Milestone had broken down completely. Milestone came to the set but refused to direct, ceding control to Brando.

Mutiny on the Bounty was perhaps the most complicated and physically demanding shoot of Milestone's career. Now sixty-six, he was required to stand for hours in blazing heat on board the ship, where many of the scenes were filmed. He was in command of a cast and crew of hundreds of people, some of whom did not speak English. The logistical challenges were daunting. It helped, certainly, that Milestone was an "old salt" who loved boats and sailing and frequently spent his leisure time in Los Angeles yachting with friends.

That it was exhausting for him is clear from a letter that Kendall (who accompanied him in Tahiti) wrote home to Los Angeles:

He is so exhausted at night he can hardly keep his eyes open. They are out on the boat from seven in the morning until sundown, it's terribly hot and the work is discouragingly slow. With Brando you are lucky to get two scenes a day, it's demoralizing to the whole troupe, when he finishes this one I guess he can cope with anything!

It's very hot and full of bugs here. There is nothing to do but bathe in the sea which is beautiful. Milly said he preferred the Australian location, that will give you a rough idea how he feels about it here. With the new jets, at least it's a fast trip both ways.[31]

MGM shot *Mutiny on the Bounty* in expensive widescreen Technicolor and Ultra Panavision 70. The cameras weighed five hundred pounds each, installed on the sides of the deck on tracks to provide panning and overhead shots. Robert Surtees's cinematography created a dynamic visual feast that captured the movement of the ship and the dramatic scale of the gorgeous South Pacific scenery. John McSweeney Jr. did a masterful editing job (surely with Milestone's guidance) on the sequence of the *Bounty*'s harrowing and unsuccessful passage around Cape Horn, combining shots done with a model with shots on board and below the freezing and flooding decks of the *Bounty* replica. Bronislau Kaper's score effectively heightens the tension of this sequence and makes ingenious use of Tahitian traditional music (drumming and singing) in later scenes. The exotic love theme for Christian and Maimiti becomes a leitmotif not only for their romance, but for Tahiti's exotic lure.

Given the nearly impossible conditions under which he had to work, Milestone's achievement impresses all the more. The scenes at sea are fresh and powerful. The epic scope, suspense, and energy of the royal reception of the *Bounty*'s crew at Tahiti by hundreds of native people and the exquisitely adorned Chief Hitihiti (Matahiarii Tama) take full advantage of the wide-screen format. Trevor Howard delivers one of the great performances of his career as Bligh—an inflexible, lonely man motivated by class resentment, sadism, and a perverted sense of duty, without the operatic excesses of Charles Laughton's 1935 interpretation. As the questioning sailor John Mills, a young Richard Harris brings pathos to a character searching for justice in a deeply unfair world. Numerous scenes of flogging and physical torture on board ship seethe with Milestone's deep understanding of the harsh realities of the lives of ordinary seaman, at the mercy of their superiors. They are cousins to the ordinary German soldiers fed to the guns in *All Quiet on the Western Front,* released thirty years earlier. By the time it happens, we understand well why Christian and most of the sailors take the grave risk of mutiny.

Sadly, the off-camera saga of Marlon Brando's sex life and woeful tales of production fiascos rather obscured *Mutiny on the Bounty's* considerable virtues. What turned out to be Milestone's last completed film brought the director little pleasure. It only served to prove what he had believed for his entire career, that causing the filmmaking enterprise to be dependent on stars debased the medium he loved so much. "I can only say that the movie industry has come to a sorry state when a thing like this can happen, but maybe this experience will bring our executives to their sense," he told the *Saturday Evening Post.* "They deserve what they get when they give a ham actor, a petulant child, complete control of an expensive picture."[32]

Brando returned the bad feelings. At the film's premiere at the Egyptian Theatre in Hollywood in November 1962, he refused to be photographed with Milestone. At the New York premiere, Brando's performance received boos. Critics were divided. Hollywood-insider critics praised Milestone's work. "Milestone's direction is magnificent, balancing the spectacle with the intimate," wrote the reviewer for the *Hollywood Reporter.* "There is a memorable and electric meeting between Brando and Tarita, the native girl, a superb example of cross-cutting by editor John McSweeney Jr., that grows and grows in power and implication. There is at all times an evidence of control on Milestone's part of the gigantic elements of this film, except perhaps in the noted inconsistencies of Brando's playing."[33] *Variety* agreed that "Milestone . . . can take pride in a job well done."[34]

Others were less charitable. Pauline Kael, usually one of Brando's defenders, denounced his performance as "more eccentric than heroic . . . like a short, flabby tenor wandering around the stage and not singing."[35]

Ironically, *Mutiny on the Bounty* received more Academy Award nominations—a total of seven—than any other film Milestone made. It lost in the Best Picture category, and in several other technical and musical categories, to another expensive historical epic, *Lawrence of Arabia,* and it failed to receive a single Oscar. Despite the recognition it received from the AMPAS, *Mutiny on the Bounty* shipwrecked MGM. It returned less than half of its colossal investment and seriously weakened the studio. Seven years later, in 1969, MGM was bought out by Kirk Kerkorian, who redirected the company away from films to other "leisure-based investments."

By the time *Mutiny on the Bounty* finally hit the screen, Milestone had already been hired and fired from another project. On this one, *PT 109,* he ironically suffered the same fate as the director he had replaced on *Mutiny,* Carol Reed. It was the first and only time in his long career that Milestone was replaced during production.

Jack Warner, the volatile head of Warner Bros. Studio, originally chose Raoul Walsh to direct *PT 109,* but he removed him in favor of Milestone during preproduction in March 1962. Warner had known Milestone for decades, and he probably selected him because of his just-completed work on a big feature set on a navy vessel. He also knew, of course, of Milestone's long history of making movies about a small group of soldiers (or sailors) carrying out a dangerous mission in wartime. Based on Robert Donovan's book about John F. Kennedy's experiences during World War II as commander of a patrol-torpedo boat in the Pacific, it was a delicate project because JFK was at the time serving as the U.S. president. The screenplay by Robert Breen focused on the story of how Kennedy led his crew of ten men to safety on an island after their boat was sunk in the Solomon Islands in 1943. In the process, Kennedy sustained serious injuries that plagued him the rest of his life. Cliff Robertson got the leading role.

Because of the film's political sensitivity, and because of his friendship with JFK and his father, Joseph, Jack Warner involved himself in all aspects of production. (It was the first commercial theatrical film ever made about a sitting U.S. president.) He and Milestone exchanged numerous detailed letters about the screenplay. Milestone found what Richard Breen had prepared lacking in many respects, as he explained in a memo to the Warner Bros. production staff.

I have thoroughly examined it and found it extremely inadequate:

1) Character development: Still non-existent
2) Inter-relationships: Still non-existent
3) Historically correct dramatic facts have been substituted by mediocre fiction.

4) In the entire time that the eleven men are shipwrecked we do not have a single sustained dramatic scene.

5) The drama of war, the fear of the enemy and general suspense are constantly destroyed by weak attempts at humor.[36]

Milestone concluded with the warning that "if this is to be a successful motion picture, both artistically and commercially, it must be a universal story of combat and the meaning of combat in terms of human experience. A story of the way men grow larger and stronger inside when caught up in the awesome, impersonal machinery of war."[37]

By late June, Milestone was shooting near Key West, Florida. Warner continued to hover over the production, anxious about negative publicity for a film involving the president. He cautioned Milestone in a long letter that "every action of the cast and crew during the making of PT 109 will be constantly scrutinized. . . . We cannot permit the actions of the usual Hollywood company good or bad as they may be on location. . . . Avoid liquor and unnecessary visitors. Above all, I do not want any stories given to reporters that can or will reflect upon the people playing in the picture, the director or anyone else."[38]

In the following weeks, Milestone and Warner continued to spar over the screenplay and what Warner regarded as the slow pace of production. It especially irritated Warner that Milestone insisted on changing the script during shooting. "Inasmuch as we are willing to put up the money, please shoot it and if it does not work after we put the picture together we can correct it with a thing known as the scissors! In fact, you can go back to your old job as a cutter on Main Street and cut it out!"[39] Warner also questioned the way Milestone was executing particular shots, demanding that he provide enough close-ups—although Milestone argued that close-ups did not work well with Panavision. By mid-July the relationship between producer and director had become so contentious that Milestone fired off a letter to Warner that concluded: "I would like to add that never before have I worked under conditions where the company shows so little trust in what I am doing."[40]

Just a few days later, on July 21, Warner fired Milestone and replaced him with Leslie Martinson. In a note to a friend on July 22, Milestone lamented, "I've been directing since 1925 and P.T. 109 is the first picture I've been fired from."[41] As justification for the abrupt action, Warner claimed "satisfactory progress was not being made." At a news conference, Milestone blamed the poor script.[42]

The cast and crew took the news of Milestone's firing hard. They had come to like and respect him, judging by a note sent to him and Kendall by one of the cast members a few weeks later. "I personally feel that, with you here, there was and would continue to be a spirit among the guys that led not just to top effort, but to top effort 'with love to Milly,' which could have helped raise the whole thing above mediocrity. That extra something is gone now, so we've lost more than just your creative, painstaking direction—we've lost a spirit that was present when you were here. It's tragic."[43]

A few months later, Milestone had to go to court to demand payment for his services from Warner. The studio released *PT 109* on June 19, 1963, to a lukewarm critical and popular reception. Milestone's name does not appear in the credits. Five months later, JFK was assassinated in Dallas.

After the exhausting work on *Mutiny* and the debacle of *PT 109*, Milestone retreated briefly into the world of television. He did not find much comfort there. His work with Richard Boone on one episode of his show (based on a Chekhov story) was pleasant enough. But in late 1963, he had a much less happy association with the series *Arrest and Trial*. He was contracted to direct a ninety-minute episode starring Ben Gazzara and Shelly Fabares called "An Echo of Conscience," for the paltry (for him) fee of $4,500. This assignment he completed, but he was not engaged for further work on the series.

That he was unexpectedly terminated is clear from a letter he received from the cast and crew of *Arrest and Trial,* signed by twenty-eight people connected with the show, including Gazzara and Chuck Connors. "Accept this letter as the mass expression of good will toward you, both professionally and personally, from the cast and crew of 'ARREST AND TRIAL.' None of us know the details of why it was necessary to discontinue your creative services as Director on our show. We all know you will go on to many new and bright successes in your chosen field."[44] What they possibly could have meant by "your chosen field" seems hard to understand.

This last bitter experience soured Milestone on the medium of television forever. In an extensive interview with Hal Humphrey of the *Los Angeles Times* in January 1964, Milestone explained what happened at *Arrest and Trial,* and why he was through with TV.

"I got in and found out what it was all about, then quit," he says, without bitterness.

The Hollywood TV film factories do not pay enough money to the creative people, and they put too much premium on speed for Milestone's taste.

"When television first started, everyone in our business was asked to work for less," he recalls. "Television was referred to then as a child being born. 'Give it a chance to live,' we were told.

"Well, it has lived—and how! Producers of TV series make millions of dollars. But," Milestone adds, "actors, writers and directors are not making any of this money unless they can demand and get a piece of the series."

In a moment of weakness recently, Milestone signed to do one of the "Arrest and Trial" episodes at Revue Productions, the colossus of TV film factories.

After four or five days of getting up at 6 in the morning and working into the night ("Arrest and Trial" has a nine-day shooting schedule), Milestone says he felt a cold coming on and asked one of the crew for an antihistamine.

"You haven't been feeling well, have you?" executive producer Frank Rosenberg asked Milestone the next day, revealing that Revue has an excellent central intelligence system working. Despite Milestone's assurance that he would be on his feet to finish the film, another director was brought in, and Milestone was told, "You are after a quality we don't need in these films."[45]

By this time, Milestone's health was declining, in part as a result of the extreme physical demands of shooting *Mutiny on the Bounty* and many years of cigarette smoking. He suffered from neuritis and had difficulty walking. Over the coming years, he considered and tried to develop various projects, but none came to fruition. He continued to be sought out for interviews and was feted at various film festivals. In Eastern Europe and the USSR he enjoyed an especially strong reputation, and he would meet with foreign directors when they visited Hollywood.

With the Czech director Jiri Weiss he developed a particularly warm friendship after their meeting at the San Francisco Film Festival in 1962. From Prague Weiss wrote to Milestone an admiring personal tribute. "Lewis Milestone will stay alive in my mind, in tuxedo but more so in a dressing gown or half dozing in bed, patient and strong and somehow incredible. Tell me, Kendall, is Lewis Milestone real, or is he only a myth? You should know, of all the people!"[46]

The death of Kendall on July 30, 1978, at the age of sixty-six, after an illness of several months, brought an end to their marriage of forty-three years. The actress he directed in *Rain,* then his companion on shoots around the globe, Kendall had also cared for him as his health deteriorated. Her departure must have been an enormous emotional and professional loss.

That same year, Milestone suffered a stroke that further impaired his movement and speech. He outlived Kendall by only a little more than two years. Not long before his eighty-fifth birthday, one of Hollywood's founding fathers passed away at the UCLA Medical Center, on September 25, 1980. He had come a long way from Kishinev.

13

A Hollywood Life

Discipline and constant application are prerequisites for a career as a
film director.

—Lewis Milestone

On July 28, 1979, about a year before his death, the Directors Guild of
America honored Milestone with a tribute at the Directors Guild Theatre
in Hollywood. As one of the eleven founders of the DGA, he held a place
of honor in the organization's long history. The group was established in
1936 as the Screen Directors Guild, and its goal was to protect the creative
rights of directors at a time when producers and studio heads could inter-
fere in the filmmaking process almost at will—something Milestone frequently experienced. Ensuring that only one director was assigned to a
film at a time held particular importance for the early members, who
were weary of the uncertainty and capricious competition between actors
and studios in the selection process. In 1960 the SDG merged with the
Radio and Television Directors Guild and took its current name, the
Directors Guild of America.

Robert Aldrich, a former president of the DGA, who had once served
as Milestone's assistant, presided over an evening that included tributes
from actors, actresses, writers, fellow directors, and other colleagues and
the screening of excerpts from his films. The list of speakers reads like a
who's who of Hollywood movers and shakers: the actors Lew Ayres, Dana
Andrews, Richard Boone, Lloyd Bridges, Burgess Meredith, and Barbara
Stanwyck; the director George Cukor; and the producer Hal Roach.
Sitting in the audience were Sam Goldwyn, the directors Rouben
Mamoulian and William Wyler, the writer Jules Stein, the composer
Bronislau Kaper, and the actors Robert Mitchum, Ethel Merman, and
Jane Wyatt, among many others.

The film historian David Parker wrote a lengthy appreciation of Milestone and his work for the evening's printed program. Here he stressed Millie's deep knowledge of cinematic tradition: "Through his work Lewis Milestone taught other directors what he had absorbed from the Russian and German filmmakers and what he had synthesized from the practices of American filmmakers." Parker reminded his audience of the incredible duration of Milestone's career, which stretched over nearly forty years, from the silent era through the advent of sound, through the golden age of the Hollywood film industry, and into the turbulent, television-obsessed 1960s. His earliest pioneering films, wrote Parker, "look forward to the classic American films of the later thirties in their speed, flexibility and social candor." Another constant was Milestone's respect for the literary works he brought to the screen, "finding apt cinematic equivalents for the author's words."

Like the great Soviet directors he emulated, especially Vsevolod Pudovkin and Sergei Eisenstein, Milestone believed film could not only entertain, but educate and enlighten. As Parker observed, "Milestone's body of work offers insight into the nature of social comment as it appears in the Hollywood film. His career indicates changes in the cultural climate of the industry over the four decades of his achievements." As for Milestone's influence on the younger generation of "socially committed filmmakers," Parker concluded that they could find inspiration in "the example of his economical, expressive story-telling; his forward-tracking camera; and his candid and ironic eye."

In his own contribution to the printed program, Milestone reminded his admirers, somewhat ruefully, that the film business is, after all, a business: "Film directors are not a breed apart. Money talks in the arts as it does everywhere; it always has."

When it came time for Milestone, confined to a wheelchair, to deliver remarks from the stage, he responded with a characteristically self-deprecating quip. "You invited me here and then robbed me of everything worthwhile to say."[1]

Around the same time, Milestone granted an interview to the journalist Arthur Lewis at his home on North Doheny Drive that reveals him in a more vulnerable light. In his book of memoirs, Lewis describes Milestone as "a big, black-haired, handsome man who radiates that quality of masculinity the Mexicans admire and call *macho*." But Milestone's modesty surprised Lewis, especially when compared to the self-promoting attitude he had encountered among his contemporaries, such as George Cukor. In their conversations, Milestone, wounded by his recent bruising encounters with corporate studio heads, had little good to say about the future of the Hollywood film industry: "It has none; all we have out here is a past; the town's got no future. And God knows it hasn't much present."[2]

Macho and modest. These two adjectives would seem to contradict each other, but they do get to something fundamental about Milestone's personality. As a poorly educated immigrant arriving in the United States, Milestone had to bluster his way to the kind of enormous success he achieved. Rough-hewn and plainspoken, he often alienated those in positions of power who had more education and sophistication. He insisted on being paid what he thought he was worth and reacted poorly to exhibitions of class privilege or snobbery (although he and his wife were famous for throwing parties attended by Hollywood's A-list). As many of his friends and collaborators had observed over the years, he did not have strong diplomatic skills in dealing with the front office. It is no coincidence that the films for which he is best remembered today (*All Quiet on the Western Front, The Front Page, Of Mice and Men, Halls of Montezuma*) celebrate ordinary people at the lower end of the economic scale, resigned to subservient jobs, having few choices to make about their future. These were the folks with whom Milestone could best identify and whose life stories inspired him.

Milestone's career did not follow a consistent upward trajectory. He did not achieve the same level of success as some of his more diplomatic contemporaries, such as George Cukor, Josef von Sternberg, William Wyler, Frank Capra, and John Ford. Early on, he gained a reputation for being difficult that made some studios wary of working with him. At some crucial moments he made questionable decisions about which projects to pursue (*Red Square, Arch of Triumph*). But the choices he made were most often governed by sincere personal passion and conviction. When Milestone arrived in Hollywood in the early 1920s, the industry valued the sort of stubborn independence and initiative he possessed. But in the 1930s, as the studio system gained control, it became more important for a successful director to be able to function smoothly as part of a larger machine. For Milestone this proved challenging, and this helps explain why he never developed the sort of strong connection with one studio that could have guaranteed more consistent success.

Milestone's close friend Norman Lloyd knew him better than almost anyone, and he has written: "There was something in Milly that was remarkable, of real size which never fully emerged. *All Quiet* was a masterpiece and in this instance he fulfilled his talent, but his career seemed to be blocked. He never achieved what he appeared to be capable of when he first started. I have to say, dear friend that he was, that this was because of his personal complications: temper, temperament, inability to get on with the front offices at all and resistance to authority."[3]

But despite these personal obstacles, Milestone managed to survive and remain productive for almost four decades in an industry known for devouring its most talented members. His best films are landmarks and monuments, and even his lesser efforts continue to impress in their attention to detail, dynamic editing, careful construction of character, and idealism. He showed more courage and integrity than many others in dealing with the HUAC inquisition, standing by his colleagues despite the real damage done to his career and self-interest.

A beloved member of the Hollywood community, of which he was a founding father, Milestone considered Hollywood his only real home. The many brilliant actors, designers, cinematographers, screenwriters, composers, and producers he worked with and nurtured over the years were his family. Like many of them, he arrived with little but dreams, some skill, and a brave faith in the future of a uniquely modern medium born of speed and light.

Acknowledgments

Among the many institutions and people who have helped me in creating this book, the Film Scholars Program of the Academy of Motion Picture Arts and Sciences (AMPAS) deserves pride of place. The generous fellowship I received under the auspices of this program in 2010 made it possible for me to conduct extensive research on Milestone's life and career. To Shawn Guthrie, grants coordinator of the Film Scholars Program, I am deeply indebted for his support and patience during the long gestation of this volume.

The most important repository for this material is the Margaret Herrick Library of the AMPAS in Beverly Hills, California, where Milestone's personal and professional archives are housed. How pleasant and exciting it was to spend many days working in the Herrick Library's Special Collections room, and in the sunny main reading room, stocked with a collection of books, periodicals, and other materials on every aspect of Hollywood history. The reception I received at the Herrick Library was unfailingly warm and welcoming, and for the expert help of the staff I will be forever grateful. In particular, I must acknowledge the assistance I received from Research Librarian Barbara Hall, a walking encyclopedia of Hollywood lore who pointed me toward many sources I would otherwise never have discovered. Faye Thompson, photograph archive coordinator, provided friendly guidance in identifying and selecting photographic materials from the library's rich holdings. John Damer, records management assistant, and Jeanie Braun, photograph archivist, converted the photos into digital files with expert skill.

In Los Angeles I also consulted valuable archival materials and films in the collections of the UCLA Film and Television Archive and the Special Collections of the Doheny Library at the University of Southern California.

Acknowledgments

For providing endless encouragement and hospitality during my many research trips to Los Angeles, I thank my dear friends Kate Amend and Johanna Demetrakas, both of them distinguished documentary film professionals.

My former home, the Department of History in the College of Social Sciences and Humanities at Northeastern University, gave me deeply appreciated financial assistance in the form of several summer research grants (from the History Department's Offenberg Fund) and two sabbatical leaves. Professor Heather Streets-Salter, chair of the History Department, supported this project with enthusiasm throughout. My friend and colleague, the late Professor Gerald Herman, prodded me along the way and allowed me to work out some of my ideas about Milestone in the course we taught together for more than a decade in the Cinema Studies Program at Northeastern.

Professor Catherine Portuges, director emerita of the Cinema Studies Program at the University of Massachusetts–Amherst, offered expert and friendly editorial and historical advice and read many drafts of the book as it progressed.

Anne Dean Dotson, my editor at the University Press of Kentucky, has cultivated and guided this project to completion. Thanks to her and to the other devoted members of her team, including copy editor *extraordinaire* Ann Twombly.

To Robert Holley—my partner of thirty-nine years and husband of sixteen years—who was present at this book's conception and nurtured it with me through its childhood, adolescence, and adulthood, I cannot begin to express the depth of my gratitude for your love, sustenance, and belief in its importance. This book is dedicated to you.

West Hollywood, California
June 2019

Filmography

Silent Films

SEVEN SINNERS (Warner Bros., 1925)
Screenplay: Lewis Milestone, Darryl F. Zanuck
Photography: David Abel
Cast: Marie Prevost, Clive Brook, John Patrick, Charles Conklin
76 mins.

THE CAVE MAN (Warner Bros., 1926)
Screenplay: Darryl F. Zanuck (from a story by Gelett Burgess)
Photography: David Abel
Cast: Matt Moore, Marie Prevost, John Patrick, Myrna Loy, Phillis Haver,
   Hedda Hopper
75 mins.

THE NEW KLONDIKE (Paramount, 1926)
Screenplay: Thomas J. Geraghty (from a story by Ring Lardner)
Photography: Alvin Wyckoff
Cast: Thomas Meighan, Lisa Lee, Paul Kelly, Hallie Manning, Robert
   Craig
83 mins.

TWO ARABIAN KNIGHTS (Caddo Company, United Artists, 1927)
Screenplay: James T. O'Donohue, Wallace Smith (from a story by Donald
   McGibney)
Photography: Tony Gaudio, Joseph August
Cast: William Boyd, Mary Astor, Louis Wolheim, Michael Vavitch, Ian Keith
92 mins.

THE GARDEN OF EDEN (United Artists, 1928)
Screenplay: Hans Kraly (from a play by Rudolf Bernauer and Rudolf
   Oesterreicher)
Photography: John Arnold
Art Direction: William Cameron Menzies
Cast: Corinne Griffith, Louise Dresser, Lowell Sherman, Maude George,
   Charles Ray
81 mins

THE RACKET (Caddo Company/Paramount, 1928)
Screenplay: Harry Behn, Del Andrews (from a play by Bartlett
   Cormack)
Photography: Tony Gaudio
Cast: Thomas Meighan, Marie Prevost, Louis Wolheim, George Stone,
   John Darrow
85 mins.

BETRAYAL (Paramount, 1929)
Screenplay: Hans Kraly (from a story by Victor Schertzinger, Nicholas
   Saussanin)
Photography: Henry Gerard
Art Director: Hans Dreier
Cast: Emil Jannings, Esther Ralston, Gary Cooper, Jada Weller, Douglas
   Haig
73½ mins.

Sound Films

NEW YORK NIGHTS (United Artists, 1929)
Milestone asked to have his name removed from this film because it was
   substantially reedited without his permission, although his name
   does appear as director.
Screenplay: Jules Furthman (from a play, *Tin Pan Alley,* by Hugh Stanislaus
   Strange)
Photography: Ray June
Cast: Norma Talmadge, Gilbert Roland, John Wray, Lilyan Tashman,
   Mary Doran, Roscoe Karns
82½ mins.

ALL QUIET ON THE WESTERN FRONT (Universal, 1930)
Production: Carl Laemmle Jr.
Screenplay: Maxwell Anderson, Del Andrews, George Abbott (from the
    novel by Erich Maria Remarque)
Dialogue Direction: George Cukor
Photography: Arthur Edeson, Karl Freund, Tony Gaudio
Music and Synchronization: David Broekman
Cast: Lew Ayres, Louis Wolheim, John Wray, Raymond Griffith, George
    "Slim" Summerville
145 mins.
This film was released in sound and silent versions, and in other edited
    versions over the years.

THE FRONT PAGE (Caddo Company/United Artists, 1931)
Production: Howard Hughes
Screenplay: Bartlett Cormack (from the play by Ben Hecht and Charles
    MacArthur)
Photography: Tony Gaudio, Hal Mohr, Glen MacWilliams
Cast: Adolphe Menjou, Pat O'Brien, Mary Brian, Walter Catlett, Edward
    Everett Horton
100 mins.

RAIN (United Artists, 1932)
Screenplay: Maxwell Anderson (from a play by John Colton and Clemence
    Randolph from a story by Somerset Maugham)
Photography: Oliver Marsh
Cast: Joan Crawford, Walter Huston, William Gargan, Matt Moore,
    Beulah Bondi, Kendall Lee, Guy Kibbee
85 mins.

HALLELUJAH, I'M A BUM (United Artists, 1933)
Screenplay: S. N. Behrman (from a story by Ben Hecht)
Musical Dialoguers: Richard Rodgers, Lorenz Hart
Photography: Lucien Andriot
Music Direction: Alfred Newman
Cast: Al Jolson, Madge Evans, Harry Langdon, Frank Morgan, Chester
    Conklin, Edgar Connor
82 mins.

THE CAPTAIN HATES THE SEA (Columbia, 1934)
Screenplay: Wallace Smith (from his own story)
Photography: Joseph August
Cast: Victor McLaglen, John Gilbert, Walter Connolly, Alison Skipworth, Wynne Gibson, Helen Vinson, the Three Stooges
92 mins.

PARIS IN SPRING (Paramount, 1935)
Screenplay: Samuel Hoffenstein, Franz Schulz, Keene Thompson (from a play by Dwight Taylor)
Photography: Ted Tetzlaff
Music: Harry Revel
Cast: Mary Ellis, Tullio Carminati, Ida Lupino, Lynne Overman, James Blakeley
83 mins.

ANYTHING GOES (Paramount, 1936)
Screenplay: Howard Lindsay, Russel Crouse, Guy Bolton, P. G. Wodehouse (from their musical comedy)
Photography: Karl Struss
Music and Lyrics: Cole Porter (with additional songs by others)
Additional Songs: Leo Robin, Richard A. Whiting, Friedrich Hollaender, Hoagy Carmichael, Edward Heyman
Cast: Bing Crosby, Ethel Merman, Charles Ruggles, Ida Lupino
92 mins.

THE GENERAL DIED AT DAWN (Paramount, 1936)
Screenplay: Clifford Odets (from a novel by Charles G. Booth)
Photography: Victor Milner
Music: Werner Janssen
Cast: Gary Cooper, Madeleine Carroll, Akim Tamiroff, Porter Hall, William Frawley, Philip Ahn
98 mins.

THE NIGHT OF NIGHTS (Paramount, 1939)
Screenplay: Donald Ogden Stewart
Photography: Leo Tover

Cast: Pat O'Brien, Olympe Bradna, Roland Young, Reginald Gardiner, George E. Stone
85 mins.

OF MICE AND MEN (Hal Roach Studios/United Artists, 1939)
Screenplay: Eugene Solow (from a novel and play by John Steinbeck)
Photography: Norbert Brodine
Art Director: Nicolai Remisoff
Music: Aaron Copland
Cast: Burgess Meredith, Betty Field, Lon Chaney Jr., Charles Bickford, Roman Bohnen, Bob Steele
106 mins.

LUCKY PARTNERS (RKO, 1940)
Screenplay: Allan Scott, John Van Druten (from Sacha Guitry's play and film *Bonne Chance*)
Photography: Robert De Grasse
Music: Dmitri Tiomkin
Cast: Ronald Colman, Ginger Rogers, Jack Carson, Spring Byington, Cecilia Loftus
101 mins.

MY LIFE WITH CAROLINE (United Producers/RKO, 1941)
Screenplay: John Van Druten, Arnold Belgard (from a play, *Train to Paris*, by Louis Verneuil, Georges Berr)
Photography: Victor Milner
Art Direction: Nicolai Remisoff
Music: Werner Heymann
Cast: Ronald Colman, Anna Lee, Charles Winninger, Reginald Gardiner, Gilbert Roland, Kay Leslie
81 mins.

OUR RUSSIAN FRONT (Russian War Relief, Inc., 1942)
Production: Joris Ivens, Lewis Milestone
Photography: Soviet frontline cameramen
Editing: Lewis Milestone
Narration: Walter Huston
37 mins.

Filmography

EDGE OF DARKNESS (Warner Bros., 1943)
Production: Henry Blanke and Jack L. Warner
Screenplay: Robert Rossen (from a novel by William Woods)
Photography: Sid Hickox
Music: Franz Waxman
Cast: Errol Flynn, Ann Sheridan, Walter Huston, Nancy Coleman, Judith
    Anderson, Helmut Dantinem, Ruth Gordon
118 mins.

THE NORTH STAR (RKO, 1943)
Production: Sam Goldwyn
Screenplay: Lillian Hellman
Photography: James Wong Howe
Music: Aaron Copland
Cast: Anne Baxter, Dana Andrews, Walter Huston, Walter Brennan, Ann
    Harding, Farley Granger, Erich von Stroheim
105 mins.

THE PURPLE HEART (20th Century Fox, 1944)
Production: Darryl F. Zanuck
Screenplay: Jerome Cady (from a story by Melville Crossman, probably a
    pen name for Darryl F. Zanuck)
Photography: Arthur Miller
Music: Alfred Newman
Cast: Dana Andrews, Richard Conte, Farley Granger, Kevin O'Shea,
    Donald Barry, Sam Levene
99 mins.

A WALK IN THE SUN (20th Century Fox, 1945)
Production: Lewis Milestone
Screenplay: Robert Rossen (from a novel by Harry Brown)
Photography: Russell Harlan
Music: Frederic Efrem Rich and Earl Robinson (ballads)
Cast: Dana Andrews, John Ireland, Richard Conte, Sterling Holloway,
    George Tyne, Norman Lloyd, Lloyd Bridges
117 mins.

THE STRANGE LOVE OF MARTHA IVERS (Paramount, 1946)
Production: Hal B. Wallis
Screenplay: Robert Rossen, from a story by John Patrick
Photography: Victor Milner
Music: Miklós Rózsa
Cast: Barbara Stanwyck, Van Heflin, Kirk Douglas, Lizabeth Scott, Judith
    Anderson
117 mins.

ARCH OF TRIUMPH (Enterprise/United Artists, 1948)
Screenplay: Lewis Milestone, Harry Brown (from the novel by Erich
    Maria Remarque)
Photography: Russell Metty
Art Direction: William Cameron Menzies
Music: Louis Gruenberg
Cast: Charles Boyer, Ingrid Bergman, Charles Laughton, Louis Calhern,
    Roman Bohnen
115 mins.

NO MINOR VICES (Enterprise/MGM, 1948)
Production: Lewis Milestone
Screenplay: Lewis Milestone and Harry Brown, from a story by Arnold
    Manoff
Art Direction: Nicolai Remisoff
Music: Franz Waxman
Cast: Dana Andrews, Lilli Palmer, Louis Jourdan, Jane Wyatt, Norman Lloyd
96 mins.

THE RED PONY (Republic, 1949)
Screenplay: John Steinbeck (from his own stories) and Lewis Milestone
Photography: Tony Gaudio (color)
Production Design: Nicolai Remisoff
Music: Aaron Copland
Cast: Myrna Loy, Robert Mitchum, Louis Calhern, Shepperd Strudwick,
    Peter Miles
89 mins.

HALLS OF MONTEZUMA (20th Century Fox, 1951)
Screenplay: Michael Blankfort (from his own story)
Photography: Winton C. Hoch, Harry Jackson (color)
Music: Sol Kaplan
Cast: Richard Widmark, Walter [Jack] Palance, Reginald Gardiner, Robert Wagner, Karl Malden
113 mins.

KANGAROO (20th Century Fox, 1952)
Screenplay: Harry Kleiner (from a story by Martin Berkeley)
Photography: Charles G. Clarke (color)
Music: Sol Kaplan
Cast: Peter Lawford, Maureen O'Hara, Finlay Currie, Richard Boone, Chips Rafferty
84 mins.

LES MISERABLES (20th Century Fox, 1952)
Screenplay: Richard Murphy (from Victor Hugo's novel)
Photography: Joseph LaShelle
Music: Alec North
Cast: Michael Rennie, Debra Paget, Robert Newton, Edmund Gwenn, Sylvia Sidney
104 mins.

MELBA (United Artists, 1953)
Screenplay: Harry Kurnitz (from his own story)
Photography: Ted Scaife (color)
Art Direction: André Andrejew
Music: Muir Mathieson (and scenes from operas)
Cast: Patrice Munsel, Robert Morley, John McCallum, John Justin, Alec Clunes, Sybil Thorndike
113 mins.

THEY WHO DARE (Mayflower Pictures/British Lion, 1953)
Screenplay: Robert Westerby
Photography: Wilkie Cooper
Music: Robert Gill

Cast: Dirk Bogarde, Denholm Elliott, Akim Tamiroff, Gérard Oury, Eric Pohlmann

101 mins.

LA VEDOVA X (THE WIDOW) (Venturini/Express, 1954)
Screenplay: Louis Stevens (from a novel by Susan York)
Photography: Arturo Gallea
Music: Mario Nascimbene
Cast: Patricia Roc, Anna Maria Ferrero, Massimo Serato, Akim Tamiroff, Leonardo Botta

89 mins.

PORK CHOP HILL (Melville/United Artists, 1959)
Production: Sy Barlett
Screenplay: James R. Webb (from a book by S. L. A. Marshall)
Photography: Sam Leavitt
Art Direction: Nicolai Remisoff
Music: Leonard Rosenman
Cast: Gregory Peck, Harry Guardino, George Shibata, Woody Strode, Robert Blake, James Edwards, Lewis Gallo, Rip Torn, George Peppard

97 mins.

OCEAN'S 11 (Dorchester/Warner Bros., 1960)
Production: Lewis Milestone
Screenplay: Harry Brown, Charles Lederer (from a story by George Clayton Johnson and Jack Golden Russell
Photography: William H. Daniels (color)
Art Direction: Nicolai Remisoff
Music: Nelson Riddle
Cast: Frank Sinatra, Dean Martin, Sammy Davis Jr., Peter Lawford, Angie Dickinson, Richard Conte

128 mins.

MUTINY ON THE BOUNTY (Arcola/MGM, 1962)
Production: Aaron Rosenberg
Screenplay: Charles Lederer (from the book by Charles Nordhoff, James Norman Hall)
Photography: Robert L. Surtees (color)

Music: Bronislau Kaper

Cast: Marlon Brando, Trevor Howard, Richard Harris, Hugh Griffith, Richard Haydn

179 mins.

Notes

Abbreviations

The following abbreviations are used in the notes for frequently cited sources.

BR   Kevin Brownlow interviews with Milestone, 1969, Lewis Milestone Archives, f. 323, Margaret Herrick Library.

GR   Joel Greenberg interviews with Milestone, Louis B. Mayer American Oral History, Project of the American Film Institute, 1971–73, Lewis Milestone Archives, f. 328, Margaret Herrick Library.

HG   Charles Higham and Joel Greenberg profile of Milestone, in *The Celluloid Muse: Hollywood Directors Speak* (1969; repr., Chicago: Regnery, 1971).

LMA   Lewis Milestone Archives, Margaret Herrick Library.

LMT   Lewis Milestone testimony to House Un-American Activities Committee investigator William Wheeler, reported by Harold M. Leibovitz, June 25, 1951, Los Angeles, National Archives and Records Administration, Center for Legislative Archives, Washington, D.C.

MC   Joseph R. Millichap, *Lewis Milestone* (Boston: Twayne, 1981).

MS   Lewis Milestone, with Donald Chase, "Milestones," uncompleted Milestone autobiography, ff. 317, 318, 319, 322, Margaret Herrick Library.

NR   Nicolai Remisoff Archives, University of Southern California Library Special Collections.

PCA   Production Code Administration files, Margaret Herrick Library.

PS   David L. Parker and Burton J. Shapiro, "Lewis Milestone," in *Close Up: The Contract Director*, ed. Jon Tuska (Metuchen, N.J.: Scarecrow, 1976).

VS   Barbara Hall interview with Albert E. Van Schmus, 1993, Oral History Program, Margaret Herrick Library.

Note: All translations from the Russian are mine unless otherwise indicated.

Introduction

1. Joseph R. Millichap, *Lewis Milestone* (Boston: Twayne, 1981). Andrew Kelly's very valuable *All Quiet on the Western Front: The Story of a Film* (New York: I. B. Tauris, 1998) focuses primarily on a single film.

2. David Parkinson, *History of Film* (New York: Thames & Hudson, 1996), 106.

3. Leonard Maltin, ed., *Leonard Maltin's Movie Encyclopedia* (New York: Plume, 1994), 608.

4. Darryl Zanuck to Milestone, June 15, 1950, *Kangaroo* production, f. 32, LMA.

5. Warren French, foreword to Millichap, *Lewis Milestone*.

6. Otto Friedrich, *City of Nets: A Portrait of Hollywood in the 1940s* (New York: Harper and Row, 1986), 304.

1. "Nobody Asked You to Go to America"

1. *Los Angeles Express,* April 21, 1930.

2. *Rochester (N.Y.) American,* April 13, 1930.

3. *New York Evening World,* April 25, 1930.

4. Lewis Milestone, with Donald Chase, "Milestones," draft autobiography (1964–65), f. 319, Lewis Milestone Archives, Margaret Herrick Library, 71.

5. Bob Fischer, draft of interview with Milestone for *Action* magazine, "Lewis Milestone Marks 50 Years in Hollywood," f. 324, LMA.

6. Louella Parsons column, *Los Angeles Examiner,* January 5, 1931.

7. Regina Crewe, "Task Done, Milestone to Go Home," *New York American,* May 4, 1930.

8. Mark Hellinger, "A Toast to Lewis Milesone," *Daily Mirror* service, undated, 1930, Milestone clipping files, LMA.

9. Milestone himself was inconsistent on the facts of his birthplace; most often he claimed to have been born in Odessa, but in testimony to a HUAC investigator in 1951 he stated that he was born in Kishinev, and elsewhere he simply said he was born "in Russia."

10. Crewe, "Task Done, Milestone to Go Home,"

11. GR, 5.

12. Ilya Ehrenburg, *Memoirs: 1921–1941,* trans. Tatiana Shebunina with Yvonne Kapp (Cleveland: World Publishing, 1963), 127.

13. *New York Times,* April 28, 1903.

14. J. J. Goldberg, "Kishinev 1903: The Birth of a Century. Reconsidering the 49 Deaths That Galvanized and Changed Jewish History," *Forward,* April 4, 2003.

15. MS, f. 317, 28–29.

16. BR, 47.

17. Ibid., 13.

18. GR, 3.

19. Ibid., 4.

20. Ibid., 6.

21. Ibid.
22. Ibid., 8.
23. Ibid., 7.
24. GR, 10.
25. MS, f. 317, 5.
26. GR, 14.
27. Ibid., 17.
28. MS, f. 321, 52.
29. Ibid.
30. Ibid.
31. MS, f. 317, 2.
32. Ibid., 4.
33. Ibid., 5-B.
34. PS, 300.
35. MS, f. 317, 22.
36. PS, 300.
37. GR, 8.
38. BR, 37.
39. MS, f. 317, 16.
40. HG, 145.
41. Ibid., 23.

2. The Constructive Cutter

1. Lucy Fischer, ed., *American Cinema of the 1920s: Themes and Variations* (New Brunswick, N.J.: Rutgers University Press, 2009), 15.

2. Halsey Stuart & Co., "The Motion Picture Industry as a Basis for Bond Financing" (1927) in *The American Film Industry*, ed. Tino Balio (Madison: University of Wisconsin Press, 1976), 176, 179.

3. Quoted in Fischer, 2.

4. Frederick Lewis Allen, *Only Yesterday: An Informal History of the Nineteen-Twenties* (1931; repr. New York: Harper and Row, 1957), 39.

5. Crewe, "Task Done, Milestone to Go Home."

6. HG, 145.

7. GR, 33.

8. MS, f. 319, 141–42.

9. GR, 38.

10. PS, 300–301.

11. GR, 35.

12. Ibid., 43.

13. Ibid., 44.

14. MC, 29.

15. Ibid., 29.

16. HG, 146.

17. GR, 44.

18. Ibid., 44.

19. Undated, unidentified review, Milestone clipping files, LMA.

20. Ibid.

21. Ibid.

22. *Cave Man* script, f. 43, LMA.

23. MS, f. 319, 72.

24. "A Significant Milestone," undated, unidentified clipping (ca. 1926), Milestone clipping files, LMA.

25. "Warner's Sue for Milestone Walkout," *Variety* (New York), August 18, 1926.

26. *Hollywood Filmograph*, September 18, 1926.

27. "Milestone Is Refused Warner Injunction," *Variety* (New York), November 3, 1926.

28. MS, f. 319, 71.

29. Ibid., 69.

30. PS, 304.

31. *Variety*, August 18, 1926.

32. MS, f. 319, 67.

33. Jim Tully, "Why I Live in Hollywood," *Hollywood Magazine*, December 1930.

34. Ibid., 147.

35. Regina Cannon, review of *The New Klondike* in unidentifed newspaper, March 24, 1926, Milestone clipping files, LMA.

36. Tully, "Why I Live in Hollywood."

37. Charles Higham, *Howard Hughes: The Secret Life* (New York: G. P. Putnam's, 1993), 38.

38. Ben Hecht, "The Boy Pirate," *Liberty*, January 1932.

39. MS, f. 319, 70.

40. Donald L. Barlett and James B. Steele, *Empire: The Life, Legend, and Madness of Howard Hughes* (New York: W. W. Norton, 1979), 178.

41. William Bates, "Howard Hughes' Lab of 'Rosebuds,'" *Los Angeles Times*, February 12, 1978.

42. HG, 39.

43. Ibid.

44. Richard Hack, *Hughes: The Private Diaries, Memos and Letters* (Beverly Hills: New Millenium Press, 2001), 63.

45. *Variety* (New York), November 28, 1927.

46. Hack, *Hughes*, 63.

47. The Bystander, "Over the Teacups: Fanny the Fan Reviews the Passing Show of the Picture Colony, Ballyhoos Two Films, and Gossips of This and That," unidentified magazine article, Milestone clipping files, LMA.

48. *Photoplay*, January 1928.

49. Sergei Bertensson, *V Khollivude s V. I. Nemirovichem-Danchenko* (Monterey, Calif.: K. Arensburger, 1964), 164.

50. PS, 306.

51. Betty Colfax, "Milestone Scores Again with Film at Paramount," *New York Graphic,* March 19, 1928.

52. *Los Angeles Record,* April 14, 1928.

53. Colfax, "Milestone Scores Again."

54. MS, f. 319, 75.

55. Ibid., 76.

56. HG, 149.

57. MS, f. 319, 77–78.

58. Ibid., 78.

59. PS, 308.

60. AMPAS to Milestone, February 19, 1929, f. 202, LMA.

3. "The Greatest Picture Ever Made"

1. E. M. Remarque, quoted in "Not All Quiet for Remarque," *Literary Digest,* October 12, 1929, 19.

2. E. M. Remarque, *All Quiet on the Western Front,* trans. A. W. Wheen (1929; repr., New York: Ballantine Books, 1982), 1.

3. Ibid., 22.

4. Ibid., 296.

5. Ibid., 149.

6. Ibid., 223.

7. Kelly, *All Quiet on the Western Front,* 66–67.

8. C. Laemmle, "*All Quiet on the Western Front,*" *Universal Weekly,* July 27, 1929.

9. C. Laemmle, "The Boy," *Photoplay,* September 1934, 38.

10. Kelly, *All Quiet on the Western Front,* 99.

11. Marguerite Tazelaar, "A Talk with the Director of 'All Quiet,'" *New York Herald Tribune,* May 4, 1930.

12. Norman Zierold, *The Moguls: Hollywood's Merchants of Myth* (Los Angeles: Silman-James Press, 1991), 111.

13. Tazelaar, "A Talk with the Director."

14. Ibid.

15. Kelly, *All Quiet on the Western Front,* 163.

16. George Abbott, *Mister Abbott* (New York: Random House, 1963), 135.

17. BR, 25.

18. MS, f. 319, 134.

19. Remarque, *All Quiet on the Western Front,* 294.

20. Ibid., 296.

21. MS, f. 319, 125.

22. Ibid.

23. Ibid., 125–31.

24. Ibid., 133–34.

25. Lesley L. Coffin, *Lew Ayres: Hollywood's Conscientious Objector* (Jackson: University Press of Mississippi, 2012), 194.

26. News item circulated to various newspapers in 1930, Milestone clipping files, LMA.

27. BR, 37.

28. Carl Laemmle Jr. to Milestone, February 26, 1930, f. 2, LMA.

29. MS, f. 319, 79–82.

30. HG, 155.

31. Ibid., 151.

32. BR, 37–38.

33. MS, f. 319, 91.

34. Ibid., 94.

35. Ibid., 96.

36. Kelly, *All Quiet on the Western Front,* 98.

37. Sergei Eisenstein "A Dialetic Approach to Film Form," *Film Form: Essays in Film Theory,* ed. and trans. Jay Leyda (New York: Harcourt, Brace, 1949), 48.

38. Kelly, *All Quiet on the Western front,* 85.

39. William Boehnel, "'Western Front' Director Follows Own System," *New York Telegram,* April 29, 1930.

40. Jesse L. Lasky quoted in an unsigned article, *Film Spectator,* May 24, 1930.

41. Ibid.

42. Yon Barna, *Eisenstein* (Bloomington: Indiana University Press, 1973), 155.

43. Sergei Eisenstein, *Beyond the Stars: The Memoirs of Sergei Eisenstein,* ed. Richard Taylor, trans. William Powell (Calcutta: Seagull, 1995), 287.

44. *Variety,* May 7, 1930.

45. Ginger Rogers, *Ginger: My Story* (New York: HarperCollins, 1991), 61.

46. Howard Hughes to Milestone, July 15, 1930, telegram, f. 2, LMA.

47. Steven Randis, "A Final Interview with Lew Ayres," *Films of the Golden Age,* Fall 1997, 20.

48. Recommendation of International Federation of Catholic Alumanae, Motion Picture Bureau, June 6, 1930, Production Code files on *All Quiet on the Western Front,* Herrick Library.

49. Frank Pease to Herbert Hoover et al., telegram, April 28, 1930, Herrick Library.

50. C. J. Carlson, regional executive, Boy Scouts of America, Region XII, September 11, 1930, Herrick Library.

51. "Col. Joy's Resume," April 8, 1930, Production Code files on *All Quiet on the Western Front,* Herrick Library.

52. Unsigned letter sent to Mr. Hays and F. L. Herron, December 6, 1930, Production Code files on *All Quiet on the Western Front,* Herrick Library.

53. Leni Riefenstahl, *The Sieve of Time* (London: Quartet, 1992), 65–66.

54. Report from Foreign Department of MPPDA, December 29, 1930, Production Code files on *All Quiet on the Western Front,* Herrick Library.

55. *Manchester Guardian,* December 12, 1930.

56. "United States Government representative in Berlin," report dated December 18, 1930, Production Code files on *All Quiet on the Western Front,* Herrick Library.

57. Report from Foreign Department of MPPDA, December 29, 1930.

58. Milestone, handwritten note, undated (ca. 1964), miscellaneous materials on *All Quiet on the Western Front*, f. 2, LMA.

59. MS, f. 319, 138.

60. HG, 155.

61. Kelly, *All Quiet on the Western Front*, 138.

62. *New York Times*, October 9, 1939.

63. Milestone to James Sheehan, March 26, 1964, miscellaneous materials on *All Quiet on the Western Front*, f. 2, LMA.

64. MS, f. 319, 138.

65. Regina Crewe, "Task Done, Milestone to Go Home," *New York American*, May 4, 1930.

66. Milestone's passport, issued May 23, 1930, f. 307, LMA.

67. Sergei Bertensson, *Pis'ma v Khollivud. Po materialam arkhiva S. L. Bertensona*, ed. K. Arenskii (Monterey, Calif.: K. Arensburger, 1968), 97.

68. *Variety*, August 13, 1930.

69. *Hollywood Filmograph*, December 6, 1930.

4. Photoplays

1. *Hollywood International Film Reporter*, November 28, 1930.

2. MS, f. 319, 149.

3. William MacAdams, *Ben Hecht: The Man behind the Legend* (New York: Scribner's, 1990), 106.

4. Ben Hecht and Charles MacArthur, *The Front Page* (New York: Covici-Friede, 1928), 31.

5. Ibid., 39.

6. Ibid., 108.

7. *New York Times*, August 19, 1928.

8. MS, f. 319, 149.

9. "Milestone Works on Percentage," *Hollywood Reporter*, October 16, 1930.

10. Milestone *The Front Page* contract, October 10, 1930, f. 21, LMA.

11. MS, f. 319, 154.

12. *The Front Page* production file, f. 23, LMA.

13. Michael Sragow, notes to the Criterion DVD release of *The Front Page*, 2017.

14. MS, f. 319, 139.

15. Ibid., 157.

16. Bertensson, *Pis'ma v Khollivud*, 117.

17. *The Front Page* production reports, f. 22, LMA.

18. *The Front Page* cost reports, f. 19, LMA.

19. MS, f. 319, 158–59.

20. Bertensson, *Pis'ma v Khollivud*, 131.

21. Ibid., 133.

22. Viktor Tourjansky (1891–1976) was a Ukrainian émigré director with whom Milestone had worked on the film *Tempest*.

23. Fyodor Chaliapin (1905–1992) was the youngest son of the Russian operatic bass Feodor Chaliapin Jr. and an actor who appeared in numerous Hollywood features, including *For Whom the Bell Tolls* and *Moonstruck*.

24. Alexander Vertinsky (1889–1957) was one of the most famous Russian popular singers of his time. He lived in Paris in the 1920s, where he sang to great acclaim in cabarets. He also appeared in numerous films, both silent and sound.

25. Ivan Mosjoukine (Mozzhukin, 1889–1939) was a Russian-born actor and film star who moved to France in 1919 and had a brilliant career in silent films.

26. Muratov was another Russian actor.

27. Bertensson, *Pis'ma v Khollivud*, 157–58.

28. Ibid., 161.

29. Ibid., 169–70.

30. Somerset Maugham, "Rain," in *Collected Short Stories*, vol. 1 (New York: Penguin, 1977), 44.

31. Ibid., 45.

32. MS, f. 319, 161.

33. Ibid., 161–62.

34. *Rain* cost reports, f. 94, LMA.

35. MS, f. 319, 163.

36. Jeffrey Meyers, *Somerset Maugham: A Life* (New York: Alfred A. Knopf, 2004),146–47.

37. MS, f. 319, 164–65.

38. Joan Crawford with Jane Kesner Ardmore, *A Portrait of Joan: The Autobiography of Joan Crawford* (Garden City, N.Y.: Doubleday, 1962), 95.

39. David Bret, *Joan Crawford: Hollywood Martyr* (New York: Carroll & Graf, 2007), 71.

40. Eileen Creelman, "Picture Plays and Players: Lewis Milestone Tells of Plans for Directing Drama of Life in Modern Russia," *New York Sun*, May 25, 1933.

41. MS, f. 319, 161.

42. Charlotte Chandler, *Not the Girl Next Door: Joan Crawford, a Personal Biography* (New York: Simon and Schuster, 2008), 72.

43. Milestone quoted in Fred Lawrence Guiles, *Joan Crawford: The Last Word* (Secaucus, N.J.: Birch Lane Press, 1995), 84.

44. Chandler, *Not the Girl Next Door*, 72.

45. *Los Angeles Times*, July 3, 1977.

46. Creelman, "Picture Plays and Players."

47. David Rothel, *Richard Boone: A Knight without Armor in a Savage Land* (Madison, N.C.: Empire Publishing, 2000), 42.

48. Milestone to Lee, October 22, 1933, telegram, f. 3, Kendall Lee Correspondence, LMA.

49. "Divorced, Will Wed Film Man," *Sunday Mirror*, May 13, 1934.

50. Ibid.

51. "Lewis Milestone Is Honeymooning," *Los Angeles Herald,* July 29, 1935.

52. Ingrid Bergman to Milestone, February 14, 1947, f. 209, LMA.

53. Norman Lloyd, *Stages: Norman Lloyd,* interviewed by Francine Parker (Metuchen, N.J.: Scarecrow Press, 1990), 96.

54. Ibid., 91.

55. Herbert G. Goldman, *Jolson: The Legend Comes to Life* (New York: Oxford University Press, 1988), 187.

56. Quoted ibid., 206.

57. MC, 77.

58. Pearl Sieben, *The Immortal Jolson: His Life and Times* (New York: Frederick Fell, 1962), 155.

59. Penelope Gilliatt, "Hot and Cold, Getting Colder," *New Yorker,* June 23, 1973.

5. Up and Down

1. Various correspondence and materials, LMA.

2. Milestone contract, f. 143, LMA.

3. Eileen Creelman, "Picture Plays and Players: Lewis Milestone Tells of Plans for Directing Drama of Life in Modern Russia," *New York Sun,* May 25, 1933.

4. Ibid.

5. Ibid.

6. Philip K. Scheuer, "Russia to Be Given in Film: Milestone, Stallings Back from Moscow with Unique Script," *Los Angeles Times,* December 10, 1933.

7. Milestone's passport, f. 307, LMA.

8. Scheuer, "Russia to Be Given in Film."

9. Ehrenburg, *Memoirs,* 239–40.

10. "Research on Russia," f. 310, LMA.

11. Milestone to Columbia, February 19, 1934, f. 143, LMA.

12. Pilnayk describes his time in Hollywood in his entertaining book *Okei: Amerikanskii roman* (*Okay: An American Novel*) (Moscow, 1933), which is unfortunately not yet available in English translation.

13. Bob Thomas, *King Cohn: The Life and Times of Harry Cohn* (New York: G. P. Putnam's Sons, 1967), 100.

14. Ibid.

15. HG, 157.

16. Eve Golden, *John Gilbert: The Last of the Silent Film Stars* (Lexington: University Press of Kentucky, 2013), 270.

17. Ibid.

18. Milestone to Lee, July 18, 1934, f. 3, Kendall Lee Correspondence, LMA.

19. "Something Went Awry," *New York Times,* November 29, 1934.

20. Milestone to Lee, May 20, 1935, f. 2, Kendall Lee Correspondence, LMA.

21. HG, 158.

22. Files on *Paris in Spring,* PCA.

23. Brian Kellow, *Ethel Merman: A Life* (New York: Viking, 2007), 47.

24. Production schedule and costs, f. 143, LMA.

25. Gary Giddins, *Bing Crosby: A Pocketful of Dreams,* vol. 1, *The Early Years 1903–1940* (Boston: Little, Brown, 2001), 393.

26. Press book materials on *Anything Goes,* LMA.

27. Kellow, *Ethel Merman,* 58.

28. Henry Herzbrun to Milestone, September 26, 1935, f. 146, LMA.

29. Herzbrun to Milestone, October 2, 1935, memo, f. 146, LMA.

30. "Cinema: New Pictures: Anything Goes," *Time,* February 3, 1936.

31. Ethel Merman, with George Eells, *Merman: An Autobiography* (New York: Simon and Schuster, 1978), 78.

32. Caryl Flinn, *Brass Diva: The Life and Legends of Ethel Merman* (Berkeley: University of California Press, 2007), 74.

6. "The Goose Hangs High"

1. HG, 158.

2. Ibid.

3. Ibid.

4. Ibid., 159.

5. Margaret Brenman-Gibson, *Clifford Odets: American Playwright: The Years from 1906 to 1940* (1981; repr., New York: Applause, 2002), 396–97.

6. Ibid., 444.

7. Lewis Milestone, "First Flight: Clifford Odets' First Essay in Pictures Brings Off a Dramatic and Moving Film," *Stage,* October 1936, 42.

8. Joseph Breen to John Hammell of Paramount Studios, April 18, 1936, PCA.

9. Milestone, "First Flight."

10. Breen to Hammell.

11. Milestone, "First Flight."

12. Milestone to Lee, Kendall Lee Correspondence, f. 3, LMA.

13. Paramount press book for *The General Died at Dawn,* LMA.

14. HG, 159.

15. Regina Crewe, "Lewis Milestone Makes a Report on a Changing Hollywood," *New York American,* September 13, 1936.

16. Brenman-Gibson, *Clifford Odets,* 407.

17. Paramount press book for *The General Died at Dawn,* LMA.

18. Quoted in Jeffrey Meyers, *Gary Cooper: American Hero* (New York: William Morrow, 1998), 122.

19. Paramount press book for *The General Died at Dawn,* LMA.

20. Brenman-Gibson, *Clifford Odets,* 421.

21. Crewe, "Lewis Milestone Makes a Report."

22. Matthew Bernstein, *Walter Wanger: Hollywood Independent* (Berkeley: University of California Press, 1994), 129.

23. Ibid.

24. Ibid., 455.

25. Brenman-Gibson, *Clifford Odets,* 455.

26. Bernstein, *Walter Wanger,* 129–31.

27. Quoted in Jan Herman, *A Talent for Trouble: The Life of Hollywood's Most Acclaimed Director, William Wyler* (New York: G. P. Putnam's Sons, 1995), 169.

28. PS, 318.

29. Ed Sullivan column, *Citizen News,* February 12, 1940.

30. MS, 121.

31. Milestone to Kendall Lee, May 20, 1938, Kendall Lee Correspondence, f. 4, LMA.

32. Milestone to Kendall Lee, January 17, 1939, Kendall Lee Correspondence, f. 4, LMA.

33. Milestone to Kendall Lee, February 13, 1939, Kendall Lee Correspondence, f. 4, LMA.

34. Jay Parini, *John Steinbeck: A Biography* (New York: Henry Holt, 1995), 218.

35. Thornton Delehanty, interview with Milestone, *New York Herald Tribune,* undated clipping, Milestone clipping files, LMA.

36. Charlotte Cook Hadella, *Of Mice and Men: A Kinship of Powerlessness* (New York: Twayne, 1995), 15.

37. Ibid.

38. Parini, *John Steinbeck,* 177.

39. Ibid., 219.

40. MS, 117.

41. "Close-up, *Of Mice and Men,*" *Life,* January 8, 1940.

42. Quentin Reynolds, "That's How Pictures Are Born," *Collier's,* January 6, 1940.

43. Ibid.

44. Interview with Gore Vidal, quoted in Parini, *John Steinbeck,* 229.

45. Milestone to Kendall Lee, June 30, 1939, f. 4, Kendall Lee Correspondence, LMA.

46. Delehanty, interview with Milestone.

47. Jackson J. Benson, *The True Adventures of John Steinbeck, Writer* (New York: Viking, 1984), 407.

48. Joseph Breen to Milestone, January 30, 1939, PCA.

49. Lewis Gannett article for studio promotional brochure, box 2, NR.

50. *Variety,* January 3, 1940.

51. "The Picture Hollywood Said 'Couldn't Be Made,'" *Variety,* December 28, 1939.

52. Steinbeck to Elizabeth Otis, December 15, 1939, in John Steinbeck, *Steinbeck: A Life in Letters,* ed. Elaine Steinbeck and Robert Wallsten (New York: Viking, 1975), 195.

53. Milestone to Kendall Lee, August 4, 1944, f. 4., Kendall Lee Correspondence, LMA.

54. Publicity brochure for *Of Mice and Men,* box 2, NR.

55. Delehanty, interview with Milestone.

56. Reynolds, "That's How Pictures Are Born."

57. Irving Hoffman, "Tales of Hoffman," *Hollywood Reporter,* n.d., Milestone clipping files, LMA.

58. Calvin Beck, *Heroes of the Horrors* (New York: Collier Books, 1975), 232.

59. B. Gelman Jackson, "The Life Story of Lon Chaney, Jr., " *Monster Fantasy,* 1975, 28.

60. Publicity brochure for *Of Mice and Men,* box 2, NR.

61. Ibid.

62. Ibid.

63. Interview with Nicolai Remisoff, undated clipping, box 17, NR.

64. Ibid.; Jerry Breitigam, untitled article on Remisoff's work on *My Life with Caroline, Hollywood Bulletin,* March 29, 1941, boxes 16, 17, NR.

65. MS, 122.

66. Quoted in Howard Pollack, *Aaron Copland: The Life and Work of an Uncommon Man* (New York: Henry Holt, 1999), 343.

67. Milestone to Kendall Lee, October 6, 1939, f. 4, Kendall Lee Correspondence, LMA.

68. Ibid.

69. Richard Griffith review, unidentified source, dated February 26, 1940, Milestone clipping files, LMA

70. *Variety,* December 23, 1939.

71. James Agate, "The Cinema," *Tatler,* April 24, 1940.

72. *New Yorker,* n.d., LMA.

73. *Hollywood Reporter,* December 23, 1939.

74. Mary Pickford to Milestone, telegram, February 18, 1940, LMA.

75. *Variety,* December 28, 1939.

76. Tom Flannery, *1939, The Year in Movies: A Comprehensive Filmography* (Jefferson, N.C.: McFarland, 1990), xiii.

77. Otto Friedrich, *City of Nets: A Portrait of Hollywood in the 1940's* (New York: Harper and Row, 1986), 14.

78. MS, 122.

7. The Home Front

1. HG, 161.

2. Juliet Benita Colman, *Ronald Colman: A Very Private Person* (New York: William Morrow, 1975), 195.

3. Ibid., 197.

4. *Hollywood Reporter,* August 14, 1940.

5. *New York Post,* undated clipping [September 1940], Milestone clipping files, LMA.

6. Lawrence J. Quirk, *The Films of Ronald Colman* (Secaucus, N.J.: Citadel Press, 1977), 209.

7. Jerry Breitigam, untitled article on Remisoff's work on *My Life with Caroline, Hollywood Bulletin,* March 29, 1941.

8. Bosley Crowther, "Critical Comment: 'My Life with Caroline,'" *New York Times,* October 30, 1941.

9. Milestone quoted in Colman, *Ronald Colman,* 198.

10. Quirk, *The Films of Ronald Colman,* 211.

11. Colman, *Ronald Colman,* 198–99.

12. Hans Schoots, *Living Dangerously: A Biography of Joris Ivens* (Amsterdam: Amsterdam University Press, 2000), 166.

13. *New York Times,* February 1, 1941.

14. Schoots, *Living Dangerously,* 167.

15. GR, 168.

16. Ibid.

17. Ibid.

18. *New York Times,* February 1, 1941.

19. Alan Casty, *Robert Rossen: The Films and Politics of a Blacklisted Idealist* (Jefferson, N.C.: McFarland, 2013), 1.

20. Ibid., 77–78.

21. MS, 181.

22. HG, 162.

23. Undated review, *Family Circle,* Milestone clipping files, LMA.

24. MS, 182.

25. André Bazin, "On *Why We Fight:* History, Documentation, and the Newsreel," trans. and ed. Bert Cardullo, *Film and History* 31, no. 1 (2001): 60.

26. Ellen Schrecker, *Many Are the Crimes: McCarthyism in America* (Boston: Little, Brown, 1998), 320–21.

27. Kenneth Lloyd Billingsley, *Hollywood Party: How Communism Seduced the American Film Industry in the 1930s and 1940s* (Rocklin, Calif.: Forum, 1998).

28. Clayton R. Koppes and Gregory D. Black, *Hollywood Goes to War: How Politics, Profits and Propaganda Shaped World War II Movies* (New York: Free Press, 1987), 221.

29. A. Scott Berg, *Goldwyn: A Biography* (New York: Alfred A. Knopf, 1989), 368.

30. Hellman quoted in Carl Rollyson, *Dana Andrews: Hollywood Enigma* (Jackson: University Press of Mississippi, 2012), 139.

31. HG, 162.

32. Lewis Milestone, "Mr. Milestone Beats a Plowshare into a Sword," *New York Times,* March 14, 1943, X3.

33. "The Author's Case: Post-Premiere Cogitations of Lillian Hellman on 'The North Star,'" *New York Times,* December 19, 1943.

34. Review of *The North Star, Look* (n.d.), Milestone clipping files, LMA.

35. Farley Granger with Robert Calhoun, *Include Me Out: My Life from Goldwyn to Broadway* (New York: St. Martin's Press, 2007), 22.

36. Ibid., 20.

37. Ibid., 11.

38. Ibid., 20–21.

39. James Agee, "So Proudly We Fail," *Nation,* October 30, 1943.

40. Lillian Hellman, *An Unfinished Woman* (Boston: Little, Brown, 1969), 125.

41. Bosley Crowther, "Missionary Zeal: The Ecstasies in 'Mission to Moscow' Raise Doubts on Political Films," *New York Times,* May 9, 1943.

42. John Dewey and Suzanne La Follette, letter to the editor, *New York Times,* May 9, 1943.

43. *New York Times,* May 19, 1943, 8.

44. *New York Times,* May 28, 1943, 4.

45. Howard Koch, letter to the editor, *New York Times,* June 13, 1943, section 2, p. 3.

46. Granger with Calhoun, *Include Me Out,* 24.

47. Neil Rau, review of *The North Star, San Francisco Examiner,* December 27, 1943, Milestone clipping files, LMA.

48. John T. McManus, review of *The North Star, PM,* November 5, 1943.

49. Manchester Boddy, editorial, *Los Angeles Daily News,* December 28, 1943.

50. VOKS to Goldwyn, Milestone, and Hellman, telegram, April 18, 1944, Milestone clipping files, LMA.

8. King of the Set

1. MS, 189.

2. MC, 126.

3. Undated clipping, Milestone clipping files, LMA.

4. HG, 163.

5. *Purple Heart* screenplay, f. 89, LMA, 12.

6. Ibid., 8.

7. Rollyson, *Dana Andrews,* 141.

8. Ibid., 144.

9. Granger, *Include Me Out,* 25.

10. Rollyson, *Dana Andrews,* 142.

11. Mary McCarthy, *Film Comment,* January–February 1976, 34.

12. Press Alliance, unidentified clipping, ca. early 1944, Milestone clipping files, LMA.

13. Eileen Creelman, "Picture Plays and Players: Lewis Milestone Talks of 'Guest in the House' and of 'The Purple Heart,'" *New York Sun,* February 26, 1944.

14. "Milestone under Hurry-Up Knife," *Variety,* May 24, 1944.

15. Ralph Bellamy, *When the Smoke Hit the Fan* (Garden City, N.Y.: Doubleday, 1979), 192.

16. PS, 327.

17. *A Guest in the House* legal documents, f. 26, LMA.

18. MS, 210.

19. Ibid., 213.

20. Lloyd, *Stages,* 97.

21. Ibid.

22. Ibid., 96, 98.

23. MS, 200.

24. Casty, *Robert Rossen,* 78.

25. Joseph Breen to Will Hays, August 2, 1945, and Hays to Breen, September 5, 1945, PCA.

26. MS, 200.

27. Ibid., 206.

28. Nicholas Cull, "Samuel Fuller on Lewis Milestone's *A Walk in the Sun* (1946): The Legacy of *All Quiet on the Western Front* (1930)," *Historical Journal of Film, Radio and Television* 20, no. 1 (2000): 80.

29. Lloyd, *Stages,* 94.

30. Rollyson, *Dana Andrews,* 179.

31. MS, 208.

32. Dana Andrews quoted in *New York Sun,* January 11, 1946.

33. Lloyd, *Stages,* 96.

34. Norman Lloyd, interview, DVD release of *A Walk in the Sun* (1998).

35. James Agee, *Agee on Film* (Boston: Beacon Press, 1958), 185–86.

36. Casty, *Robert Rossen,* 78.

37. Harry Crocker, "Around the Town," *Los Angeles Examiner,* August 2, 1945.

38. Clipping from unidentified newspaper, dated September 1945, Milestone clipping files, LMA.

39. "Red Cross Unit Launched into Show Business," clipping from unidentified newspaper, July 29, 1945, Milestone clipping files, LMA.

40. Claire McAloon quoted in David Rothel, *Richard Boone: A Knight without Armor in a Savage Land* (Madison, N.C.: Empire Publishing, 2000), 42–43.

41. Mark Bould, *Film Noir: From Berlin to Sin City* (New York: Wallflower, 2005), 40.

42. David Thomson, *The Whole Equation: A History of Hollywood* (New York: Alfred A. Knopf, 2004), 261.

43. Joseph Breen to Hal Wallis, August 2, 1945, Hal Wallis Archives, f. 235, Herrick Library.

44. Manny Farber quoted in Casty, *Robert Rossen,* 84.

45. Paramount press book for *The Strange Love of Martha Ivers,* 5, LMA.

46. Harold Heffernan, "Van Heflin, Ex-Serviceman, Adjusts to Postwar Career," *Miami Daily News,* October 14, 1945, 4.

47. Lauren Bacall quoted in Axel Madsen, *Stanwyck* (New York: HarperCollins, 1994), 234.

48. Kirk Douglas, *The Ragman's Son: An Autobiography* (New York: Simon and Schuster, 1988), 132.

49. Joseph McBride, *Kirk Douglas* (New York: Pyramid, 1976), 23.

50. Douglas, *The Ragman's Son,* 135.

51. Paramount press book for *The Strange Love of Martha Ivers,* 7.

52. MS, 220.

53. Douglas, *The Ragman's Son,* 153.

54. Madsen, *Stanwyck,* 141.

55. Bernard Dick, *Hal Wallis: Producer to the Stars* (Lexington: University Press of Kentucky, 2004), 95.

56. HG, 331.

57. Ibid.

58. Paramount press book for *The Strange Love of Martha Ivers,* 7.

59. Dan Callahan, *Barbara Stanwyck: The Miracle Woman* (Jackson: University Press of Mississippi, 2012), 152.

60. Douglas, *The Ragman's Son,* 136.

61. Thomas Schatz, *Boom and Bust: The American Cinema in the 1940s,* vol. 6 of *History of the American Cinema,* ed. Charles Harpole (New York: Charles Scribner's Sons, 1997), 306.

9. Fallen Arch

1. MS, 263.

2. *Picturegoer* (London), November 9, 1946.

3. Hilton Tims, *Erich Maria Remarque: The Last Romantic* (New York: Carroll and Graf, 2003), 146.

4. PS, 332.

5. Lloyd, *Stages,* 100.

6. *Arch of Triumph* screenplay, dated January 13, 1947, f. 4, LMA.

7. Larry Swindell, *Charles Boyer: The Reluctant Lover* (Garden City, N.Y.: Doubleday, 1983), 210.

8. Lloyd, *Stages,* 101.

9. Ingrid Bergman and Alan Burgess, *Ingrid Bergman: My Story* (New York: Delacorte, 1972), 164–65.

10. Mary Morris, "Breakfast with Lewis Milestone," *Los Angeles Times Magazine,* 1947 (undated), Milestone clipping files, LMA.

11. Donald Spoto, *Notorious: The Life of Ingrid Bergman* (New York: HarperCollins, 1997), 214.

12. Tims, *Erich Maria Remarque,* 149.

13. HG, 165.

14. Lloyd, *Stages,* 102.

15. Ibid., 108.

16. VS, 77.

17. Ibid.

18. Ibid.

19. Morris, "Breakfast with Lewis Milestone."

20. Lloyd, *Stages,* 105.

21. Ibid., 107.

22. HG,165.

23. PS, 332.

24. VS, 78.

25. Swindell, *Charles Boyer,* 215.

26. David O. Selznick, *Memo from David O. Selznick,* ed. Rudy Behlmer (New York: Viking, 1972), 392.

27. Bosley Crowther, "Ingrid Bergman and Charles Boyer Are Seen in 'Arch of Triumph' at Globe," *New York Times,* April 21, 1948.

28. Simon Callow, *Charles Laughton: A Difficult Actor* (London: Methuen, 1987), 181.

29. Casty, *Robert Rossen,* 78.

30. Jennifer Frost, *Hedda Hopper's Hollywood: Celebrity Gossip and American Conservatism* (New York: New York University Press, 2011), 78–79.

31. LMT, 14.

32. Ibid., 61.

33. Alan L. Gansberg, *Little Caesar: A Biography of Edward G. Robinson,* Scarecrow Press, 2004, 118.

34. GR, 75.

35. LMT, 9.

36. Edward Dmytryk, *It's a Hell of a Life but Not a Bad Living* (New York: Times Books, 1978), 95.

37. Larry Parks, "Betty Darling . . . ," *Modern Screen,* March 1948, 93.

38. LMT, 16.

39. Larry Ceplair and Christopher Trumbo, *Dalton Trumbo: Blacklisted Hollywood Radical* (Lexington: University Press of Kentucky, 2015), 190–91.

40. Bruce Cook, *Dalton Trumbo* (New York: Scribner, 1977), 175.

41. LMT, 14.

42. Ibid., 13.

43. Ibid., 12.

44. *Daily Variety,* October 16, 1947, 8–9, and *Hollywood Reporter,* October 16, 1947, 8–9.

45. GR, 74.

46. LMT, 14.

47. Ceplair and Trumbo, *Dalton Trumbo,* 197.

48. GR, 74.

49. Gary Crowdus, ed., *The Political Companion to American Film* (Chicago: Lake View Press, 1994), 243.

50. LMT, 17.

51. Cook, *Dalton Trumbo,* 179.

52. *Hollywood Reporter,* November 26, 1947, 1, 7.

53. GR, 76.

54. "Directors at Work—unedited soundtrack," interview with Lewis Milestone and John Cromwell, n.d., Canadian Broadcasting Corporation, UCLA Film and Television Archives.

55. Lloyd, *Stages,* 106.

56. MS, 227.

57. Lloyd, *Stages,* 107.

58. Ibid., 109.

59. *The Red Pony* legal files, f. 99, LMA.

60. Ibid.

61. VS, 58.

62. Milestone to John Hersey, n.d., *The Red Pony* production files, f. 100, LMA.

63. GR, 77.

64. VS, 59.

65. James Kotsilibas-Davis and Myrna Loy, *Myrna Loy: Being and Becoming* (New York: Alfred A. Knopf, 1987), 212–13.

66. VS, 59.

67. Aaron Copland and Vivian Perlis, *Copland: Since 1943* (New York: St. Martin's Press, 1989), 88–89.

68. Ibid., 88–89.

69. Steinbeck quoted ibid., 91.

70. Bosley Crowther, "The Screen in Review: 'Red Pony,' Based on Steinbeck Novel, New Bill at Mayfair—Mitchum, Loy in Cast," *New York Times,* March 9, 1949.

71. VS, 59.

10. On the Graylist

1. Norma Barzman, *The Red and the Blacklist: The Intimate Memoir of a Hollywood Expatriate* (New York: Thunder's Mouth Press/Nation Books), 2003.

2. Milestone to Kendall Lee, September 9, 1950, f. 32, LMA.

3. Brenda Helser to Hedda Hopper, February 2, 1950, Brenda Helser Archives, f. 1082, Herrick Library.

4. Helser to Hopper, February 15, 1950, Helser Archives, f. 1082.

5. *Hollywood Reporter,* August 20, 1957.

6. Breen to Jason S. Joy, Director of public relations for Twentieth Century Fox, January 18, 1950, *Halls of Montezuma* files, PCA.

7. Darryl Zanuck to Milestone, June 15, 1950, *Kangaroo* archives, f. 32, LMA.

8. Ibid.

9. *Kangaroo* archives, f. 31, LMA.

10. Milestone to Kendall Lee, September 25, 1950, f. 32, LMA.

11. Milestone to Kendall Lee, n.d., f. 32, LMA.

12. Milestone to Kendall Lee, August 28, 1950, f. 32, LMA.

13. Ibid.

14. Milestone to Darryl Zanuck, memo, January 2, 1951, f. 32, LMA.

15. Zanuck to Milestone, memo, January 27, 1951, f. 32, LMA.

16. HG, 166.

17. Rothel, *Richard Boone,* 45.

18. Bosley Crowther, "The Screen in Review; 'Halls of Montezuma,' Realistic Depiction of Goriness of War, Presented at Roxy Theatre," *New York Times,* January 6, 1951.

19. Spyros Skouras to Zanuck, memo, November 30, 1950, f. 32, LMA.

20. 20th Century Fox press release, LMA.

21. Peter Lev, *History of the American Cinema,* vol. 7, *Transforming the Screen, 1950–1959* (New York: Scribner's, 2003), 69.

22. *Alert: A Weekly Confidential Report on Communism and How to Combat It,* January 4, 1951.

23. Zanuck to Milestone, January 10, 1951, f. 280, LMA.

24. Milestone to Zanuck, February 1, 1951, f. 280, LMA.

25. Milestone to Felix Ferry, January 24, 1951, f. 31, LMA.

26. LMT, 67.

27. Lev, *Transforming the Screen,* 70.

28. MS, 225.

29. LMT, 67.

30. Ibid., 57.

31. Ibid., 66.

32. MS, 264.

33. GR, 80.

34. HG, 167–68.

35. *Variety,* May 19, 1952.

36. *Hollywood Reporter,* May 19, 1952.

37. MS, 247.

38. PS, 68.

39. MS, 247.

40. Howard McClay, *Daily News* (unspecified location), February 5, 1952, Milestone clipping files, LMA.

41. Ibid.

42. Richard Murphy to Milestone, February 19, 1952, f. 34, LMA.

11. Abroad

1. HG, 168.

2. Patrice Munsel to Milestone, October 1, 1976, f. 38, LMA.

3. HG, 168.

4. *Hollywood Reporter,* June 24, 1953.

5. Contract signed August 14, 1952, and Milestone to attorneys Gang, Kopp, and Tyre, December 17, 1954, f. 40, LMA.

6. Dirk Bogarde, *Snakes and Ladders* (New York: Holt, Rinehart and Winston, 1978), 136.

7. Gerald Bowman, *London Evening News,* June 10, 1953.

8. Bogarde, *Snakes and Ladders,* 136.

9. Ibid., 137.

10. Ibid.

11. Milestone to André Hakim, March 30, 1953, *They Who Dare* production files, f. 110, LMA.

12. Westerby quoted in Bowman, *London Evening News,* June 10, 1953.

13. MS, 268.

14. *Globe and Mail,* October 11, 1954.

15. Milestone to Rex Cole, December 31, 1954, f. 220, LMA.

16. MS, 268.

17. Rex Cole to Milestone, February 21, 1955, f. 220, LMA.

18. Milestone to Rex Cole, February 21, 1955, f. 220, LMA.

19. *Hollywood Reporter,* August 20, 1957.

20. "Have Gun Will Travel," f. 182, LMA.

21. North American Newspaper Alliance, August 26, 1958, *Pork Chop Hill* production files, f. 83, LMA.

22. Gary Fishgall, *Gregory Peck: A Biography* (New York: Scribner, 2002), 206.

23. PS, 343.

24. Fishgall, *Gregory Peck,* 206–7.

25. HG, 169.

26. Fishgall, *Gregory Peck,* 207.

27. MC, 180.

28. Viraj Amonsin to Gregory Peck, November 24, 1958, *Pork Chop Hill* correspondence, f. 566, Gregory Peck Archives, Herrick Library.

29. *Variety,* May 5, 1959.

12. "Where the Devil Has He Been?"

1. James Spada, *Peter Lawford: The Man Who Kept the Secrets* (New York: Bantam, 1991), 213.

2. Ibid.

3. MS, 275.

4. Milestone contract, November 18, 1958, *Ocean's 11* legal file, LMA.

5. Shawn Levy, *Rat Pack Confidential: Frank, Dean, Sammy, Peter, Joey and the Last Great Showbiz Party* (New York: Doubleday, 1998), 107.

6. Harold Hildebrand, "Names Make the News," *Los Angeles Examiner,* August 7, 1960, sec. 5, 1.

7. Ibid.

8. Manohla Dargis, review of *Ocean's 8, New York Times,* June 8, 2018, C8.

9. Levy, *Rat Pack Confidential,* 6.

10. Spada, *Peter Lawford,* 214.

11. Scott Allen Nollen, *The Cinema of Sinatra: The Actor, on Screen and in Song* (Baltimore: Luminary Press, 2003), 205.

12. Hildebrand, "Names Make the News," 1–2.

13. Michael Freedland, *All the Way: A Biography of Frank Sinatra* (New York: St. Martin's Press, 1997), 287.

14. Peter J. Levinson, *September in the Rain: The Life of Nelson Riddle* (New York: Billboard Books, 2001), 142.

15. Jan-Christopher Horak, *Saul Bass: Anatomy of Film Design* (Lexington: University Press of Kentucky, 2014), 253.

16. Levy, *Rat Pack Confidential,* 118.

17. Hildebrand, "Names Make the News."

18. Bill Feeder to Milestone, August 8, 1960, *Ocean's 11* publicity files, f. 65, LMA.

19. *Variety,* August 10, 1960.

20. *Hollywood Reporter,* August 5, 1960.

21. Peter Manso, *Brando: The Biography* (New York: Hyperion, 1994), 515.

22. Nicholas Wapshott, *The Man Between: A Biography of Carol Reed* (London: Chatto and Windus, 1990), 308.

23. Milestone contract, March 27, 1961, legal file for *Mutiny on the Bounty,* f. 45, LMA.

24. Manso, *Brando,* 518.

25. Ibid., 537.

26. Bill Davidson, "The Mutiny of Marlon Brando," *Saturday Evening Post,* June 16, 1962, 21.

27. Ibid., 22.

28. Manso, *Brando,* 536.

29. Geoffrey Shurlock of the Production Code Administration to Robert Vogel of MGM, June 23, 1960, PCA.

30. Manso, *Brando,* 545–46.

31. Kendall Lee Milestone to Harry Kleiner, May 10, 1961, f. 235, LMA.

32. Davidson, "The Mutiny of Marlon Brando."

33. *Hollywood Reporter,* November 8, 1962.

34. *Variety,* November 8, 1962.

35. Pauline Kael, "Marlon Brando: An American Hero," *Atlantic Monthly,* March 1966, 74.

36. Milestone to Warner Bros., April 30, 1962, *PT 109* production files, f. 78, LMA.

37. Ibid.

38. Jack Warner to Milestone, June 26, 1962, f. 78, LMA.

39. Warner to Milestone, July 6, 1962, f. 78, LMA.

40. Milestone to Warner, July 15, 1962, f. 78, LMA.

41. Milestone to Henry Barnard, July 22, 1962, f. 78, LMA.

42. PS, 344.

43. Unidentified member of the film crew to Milestone and Kendall, July 31, 1962, f. 78, LMA.

44. Cast and crew of *Arrest and Trial* to Milestone, December 10, 1963, *Arrest and Trial* file, f. 180, LMA.

45. Hal Humphrey, "Why Milestone Avoids TV Jobs," *Los Angeles Times,* Calendar, January 12, 1964, 27.

46. Jiri Weiss to Milestone, August 19, 1965, f. 277, LMA.

13. A Hollywood Life

1. "Directors Guild Pays Tribute to Lewis Milestone," *Variety,* July 30, 1979.

2. Arthur H. Lewis, *It Was Fun While It Lasted* (New York: Trident, 1973), 138.

3. Lloyd, *Stages,* 95.

Selected Bibliography

Primary Sources

Higham, Charles, and Joel Greenberg. "Lewis Milestone." In *The Celluloid Muse: Hollywood Directors Speak.* 1969. Reprint, Chicago: Regnery, 1971.

Lewis Milestone Archives. Margaret Herrick Library, Academy of Motion Picture Arts and Sciences, Beverly Hills, Calif.

Milestone, Lewis. Interviews with Kevin Brownlow, 1969. Lewis Milestone Archives, f. 323, Margaret Herrick Library

———. Interviews with Joel Greenberg. Louis B. Mayer American Oral History, Project of the American Film Institute, 1971–73. Lewis Milestone Archives, f. 328, Margaret Herrick Library.

———. Joint interview with John Cromwell. "Directors at Work—unedited soundtrack." Canadian Broadcasting Corporation, audio tape. UCLA Film and TV Archives, n.d.

———. Testimony to the House Un-American Activities Committee investigator William Wheeler, reported by Harold M. Leibovitz, June 25, 1951, Los Angeles. National Archives and Records Administration, Center for Legislative Archives, Washington, D.C.

Milestone, Lewis, with Donald Chase. "Milestones" (unfinished autobiography), 1964–65. Manuscript, Lewis Milestone Archives, ff. 317, 318, 319, 322, Margaret Herrick Library.

Nicolai Remisoff Archives, University of Southern California Library Special Collections.

Parker, David L., and Burton J. Shapiro. "Lewis Milestone." In *Close Up: The Contract Director,* ed. Jon Tuska. Metuchen, N.J.: Scarecrow Press, 1976.

Production Code Administration files, Margaret Herrick Library.

Van Schmus, Albert E. Interview with Barbara Hall, 1993. Oral History Program, Margaret Herrick Library.

Secondary Sources

Barlett, Donald L., and James B. Steele. *Empire: The Life, Legend, and Madness of Howard Hughes*. New York: W. W. Norton, 1979.

Barzman, Norma. *The Red and the Blacklist: The Intimate Memoir of a Hollywood Expatriate*. New York: Thunder's Mouth Press/Nation Books, 2003.

Berg, A. Scott, *Goldwyn: A Biography*. New York: Alfred A. Knopf, 1989.

Bergman, Ingrid, and Alan Burgess. *Ingrid Bergman: My Story*. New York: Delacorte, 1972.

Bernstein, Matthew. *Walter Wanger: Hollywood Independent*. Berkeley: University of California Press, 1994.

Bertensson, Sergei. *Pis'ma v Khollivud. Po materialam arkhiva S. L. Bertensona* (*Letters to Hollywood: From Materials of the Archives of S. L. Bertensson*), ed. K. Arenskii. Monterey, Calif.: K. Arensburger, 1968.

Billingsley, Kenneth Lloyd. *Hollywood Party: How Communism Seduced the American Film Industry in the 1930s and 1940s*. Rocklin, Calif.: Forum, 1998.

Bogarde, Dirk. *Snakes and Ladders*. New York: Holt, Rinehart and Winston, 1978.

Brenman-Gibson, Margaret. *Clifford Odets: American Playwright: The Years from 1906 to 1940*. 1981. Reprint, New York: Applause, 2002.

Bret, David. *Joan Crawford: Hollywood Martyr*. New York: Carroll & Graf, 2007.

Callahan, Dan. *Barbara Stanwyck: The Miracle Woman*. Jackson: University Press of Mississippi, 2012.

Callow, Simon. *Charles Laughton: A Difficult Actor*. London: Methuen, 1987.

Casty, Alan. *Robert Rossen: The Films and Politics of a Blacklisted Idealist*. Jefferson, N.C.: McFarland, 2013.

Ceplair, Larry, and Christopher Trumbo. *Dalton Trumbo: Blacklisted Hollywood Radical*. Lexington: University Press of Kentucky, 2015.

Chandler, Charlotte. *Not the Girl Next Door: Joan Crawford, a Personal Biography*. New York: Simon and Schuster, 2008.

Coffin, Lesley L. *Lew Ayres: Hollywood's Conscientious Objector*. Jackson: University Press of Mississippi, 2012.

Colman, Juliet Benita. *Ronald Colman: A Very Private Person*. New York: William Morrow, 1975.

Copland, Aaron, and Vivian Perlis. *Copland: Since 1943*. New York: St. Martin's Press, 1989.

Crawford, Joan, with Jane Kesner Ardmore. *A Portrait of Joan: The Autobiography of Joan Crawford*. Garden City, N.Y.: Doubleday, 1962.

Crowdus, Gary, ed. *The Political Companion to American Film*. Chicago: Lake View Press, 1994.

Dick, Bernard. *Hal Wallis: Producer to the Stars*. Lexington: University Press of Kentucky, 2004.

Dmytryk, Edward. *It's a Hell of a Life but Not a Bad Living*. New York: Times Books, 1978.

Selected Bibliography

Doherty, Thomas. *Hollywood and Hitler, 1933–1939.* New York: Columbia University Press, 2015.

———. *Show Trial: Hollywood, HUAC and the Birth of the Blacklist.* New York: Columbia University Press, 2018.

Douglas, Kirk. *The Ragman's Son: An Autobiography.* New York: Simon and Schuster, 1988.

Ehrenburg, Ilya. *Memoirs: 1921–1941.* Translated by Tatiana Shebunina with Yvonne Kapp. Cleveland: World Publishing, 1963.

Fischer, Lucy, ed. *American Cinema of the 1920s: Themes and Variations.* New Brunswick, N.J.: Rutgers University Press, 2009.

Fishgall, Gary. *Gregory Peck: A Biography.* New York: Scribner, 2002.

Friedrich, Otto. *City of Nets: A Portrait of Hollywood in the 1940s.* New York: Harper and Row, 1986.

Frost, Jennifer. *Hedda Hopper's Hollywood: Celebrity Gossip and American Conservatism.* New York: New York University Press, 2011.

Giddins, Gary. *Bing Crosby: A Pocketful of Dreams,* vol. 1, *The Early Years, 1903–1940.* Boston: Little, Brown, 2001.

Goldberg, Anatol. *Ilya Ehrenburg: Revolutionary, Novelist, Poet, War Correspondent, Propagandist: The Extraordinary Epic of a Russian Survivor.* New York: Viking, 1984.

Golden, Eve. *John Gilbert: The Last of the Silent Film Stars.* Lexington: University Press of Kentucky, 2013.

Goldman, Herbert G. *Jolson: The Legend Comes to Life.* New York: Oxford University Press, 1988.

Granger, Farley, with Robert Calhoun. *Include Me Out: My Life from Goldwyn to Broadway.* New York: St. Martin's Press, 2007.

Guiles, Fred Lawrence. *Joan Crawford: The Last Word.* Secaucus, N.J.: Birch Lane Press, 1995.

Hadella, Charlotte Cook. *Of Mice and Men: A Kinship of Powerlessness.* New York: Twayne, 1995.

Hecht, Ben, and Charles MacArthur. *The Front Page.* New York: Covici-Friede, 1928.

Hellman, Lillian. *An Unfinished Woman: A Memoir.* Boston: Little, Brown, 1969.

Higham, Charles. *Howard Hughes: The Secret Life.* New York: G. P. Putnam's Sons, 1994.

Horak, Jan-Christopher. *Saul Bass: Anatomy of Film Design.* Lexington: University Press of Kentucky, 2014.

Kellow, Brian. *Ethel Merman: A Life.* New York: Viking, 2007.

Kelly, Andrew. *All Quiet on the Western Front: The Story of a Film.* New York: I. B. Tauris, 1998.

Koppes, Clayton, and Gregory D. Black. *Hollywood Goes to War: How Profits, Politics and Propaganda Shaped World War II Movies.* New York: Free Press, 1987.

Kotsilibas-Davis, James, and Myrna Loy. *Myrna Loy: Being and Becoming.* New York: Alfred A. Knopf, 1987.

Laurents, Arthur. *Original Story By: A Memoir of Broadway and Hollywood*. New York: Applause, 2000.

Lev, Peter. *History of the American Cinema*, vol. 7, *Transforming the Screen, 1950–1959*. New York: Scribner's, 2003.

Levinson, Peter J. *September in the Rain: The Life of Nelson Riddle*. New York: Billboard, 2001.

Levy, Shawn. *Rat Pack Confidential: Frank, Dean, Sammy, Peter, Joey and the Last Great Showbiz Party*. New York: Doubleday, 1998.

Lloyd, Norman. *Stages: Norman Lloyd*. Interviewed by Francine Parker. Metuchen, N.J.: Scarecrow Press, 1990.

MacAdams, William. *Ben Hecht: The Man behind the Legend*. New York: Scribner's, 1990.

Malone, Aubrey. *Maureen O'Hara: The Biography*. Lexington: University Press of Kentucky, 2013.

Manso, Peter. *Brando: The Biography*. New York: Hyperion, 1994.

Maugham, Somerset. "Rain." In *Collected Short Stories*, vol. 1. New York: Penguin, 1977.

Meyers, Jeffrey. *Gary Cooper: American Hero*. New York: William Morrow, 1998.

———. *Somerset Maugham: A Life*. New York: Alfred A. Knopf, 2004.

Millichap, Joseph R. *Lewis Milestone*. Boston: Twayne, 1981.

Parini, Jay. *John Steinbeck: A Biography*. New York: Henry Holt, 1996.

Remarque, Erich Maria. *All Quiet on the Western Front*. Translated by A. W. Wheen. New York: Ballantine Books, 1982.

———. *Arch of Triumph*. Translated by Walter Sorell and Denver Lindley. New York: Random House, 1972.

Rollyson, Carl. *Dana Andrews: Hollywood Enigma*. Jackson: University Press of Mississippi, 2012.

Rubinstein, Joshua. *Tangled Loyalties: The Life and Times of Ilya Ehrenburg*. New York: Basic Books, 1996.

Schatz, Thomas. *Boom and Bust: The American Cinema in the 1940s*. New York: Scribner's, 1997.

Selznick, David O. *Memo from David O. Selznick*. Edited by Rudy Behlmer. New York: Viking, 1972.

Sieben, Pearl. *The Immortal Jolson: His Life and Times*. New York: Frederick Fell, 1962.

Spada, James. *Peter Lawford: The Man Who Kept the Secrets*. New York: Bantam, 1991.

Spoto, Donald. *Notorious: The Life of Ingrid Bergman*. New York: HarperCollins, 1997.

Steinbeck, John. *Of Mice and Men*. 1937. Reprint, New York: Penguin, 1994.

———. *The Red Pony*. 1937. Reprint, New York: Penguin, 1992.

———. *Steinbeck: A Life in Letters*. Edited by Elaine Steinbeck and Robert Wallsten. New York: Viking, 1975.

Swindell, Larry. *Charles Boyer: The Reluctant Lover*. Garden City, N.Y.: Doubleday, 1983.

Thomas, Bob. *King Cohn: The Life and Times of Harry Cohn*. New York: G. P. Putnam's Sons, 1967.

Tims, Hilton. *Erich Maria Remarque: The Last Romantic*. New York: Carroll and Graf, 2003.

Index

Index

Anderson, Judith, 2, 164

Anderson, Maxwell, 29, 41–42, 72, 173

Andrejew, André, 208

Andrews, Dana, 2, 238; in *A Walk in the Sun*, 153–54; in *No Minor Vices*, 185; in *The North Star*, 139–40; in *The Purple Heart*, 146, 147–48

Andrews, Del, 41

Andriot, Lucien, 21

Anna Christie (film), 58

anti-Communism, 7, 61, 133; Eisenstein's visit to America and, 51–52; of Howard Hughes, 29; Red Scare after World War I, 20; Senator McCarthy's campaign, 201; *The North Star* attacked by anti-Communist press, 142–43. *See also* blacklist; HUAC

anti-Semitism, 11, 13, 50, 51, 161; Kishinev pogrom (1903), 9–10, 59; Nazi policies of, 132

antitrust court decisions, film studios and, 174

Anything Goes (Milestone film, 1936), 3, 4, 92, 93–95, 96

Applause (film, 1926), 36

Arch of Triumph (Milestone film, 1948), 4, 76, 184, 189, 191, 196, 240; casting, 169, 171–72; critical failure of, 176–77; editing of, 175–76; musical score, 169; prewar Paris underworld recreated in, 177; screenplay, 169–70; shooting of, 173–75

Arch of Triumph (Remarque novel), 167–69

Arrest and Trial (TV series), 235, 236

Association of Motion Picture Producers and Exhibitors, 54

Astor, Mary, 30–31

Atkinson, Brooks, 61

Auer, Mischa, 117

Avengers, The (film, 1942), 131

Awake and Sing! (Broadway play, 1935), 97

Ayres, Lew, 2, 44, 45, 53, 59, 178, 238

Babel, Isaac, 8

Bacall, Lauren, 156, 163, 182

Barrymore, John, 6, 33

Bartlett, Sy, 214, 216, 218

Bass, Saul, 224

Battle of Russia, The (film, 1943), 132–33, 135

Battleship Potemkin (film, 1925), 50

Baxter, Anne, 2, 139, 140, 149

Bazin, André, 133

Behrman, S. N., 78

Bellamy, Ralph, 149

Benedict, Richard, 221

Bennett, Charles, 105

Benny, Jack, 117

Bergman, Ingrid, 2, 131, 185; in *Arch of Triumph*, 171–72, 173, 176, 177; on Kendall Lee's first husband, 76

Berkeley, Martin, 198

Bernstein, Leonard, 217

Berr, Georges, 123

Bertensson, Sergei, 59, 64, 65, 82; Russian émigré milieu described in diary, 67–69; on *The Front Page*, 66

Best Years of Our Lives, The (film, 1946), 139

Betrayal (Milestone film, 1929), 35, 36

Big Boy (film, 1930), 78

Big Parade, The (film, 1925), 40, 82, 89

Big Town, The (Lardner), 185

Billingsley, Lloyd, 134

Birell, Tala, 90, 146

Bishop, Joey, 220, 221, 223

Black, Gregory D., 134

blacklist, 26, 97, 117, 179, 213. *See also* anti-Communism; HUAC

Blake, Robert, 215

Blankfort, Michael, 193, 201

Bligh, Captain William, 226–27, 230, 231

Blockade (film, 1938), 105

Blue Angel, The (film, 1930), 74

Bobbed Hair (film, 1925), 23

Boehnel, William, 50–51

Bogarde, Dirk, 2, 209–10, 211

Bogart, Humphrey, 156, 157, 171, 182

Boleslawski, Richard, 205

Bolshevik Revolution (1917), 4, 9, 20, 33, 50, 86; ideological conflict and, 127; U.S.–Soviet diplomatic relations and, 88; White Russian refugees from, 169. *See also* Communism; Soviet Union

Bondi, Beulah, 71–72

Index

288

Screen Classics

Screen Classics is a series of critical biographies, film histories, and analytical studies focusing on neglected filmmakers and important screen artists and subjects, from the era of silent cinema through the golden age of Hollywood to the international generation of today. Books in the Screen Classics series are intended for scholars and general readers alike. The contributing authors are established figures in their respective fields. This series also serves the purpose of advancing scholarship on film personalities and themes with ties to Kentucky.

Series Editor

Patrick McGilligan

Books in the Series

Olivia de Havilland: Lady Triumphant
Victoria Amador

Mae Murray: The Girl with the Bee-Stung Lips
Michael G. Ankerich

Hedy Lamarr: The Most Beautiful Woman in Film
Ruth Barton

Rex Ingram: Visionary Director of the Silent Screen
Ruth Barton

Conversations with Classic Film Stars: Interviews from Hollywood's Golden Era
James Bawden and Ron Miller

Conversations with Legendary Television Stars: Interviews from the First Fifty Years
James Bawden and Ron Miller

You Ain't Heard Nothin' Yet: Interviews with Stars from Hollywood's Golden Era
James Bawden and Ron Miller

Von Sternberg
John Baxter

Hitchcock's Partner in Suspense: The Life of Screenwriter Charles Bennett
Charles Bennett, edited by John Charles Bennett

Hitchcock and the Censors
John Billheimer

A Uniquely American Epic: Intimacy and Action, Tenderness and Violence in Sam Peckinpah's The Wild Bunch
Edited by Michael Bliss

My Life in Focus: A Photographer's Journey with Elizabeth Taylor and the Hollywood Jet Set
Gianni Bozzacchi with Joey Tayler

Hollywood Divided: The 1950 Screen Directors Guild Meeting and the Impact of the Blacklist
Kevin Brianton

He's Got Rhythm: The Life and Career of Gene Kelly
Cynthia Brideson and Sara Brideson

Ziegfeld and His Follies: A Biography of Broadway's Greatest Producer
Cynthia Brideson and Sara Brideson

The Marxist and the Movies: A Biography of Paul Jarrico
Larry Ceplair

Dalton Trumbo: Blacklisted Hollywood Radical
Larry Ceplair and Christopher Trumbo

Warren Oates: A Wild Life
Susan Compo

Improvising Out Loud: My Life Teaching Hollywood How to Act
Jeff Corey with Emily Corey

Crane: Sex, Celebrity, and My Father's Unsolved Murder
Robert Crane and Christopher Fryer

Jack Nicholson: The Early Years
Robert Crane and Christopher Fryer

Anne Bancroft: A Life
Douglass K. Daniel

Being Hal Ashby: Life of a Hollywood Rebel
Nick Dawson

Bruce Dern: A Memoir
Bruce Dern with Christopher Fryer and Robert Crane

Intrepid Laughter: Preston Sturges and the Movies
Andrew Dickos

Miriam Hopkins: Life and Films of a Hollywood Rebel
Allan R. Ellenberger

John Gilbert: The Last of the Silent Film Stars
Eve Golden

Stuntwomen: The Untold Hollywood Story
Mollie Gregory

Saul Bass: Anatomy of Film Design
Jan-Christopher Horak

Hitchcock Lost and Found: The Forgotten Films
Alain Kerzoncuf and Charles Barr

Pola Negri: Hollywood's First Femme Fatale
Mariusz Kotowski